autho... ...ally acclaimed and bestselling ... ...-
ing *Fighter Boys*, *Bomber Boys*, *3 Para* and *Air Force Blue*. Previously,
he was a foreign correspondent for over thirty years, reporting from
conflicts all over the world.

Praise for

THE MAN WHO WAS SATURDAY

'Neave was a brave, modest and decent man. Bishop shows him also
to be complex, sometimes troubled, and more interesting than
many who did not know him understood. He deserves a first-rate
biography, and Bishop has written it'   *Daily Telegraph*

'Airey Neave lived one of those extraordinary English twentieth-
century lives that reads like a subplot in an Anthony Powell novel,
but it ended in a murder-mystery … A sympathetic, magnificent
biography … This exemplary biography is a timely corrective when
the fashion is for politicians to run away after they suffer a setback'
                                                            The Times

'Timely … One reads the final pages in a state of horrified disbelief
… I clapped the book shut with a renewed sense of loss, and respect'
                                                        Financial Times

'It succ... ...tters, sympathetic, ... *...nday Telegraph*

'Highly readable ... Bishop presents a rounded and well researched picture of his subject'   *Literary Review*

'The story of Neave's escape from Colditz has been told many times, but it never loses its nerve-jangling excitement ... [Bishop] frames Neave's story as a cloak-and-dagger thriller ... Yet the small print of Bishop's narrative tells a more complicated story ... Bishop writes with admirable brevity and insight'   *Sunday Times*

'Perceptive'   *Daily Mail*

'Much of this biography reads like a Boys' Own version of a John le Carré novel, and works on that level as a pacy, absorbing read ... Neave emerges from these pages as a fascinatingly complex man, a sepia-toned throwback to a not-too-distant era in British politics when Conservatives could still be described as compassionate, public servants put their lives on the line for the greater good, and patriotism wasn't necessarily the last refuge of a scoundrel'   *Irish Times*

'Bishop is at his best describing Neave's wartime exploits ... Gives us an interesting snapshot of a Tory backbencher of his time'   *Tablet*

'In this remarkable biography, the brilliant historian Patrick Bishop reveals Airey Neave to have been a man of varied parts and multiple talents ... Not only a superb biography of a hardly seen hero. It holds up a mirror to a period of our national history seen through the eyes of one who was there'   FREDERICK FORSYTH, *Oldie*

'Tells the story of Neave's life with shrewdness and sympathy, although not uncritically and with great pace'   *Country Life*

THE MAN
WHO WAS
SATURDAY

Also by Patrick Bishop

PATRICK BISHOP

THE MAN WHO WAS SATURDAY

The Extraordinary Life of Airey Neave

SOLDIER, ESCAPER,
SPYMASTER, POLITICIAN

WILLIAM
COLLINS

William Collins
An imprint of HarperCollins*Publishers*
1 London Bridge Street
London SE1 9GF

WilliamCollinsBooks.com

First published in Great Britain in 2019 by William Collins
This William Collins paperback edition published in 2020

1

Maps by Martin Brown

A catalogue record for this book is
available from the British Library

ISBN 978-0-00-830908-4

Set in ITC Giovanni
Printed and bound in Great Britain by
CPI Group (UK) Ltd, Croydon

MIX
Paper from
responsible sources
FSC
www.fsc.org   FSC™ C007454

TO MARY JO, THOMAS AND MARTHA ROSE

Contents

Maps

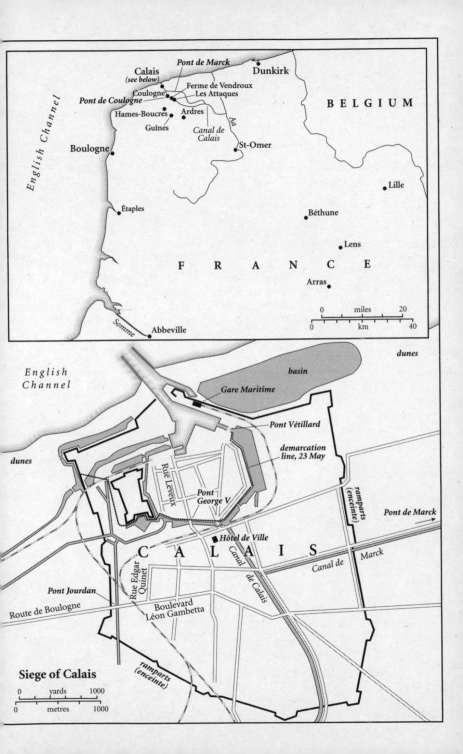

English Channel

BELGIUM

Pont de Marck ● Dunkirk

Calais
(see below)
● Coulogne — Ferme de Vendroux
Pont de Coulogne — Les Attaques
Hames-Boucres ● Ardres
Guines ● *Canal de Calais*
● St-Omer

Boulogne ●

● Lille

● Béthune

● Étaples

FRANCE

● Lens

Arras ●

Aa

0	miles	20
0	km	40

Somme
● Abbeville

English Channel

dunes

basin

Gare Maritime

Pont Vétillard

demarcation line, 23 May

dunes

Rue Leveux

Pont George V

ramparts *(enceinte)*

Pont de Marck

■ *Hôtel de Ville*

C A L A I S

Canal de Marck

Canal de Calais

Pont Jourdan

Rue Edgar Quinet

Route de Boulogne

Boulevard Léon Gambetta

ramparts *(enceinte)*

Siege of Calais

0	yards	1000
0	metres	1000

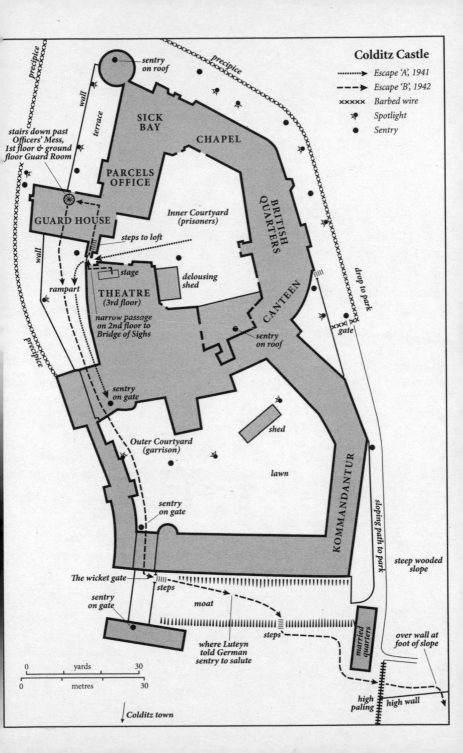

Colditz Castle

········· *Escape 'A', 1941*
--- --- --- *Escape 'B', 1942*
×××××× *Barbed wire*
⚝ *Spotlight*
● *Sentry*

precipice

precipice

sentry on roof

wall

terrace

SICK BAY

CHAPEL

stairs down past Officers' Mess, 1st floor & ground floor Guard Room

PARCELS OFFICE

GUARD HOUSE

Inner Courtyard (prisoners)

BRITISH QUARTERS

wall

steps to loft

rampart

stage

THEATRE (3rd floor)

delousing shed

precipice

narrow passage on 2nd floor to Bridge of Sighs

CANTEEN

drop to park

gate

sentry on roof

sentry on gate

shed

Outer Courtyard (garrison)

lawn

KOMMANDANTUR

sentry on gate

sloping path to park

steep wooded slope

The wicket gate

steps

sentry on gate

moat

where Luteyn told German sentry to salute

steps

married quarters

over wall at foot of slope

0 ___ yards ___ 30
0 ___ metres ___ 30

high paling *high wall*

↓ *Colditz town*

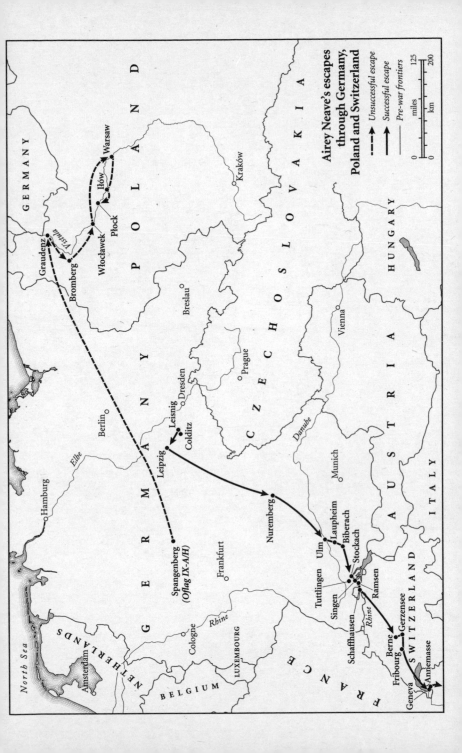

Airey Neave's escapes
through Germany,
Poland and Switzerland

Unsuccessful escape
Successful escape
Pre-war frontiers

miles   125
km   200

GERMANY

POLAND

CZECHOSLOVAKIA

HUNGARY

AUSTRIA

ITALY

SWITZERLAND

FRANCE

BELGIUM

LUXEMBOURG

NETHERLANDS

North Sea

Warsaw
Iłów
Płock
Włocławek
Bromberg
Graudenz
Vistula

Kraków

Breslau

Vienna

Dresden
Leisnig
Colditz
Leipzig

Berlin

Hamburg

Elbe

Amsterdam

Prague

Danube

Munich

Nuremberg

Laupheim
Ulm   Biberach
Tuttlingen   Stockach
Singen   Ramsen
Schaffhausen   Rhine

Spangenberg
(Oflag IX-A/H)

Frankfurt

Rhine

Cologne

Berne   Gerzensee
Fribourg
Geneva   Annemasse

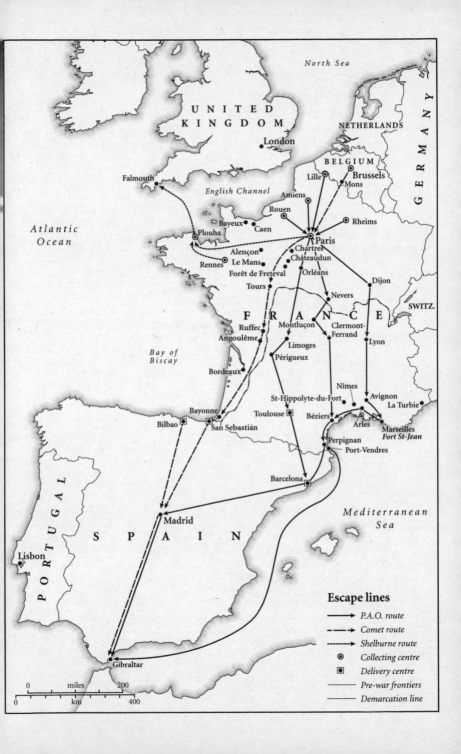

UNITED
KINGDOM

London

NETHERLANDS

BELGIUM

Lille
Brussels
Mons

Falmouth

English Channel

Amiens

North Sea

GERMANY

Atlantic
Ocean

Plouha

Rouen

Bayeux
Caen

Alençon

Rennes Le Mans

Forêt de Freteval

Tours

Rheims

Paris

Chartres
Châteaudun

Orléans

Nevers

Dijon

SWITZ.

F R A N C E

Ruffec
Angoulême

Montluçon

Clermont-
Ferrand

Bay of
Biscay

Limoges

Périgueux

Lyon

Bordeaux

St-Hippolyte-du-Fort

Nîmes

Avignon

La Turbie

Bayonne

Toulouse

Béziers

Arles

Bilbao

San Sebastián

Perpignan

Marseilles
Fort St-Jean

Port-Vendres

Barcelona

Madrid

Mediterranean
Sea

PORTUGAL

Lisbon

S P A I N

Gibraltar

miles

0   200

0   400
km

Escape lines

→ *P.A.O. route*

⤍ *Comet route*

⋯→ *Shelburne route*

◉ *Collecting centre*

▣ *Delivery centre*

— *Pre-war frontiers*

— *Demarcation line*

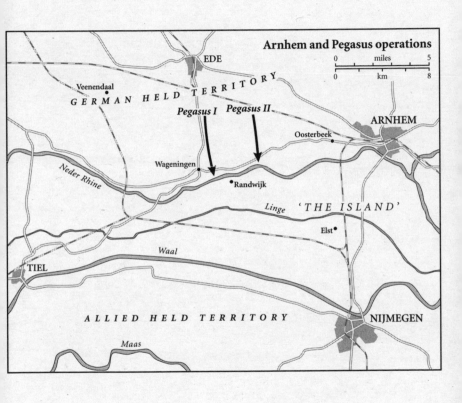

Arnhem and Pegasus operations

0 miles 5
0 km 8

GERMAN HELD TERRITORY

EDE

Veenendaal

ARNHEM

Pegasus I *Pegasus II*

Oosterbeek

Neder Rhine

Wageningen

Randwijk

Linge 'THE ISLAND'

Elst

Waal

TIEL

ALLIED HELD TERRITORY

NIJMEGEN

Maas

Preface

Biography masquerades as history but is often a species of fiction. That is not necessarily the fault of the biographer. Establishing the external facts of a public life in modern, well-documented times is fairly straightforward. It is charting the inner landscape that is the problem. How can we know what someone really thought, what drove him or her to do this or that? Letters and diaries open a window on these processes, of course, but can we be sure the motives and feelings they reveal are genuine, and not retouched with an eye to the good opinion of posterity?

In tackling the life of Airey Neave I have leaned on two versions of who he was. The public one is laid out in the several memoirs he published based on his service in the Second World War. The other is contained in the voluminous diaries he kept covering crucial years in the last period of his political career. The frequent introspective and unsparing passages make it hard to believe they were written for anyone but himself. Thus I felt I had the basis for something like a reasonably authentic portrait: Neave as he would like to be seen – and Neave as he saw himself.

There is another very important viewpoint – Neave as he appeared to everyone else. Neave struck many of his contemporaries as inscrutable. The face he presented to the world was conventional and confident. This was to some extent an act. Behind the bland mask lay a very different personality: racked by insecurities, plagued by doubts and depressions and haunted by a sense of failure and underachievement. Studying his life confirmed for me the truth of the words of the country priest whom André Malraux met when serving with the Maquis in the mountains of south-eastern France. Asked what he had learned about humanity from the many confessions he had heard over the years, he gave the answer 'The fundamental fact is that there is no such thing as a grown-up person.'

I find that answer moving and heartening. It is said to be a hazard of writing biography that familiarity breeds contempt and in the course of the research the author comes to loathe the relative stranger they blithely shacked up with at the start of the project. I am happy to say that for me the experience had the opposite effect. I came to like Neave a lot. He had his faults: vanity, touchiness, a dissatisfied nature. But they are greatly outweighed by his virtues: physical bravery – not in short supply among his generation – but also moral courage, quiet patriotism and a basic decency.

All came to an end in a shocking death at the hands of the forces he had been opposing in one way or another all his life. He led an interesting one, and his story has a satisfying curve. The adventures and achievements of his early career seemed to promise a glowing future. Instead, there followed years of frustration that sometimes brought him close to despair. Then, unexpectedly, the stars aligned to deliver a success that was all the more satisfying for its late arrival. He lived through a period of history which, though fairly recent, now feels curiously remote. What follows is an attempt to reanimate both him and his time.

THE MAN
WHO WAS
SATURDAY

Prologue

'Some Devils Got Him'

On Friday, 30 March 1979, change was in the air. For much of the month the weather had been cold and wet, but lately it had warmed up and in London the trees were in bud. The change of season matched a great political climacteric. Two days before, the Labour administration of James Callaghan had finally stumbled to an end after months of public-service strikes, already notorious as the 'Winter of Discontent'. In five weeks, a general election would in all probability elect a Conservative government with, for the first time in British history, a woman at its head.

When Airey Neave woke up that morning he had every reason to savour the atmosphere of promise and renewal. As the man who had engineered Margaret Thatcher's accession to the Conservative leadership, he had played a crucial part in great events. At the age of sixty-three, after a long wait and many disappointments, he was about to taste real power.

As a reward for his services, Mrs Thatcher had offered him any shadow portfolio he wanted. To the bafflement of many, he picked Northern Ireland. Political progress in Ulster was at a standstill and political violence a fact of everyday life. It seemed a masochistic choice. Neave saw it as a challenge – a last chance to bring off an achievement that would leave his mark in history. Since adolescence he had been opposing those he saw as the enemies of democracy – as a soldier, a prisoner of war, a Colditz escapee and an intelligence officer. The position of Secretary of State for Northern Ireland would put him in command of the latest phase of the struggle – Britain's war against Irish terrorism. The thought gave him great satisfaction.

A pleasant weekend lay ahead. He would be spending it in his Abingdon constituency with his wife Diana in the Oxfordshire village of Hinton Waldrist, where they rented a wing of the Old Rectory. Before leaving, he had some business to attend to at his office in the House of Commons. At 9.30 a.m., he left the family flat at 32 Westminster Gardens, in Marsham Street SW1, telling Diana he would be back to collect her at 3.30 p.m. The big nine-storey block was built in the 1930s and the apartments were spacious and comfortable, an ideal London base for politicians and senior civil servants.

It was half a mile from the House, but Neave chose to drive. He had long since given up smoking and drinking, following a heart attack, but was notoriously averse to exercise and his health had given his wife and children frequent cause for concern. The car, a modest Vauxhall Cavalier supplied by the engineering firm whose interests he represented in parliament, was parked in a lot beside the flats.

The journey took a few minutes. He drove through the gates of New Palace Yard, next to Big Ben, then down the entry ramp to the underground car park. Having found a space, he took the lift to the ground floor and made his way to the offices of the Leader of the Opposition, a collection of cramped rooms in a corridor behind the Speaker's chair in the House of Commons, for a 10 a.m. meeting of the Shadow Cabinet. At 11.40 a.m. he went back to his room together with Richard Ryder, the young de facto head of Mrs Thatcher's private office, and they spent some time discussing the election campaign.* Ryder left, and for an hour and a half Neave and his secretary, Joy Robilliard, 'discussed constituency weekend business, Saturday morning surgery, diary dates for the next month'.[1] Then

---

* Richard Ryder (1949–), educated Radley and Magdalene College, Cambridge; Conservative MP for Mid Norfolk, 1983–97; Government Chief Whip, 1990–95; created Lord Ryder of Wensum, 1997.

Neave asked her to inform the Special Branch of the Metropolitan Police that 'he would be leaving town at 3.30 p.m. for Hinton Waldrist.' The Special Branch were kept informed of all his movements. However, that was the extent of his personal security arrangements, and he had turned down the offer of a police bodyguard.

At 1.30 he 'announced that he would have something to eat in the House and then take a cab to his tailor.' This was Tom Brown in Princes Street, Mayfair, where he had a 2 p.m. appointment. Neave had been getting his suits from the same venerable establishment since his schooldays at Eton, where the original shop sits in the High Street. Today he was having the first fitting for two suits he had ordered a few weeks before.

The measuring over, he took a taxi back to the House, then descended to the underground car park to collect his car. Miss Robilliard's evidence to the police suggests it was unlikely that he inspected it before getting in, because although he was 'fairly good about security of the vehicle', he would 'not be troubled by anything lying on the floor of the car. He never checked the exterior of the vehicle.'

He climbed behind the wheel of the light-blue company Cavalier, switched on the ignition and moved off towards the ramp that led up to the cobbles of New Palace Yard. At 2.58 p.m., the Palace of Westminster was shaken by a great explosion. Richard Ryder ran to the window of Mrs Thatcher's office. Immediately below lay the smoking remnants of Neave's Vauxhall, 'just blown to smithereens'.[2]

Policemen and parliamentary journalists ran to the wreckage. Neave was lying back in the driver's seat. His face was blackened and his clothing charred. The explosion had removed his right leg below the knee and shattered the left leg. His face was well known in the Westminster village. One of the journalists had been with him only the night before. Neave's injuries were so bad that for a while no one recognised him. It took almost half an hour to free him from the debris and load him into an ambulance, which took him to Westminster Hospital, a mile away. He died eight minutes after getting there, just before Diana arrived.

The other woman in his life was at an event in her Finchley constituency when the bomb went off. It was a while before she learned the identity of the victim. As dusk fell, London looked wintry again. Returning to her home in Flood Street, Chelsea, with grief and shock still etched on her face, she paid her first tributes to her friend. 'He was one of freedom's warriors,' she told one camera crew. 'No one knew what a great man he was … except those nearest to him. He was staunch, brave, true, strong. But he was very gentle and kind and loyal.' To another she vented her feelings about those who had killed him. 'Some devils got him,' she said. 'And they must never, never, never be allowed to triumph. They must never prevail. Those of us who believe in the things that Airey fought for must see that our views are the ones which continue to live on in this country.'

For those of a certain age, the death of Airey Neave was a JFK moment. They can remember where they were and how they felt when the news reached them. This author was a young newspaper reporter and heard it on the radio while driving up from the West Country, where he was covering the Jeremy Thorpe affair. At that time political assassinations were scarcely unusual. Killing British public figures was a major part of Irish Republican strategy. There were two reasons, though, why Neave's death felt different. One was where it had happened. If the House of Commons car park wasn't safe from Irish terrorists, where was? The other concerned who he was. Neave was known as a right-hand man of the woman who seemed likely to be the next prime minister. The message the killers wanted to send was clear. Nowhere and no one was beyond their reach.

For all the shock of the killing, most people outside politics would have found it difficult to put a personality or even a face to the dead man. His name stuck in the mind because it was unusual. Older people might have remembered him as a war hero, the first British officer to escape from Colditz. Even inside the Westminster stockade, he was seen as rather enigmatic, detached and unknowable.

To Jonathan Aitken,* then a young backbencher, he was 'the cat who walks alone ... a sphinx'.[3] Aitken's first impression of him was of a man who 'shimmered' and 'seemed to hover around the edge of corridors, as though he were trying to vanish. If you tried to guess what his occupation might have been, you might have said "spook" or "ghost", because he moved in a funny way ... He was unobtrusive ... I think he cultivated an air of mystery and spookiness ... I remember being struck by his air of ghostliness or secretiveness.'

It is a sentiment echoed by several people I interviewed. 'I can see him walking along,' recalled Tom King.†[4] 'He seemed to make no sound and leave no impression as he went by. I always thought he was a natural conspirator ... I don't mean in an unkind sense. But he was quite a schemer, and clever.'

At first glance he looked completely conventional. He was five feet eleven inches tall and weighed fourteen stone. He looked very English. His face was round and rosy, his pouched eyes a hazy blue, his skin smooth and his light hair sparse. The new Tom Brown suits he was measured up for that afternoon were just like those he had always ordered: both grey worsted, one with a faint check, the other with a discreet stripe and each with an extra pair of trousers.[5] Even in 1979 such garments looked old-fashioned.

They marked him out as a member of the wartime generation. There were still plenty of them around on both sides of the House, but the world they were familiar with had changed. To some, it seemed that informality was becoming the norm, thrift had fallen to mass consumerism, and lingering wartime-era notions of a communal investment in shared goals and ideals had given way to

---

* Jonathan Aitken (1942–), educated Eton and Christ Church, Oxford; Conservative MP for Thanet East, 1974–83; Minister for Defence Procurement, 1992–94; Chief Secretary to the Treasury, 1994–95; imprisoned for perjury and perverting the course of justice, 1999.

† Tom King (1933–), educated Rugby and Emmanuel College, Cambridge; Conservative MP for Bridgwater, 1970–2001; from 1983, successively Secretary of State for Environment, Transport, Employment, Northern Ireland and Defence; created Lord King of Bridgwater, 2001.

the pursuit of individual and sectional interests. Older Britons complained that the rising generation seemed to believe that what to them were almost decadent luxuries were a natural right: cars, washing machines, restaurant meals, foreign holidays. And they did not expect to have to work very hard to get them.

Looking back, these aspirations seem modest and notions of what constituted a good time or a treat touchingly simple. In 1979, no one had heard of prosecco. In that morning's *Daily Mail*, the Victoria Wine company advertised Easter bargains including Martini Bianco at £1.39 a bottle and Olé medium sherry at £1.47. The television page carried the schedule for the three national channels. At 8 p.m. – prime time – viewers could choose between half an hour of the comedian Les Dawson (BBC1), a documentary on the Bengali community of Brick Lane (BBC2), or *Flambards*, a country-house mini-series set in the early years of the century (ITV). If you missed a programme, you might capture it on the new video recorders that were now in the shops. It meant a significant investment. A Philips N1700 carried by Currys cost £499, the equivalent of the monthly average wage.

Even for trendy, well-heeled Londoners looking for a sophisticated meal out, choices were, to today's eyes, either circumscribed or unappetising. At Bumbles, in Buckingham Palace Road, a short stroll from the Neaves' flat, the choices included cold lettuce soup, kidneys in champagne with saffron rice, and mushrooms stuffed with prawns and grilled with Stilton.

Neave was sometimes irritated by modern life and could get furious at displays of modern bad manners. But he was in many ways a progressive, far from the popular notion of an Eton and Oxford Tory. His voice was not loud and assertive but soft, sometimes almost inaudible. He hated country pursuits and, when compelled to stay with his wife's family at their Palladian mansion in Staffordshire, preferred to sit in an armchair reading rather than going shooting or riding to hounds.

He went to gentlemen's clubs but was not 'clubbable'. He no longer drank, and he breathed the atmosphere of cigar smoke, brandy and leather armchairs out of duty rather than pleasure. He preferred the company of clever women to pompous men. His experience of running female agents in occupied Europe in the war could be said to have turned him into a quasi-feminist, convinced that women were just as quick, resourceful and physically and mentally courageous as males. The one person he was truly himself with was Diana, who came equipped with all that he admired in a woman: intelligence, energy and good looks. Their marriage was a partnership and his story is to a considerable extent also hers.

The circumstances of his death gave a military quality to his funeral. It took place eight days after the explosion, in the church of St Mary at Longworth, near the Neaves' home in Hinton Waldrist. Margaret and Denis Thatcher led the mourners, hemmed in by a phalanx of armed police. The narrow nave and old oak pews were far too small for the hundreds who had turned up, and the service had to be relayed by loudspeaker to the crowd outside. Standing among the gravestones in the April sunshine, they heard the rector, Jim Smith, praise a 'supremely loyal subject of the Queen, a true patriot, and a good citizen of the world'.[6]

Given Neave's prominence and the shocking way in which he had been killed, interest in the story faded remarkably quickly. The election campaign, followed by Margaret Thatcher's victory, dominated the media agenda. Coverage of the hunt for his killers soon moved to the inside pages and then disappeared. There was nothing much to report. A number of suspects were rounded up, only to be released. Photofit images of possible perpetrators appeared in the press, but the faces they showed could have fitted half the young males in the British Isles. Over the years, there were a few minor flurries of excitement when arrests seemed to promise a possible prosecution. They came to nothing and, eight years after the killing, a Home Office minister told the House of Commons, 'I very much regret to say that nobody has been charged in connection with the murder and it would be misleading for me to say that I have any information to suggest that a charge is likely to be made in the immediate or near future.'[7]

Nothing more was revealed by the authorities about who killed Airey Neave or how they did it. Despite an official policy of peace and reconciliation, the relevant Home Office and Metropolitan Police files remain closed, and all my attempts to gain access to them through the Freedom of Information Act were refused on, among other grounds, those of 'national security'.

However, using private and unofficial sources I have been able to put together a picture of the circumstances behind the plot as well as learning the identities of two of those suspected of close involvement in its execution. By a curious coincidence, one of them had, like the victim, pulled off a daring and minutely planned escape from captivity, tunnelling out of the Maze prison near Belfast.

The publicity generated by the book has placed his name in the public domain, as well as helping to prompt a police decision, forty years after the event, to reopen the murder investigation. So it may just be that after all this time, the many unanswered questions about the event will be answered and peace will finally settle on Airey Neave's unquiet grave.

The mystery around Airey Neave's death is perhaps in keeping with the air of secrecy that attached to him in life and would continue to hang around for decades after he departed it. Forty years on, it is time he stepped out of the penumbra and into the light.

I

A Question of Upbringing

British boys at school in the 1920s grew up in the shadow of death. This is not a metaphor but a fact. During the decade, memorials went up at every school, ancient or modern, bearing the details of former pupils who had gone off to the Great War and not come back. Eton already had a major memorial, built to honour the fallen of the 'Second Boer War' of 1899–1902. It was on a grand scale and included a library and an assembly hall. One hundred and twenty-nine names were listed on stone tablets. When the time came to consider another memorial, the scale of the loss was very different.

Between 1914 and 1918, the trenches of the Western Front, the grey wastes of the North Sea, the heights of Gallipoli and the baked earth of Palestine and Mesopotamia swallowed 1,157 Old Etonians. Various grand schemes were examined, including a tower in the style of the era of the school's founder, Henry VI. In the end, the enormity of the loss defeated imagination. The death toll amounted to more than the number of boys at the school when war broke out (in 1914 there were 1,028 pupils). The authorities settled on a frieze of plain bronze plaques listing name, rank and date of departure. It runs the entire length of the cloisters along the western wall of School Yard.

When Airey Neave arrived at Eton in 1929 the bronze tablets were still shiny. In addition, grieving parents had commissioned their own small plaques commemorating their lost sons. So it was that Neave and his classmates passed their days moving between house, classroom, library and refectory, constantly overlooked by reminders of war and death, sacrifice and duty.

In the first years of his school career, this burden of expectation seems to have weighed lightly, if at all, on his concerns. We can glimpse his thoughts in a surviving diary from 1931, when he was fifteen. The pages are full of the routine preoccupations of a boy of his class and time, with little that hints of the extraordinary life to come. The overall tone is assured, befitting his membership of an elite which had, until recently, taken its continued power, status and prosperity for granted. Both his father and grandfather had been at Eton before him. Among his forebears were two governors of the Bank of England and a number of high-ranking soldiers. His father was descended from a baronet.

The Neaves, and the women they married, seemed the warp and weft of the British Establishment, comfortably off, confident and used to exercising authority and receiving automatic respect. However, they also had an inquiring streak, lively minds and a history of striking out down unconventional paths. One female ancestor, Caroline Neave (1781–1863), was a philanthropist and prison reformer. His grandfather, Sheffield Henry Morier Neave (1853–1936), inherited a fortune while at Eton, and after Balliol College, Oxford, seemed set on a life of pleasure. A trip to Africa in pursuit of big game brought about a conversion to seriousness. He became interested in the eradication of the tsetse fly, which carried sleeping sickness and malaria. In middle age, he trained as a doctor and he ended up Physician of the Queen's Hospital for Children in the East End of London.

His interests were inherited by his son, Sheffield Airey Neave, born in 1879. After Eton, he went to Magdalen College, Oxford, to read natural sciences. His speciality was entomology, the study of insects, the importance of which to public health and agriculture in the British Empire was starting to be appreciated.[1] In the early years of the century, he worked for the Colonial Office on scientific surveys in Northern Rhodesia and served as an entomologist on a commission investigating sleeping sickness in the Congolese province of Katanga. In 1913, he was appointed assistant director of the Imperial Institute of Entomology, and stayed in the post for thirty years before taking over as director.

Sheffield married Dorothy Middleton, a colonel's daughter, and on 23 January 1916, at 24 De Vere Gardens, a tall London brick house in Knightsbridge, she gave birth to a son. In keeping with Neave tradition, he was christened with a basket of surnames plucked from the family tree. In his youth, Airey Middleton Sheffield Neave hated the handle he had been lumbered with. For a period in the Second World War, he took to referring to himself as 'Tony'. But the name on the birth certificate stuck, and with it all the jokey and embarrassing permutations that schoolboy and service wit could devise.

Shortly after the birth, the family moved to Beaconsfield in Buckinghamshire. Their new home, Bishop's House, was large and comfortable, with steep-pitched red-tile roofs and mullioned windows, surrounded by lawns and flower beds, and only a short walk from the station, where there were regular services to Sheffield's work in London. Airey went to the local Montessori school, an enlightened choice at a time when the Italian educationalist's ideas were just taking hold in Britain. Then, aged nine, he was sent away to St Ronan's, an academically inclined prep school on the coast at Worthing, before arriving at Eton in the spring of 1929.

The school was undergoing the same painful transformation as the rest of the country as it adjusted to the post-war world. However, the curriculum would have been familiar to a boy from the previous century. Classics still ruled and an extraordinary amount of the boys' time was spent construing Greek and Latin poetry and prose. Games were exalted and the stars of the river and cricket pitch were gilded demigods. Outside the classroom and the playing field, though, the atmosphere was stimulating, and independent thought was encouraged under the leadership of the lively and well-connected headmaster, Dr Cyril Alington, who as well as hymns wrote detective novels.

Neave had just turned fifteen when the surviving pages of his diary open. He comes across as earnest and hard-working, recording in detail all the homework he is set and the marks he receives. Mostly he was in the top half of the class, but his efforts seem to have been conscientious rather than inspired. It was the same story at games. He spent the afternoons kicking and knocking balls around, panting along muddy paths on cross-country runs or heaving an oar on the river.

All this effort brought little reward, not even the ephemeral pleasure of 'a ribboned coat' or 'a season's fame'. In one cricket match, he struggled for seventy-five minutes to make nine runs. Though fairly robust, he seems to have been ill frequently. He suffered from a skin complaint and some other unspecified ailment which required regular physiotherapy sessions with a nurse called Miss Dempster, who 'weighed and measured me and made various uncomplimentary remarks about the shape of my figure'.[2]

He showed an early interest in soldiering and joined the Eton army cadet corps, but found the drill a challenge. 'I am rather vague about bayonets still,'[3] he recorded a few months after joining up. Then, a day later, 'We learned field signals etc of which I understood little.'[4] Thus, an early pattern was established. Young Airey's zeal was not matched by natural aptitude, and much as he would have liked to, he did not cut a very convincing martial figure. He left school with the rank of lance corporal.

Eton encouraged a strong interaction with the world outside its walls, hosting a stream of distinguished visitors who came to address the boys. Many were former pupils. Others, such as Mohandas Gandhi, were internationally famous. By the time he visited in October 1931, he was well embarked on his campaign to liberate India from British rule. The invitation had come from the Political Society run by the boys, an initiative of Jo Grimond, who went on to lead the Liberal Party.* He wrote that when the school authorities learned of it, they were 'vexed … However, they soon recovered their poise and fended off the indignant letters fired by

---

* Joseph Grimond (1913–93), educated Eton and Balliol College, Oxford; Liberal MP for Orkney and Shetland, 1950–83; leader of the Liberal Party, 1956–67; created Lord Grimond, 1983.

blimpish Old Etonians.' Gandhi, who wore his familiar loincloth as protection against the dank October Thames Valley weather, was 'only a modified success. Mr Gandhi was long-winded and shuffled round all direct questions. He did not impress the boys.'[5] Airey Neave noted in his diary that the Mahatma rose from his bed in the headmaster's house long before dawn and 'prayed from 4–5 a.m. in the garden'.[6]

That is as far as the entry goes. Politics barely get a mention in the diary at this stage. There is a reference to the political crisis of August 1931. It resulted in a new National Government, headed by Ramsay MacDonald, which saw taxes rise. As far as Neave was concerned, the main consequence was the economies that resulted at Bishop's House. 'The new budget has made Daddy sack John,' he wrote, a reference to the gardener Airey sometimes helped with his chores, washing the car and rolling the lawn.[7] It is an interesting choice of words. The suggestion is that it is the Prime Minister's fault that John has lost his job, rather than a failure on his father's part to make the economies necessary to keep the gardener on.

The only hint of interest in another realm that would later absorb so much of his energy comes when he mentions borrowing a book called *Twenty-Five Years in the Secret Service* from the college library. The author was Henri Le Caron, the pseudonym of Thomas Miller Beach, born in Colchester in 1841, who as a young man emigrated first to Paris and then the United States. The story he told combined two themes that would come to play a large part in the destiny of Airey Neave. One was the secret intelligence world. The other was violent Irish Republicanism. While living in Illinois, Beach saw the first stirrings of the Fenian movement. In 1866, the Brotherhood launched raids across the nearby border of Canada, the closest piece of British territory within reach. The rebels, some of them veterans of the Civil War, carried a banner declaring themselves to be the 'Irish Republican Army'. They were easily defeated but the episode set in train the long campaign against British rule at home and abroad that continued with only temporary interruptions until the signing of the Good Friday Agreement in 1998.

Beach wrote about these events in letters home. His father notified his MP, who contacted the authorities. When Beach returned to England on a visit in 1867, he received 'an official communication requesting me to attend at 50 Harley Street'. There it was agreed that 'I should become a paid agent of the Government, and that on my return to the United States I should ally myself to the Fenian organisation, in order to play the role of spy in the rebel ranks.'[8]

According to his account, Beach wormed his way into the heart of the movement, rising to the post of Inspector General of the Fenian Brotherhood. He sent back a stream of reports on funding, operations and political lobbying – then, as later, a source of alarm to the British government. Beach's view of the Irish rebels was very English, a mixture of alarm and amused condescension. 'What a sight!' he wrote, describing a whiskey-fuelled gathering in Chicago in 1881. 'What a babel of voices and a world of smoke … as for hearing, your ears are deafened by the din and clatter of many tongues and stamping feet [assembled] to clamour for dynamite as the only means of achieving their patriotic ends.'[9] Yet the rhetoric, he told his readers, was not to be taken entirely seriously: 'Always you must remember that you are dealing with Irishmen, who in their wildest and most ferocious of fights still retain [a] substratum of childishness of character and playfulness of mood, with its attendant elements of exaggeration and romance.'[10]

Neave did not record his reaction to Beach's book. He was, though, greatly impressed by *Within Four Walls*, published in 1930, a personal account of the exploits of Colonel Henry Antrobus Cartwright, who had been captured by the Germans in the 1914–18 war and succeeded in escaping at his fifth attempt. 'I greatly respected him,' he wrote. 'His book was a classic … As a small boy, I had read it with romantic pleasure, and it played a great part in forming my philosophy of escape.'[11]

Judged by the 1931 diary, Neave at fifteen was an unremarkable boy, an adolescent apparently free of angst. He seems cool and disengaged. There are no close friendships in evidence, no extracurricular enthusiasms except for an interest in collecting old books ('I went to Mrs Browns and bought a very nice prayer book, 1811, with good plates for 4s 6d. I think it was worth it.')[12] When the odd emphatic remark does pop up, it is often about school meals. He enjoyed his food and noted the menus with as much detail as his performance in class. The fare was not to his liking. 'Lunch at 1.30,' he wrote on 6 July, 'veal and ham pie and jam sponge and custard. Awful.' On 26 September, they were offered 'for boys' dinner the usual type of cat's meat'. In this respect, school was a preparation for the prison-camp privations that would follow.

Neave's education also provided another lesson in how to cope with incarceration. The boys had a complicated relationship with authority. From the outside, the regime seemed strictly hierarchical, with the masters and seniors giving orders which those under them obeyed or suffered the consequences. The reality was more subtle and interesting. Neave's eagerness to do well did not preclude a bolshie streak. By now, he was well used to English institutional life and aware of its absurdities and injustices. Like his peers, he enjoyed finding ways to get round irritating restrictions. He also liked to challenge authority when the chance arose and the odds of getting away with it were favourable. It was good for morale, a reminder that those who ruled the school did not have it all their own way.

There are frequent references in the diary to 'mobbing': semi-spontaneous outbreaks of high jinks which could erupt at mealtimes and even in chapel. 'After tea there was a great mob which m'tutor came up and stopped,' he wrote on 26 September. 'M'tutor' was his housemaster, John Foster Crace, a classicist who had been at the school since 1901 and had married late and recently become father to a girl. Then, a few hours later, 'the captain of house got mobbed at supper.' According to Neave, when Crace appeared to break it up again the boys ran off, but after prayers the housemaster's tone was almost apologetic, telling them, '"I lose my temper sometimes [titters] but I am not really so bad as you may think" [laughter]. He did not see anything wrong with the mobs but they were rather near his family.' Crace's cautious reaction to the shenanigans was perhaps a recognition of the truth that, as in prisons, without recourse to brute force, order in school essentially depended on the consent of the inmates. Imposing authority was a tricky business. The boys could spot – and instantly exploit – any perceived chink in the armour. When the class was assigned a new master called Mr Kitchen Smith, Neave's first impression was that he was 'quite nice but rather weak'.[13] This assessment must have been shared by the others, because when asked, they assured the teacher that they had no outstanding homework to do. It was a fib that was soon discovered, but it had been worth a try.

It is an insignificant episode in itself, yet indicative of the spirit that prevailed among a section of the British prisoners held in German camps in the war to come. The camp guards were uniformed versions of the beaks and prefects they had known at school, and their instinct was to defy them, test them, rag them and keep them off balance whenever possible.

Neave's school and home life meshed easily. Beaconsfield was only eleven miles from Eton and his mother often visited him at weekends, turning up to chapel or dropping off treats such as baskets of eggs. Neave seems to have been close to her, and sympathetic to her frequent indispositions, when she would retreat to bed with unexplained illnesses. Family lore represents Sheffield Neave as a Victorian father, large and imposing, but absorbed in his work, neglectful of his wife and distant towards his children. By the summer of 1931 there were four of them. After Airey came Iris Averil, 13, Rosamund, 10, Viola, 6, and a brother, Digby, 3. According to Airey's eldest child, Marigold, 'He didn't have a great relationship with his father … He was not a very warm man, I think. This was his problem. He was quite difficult to warm to, quite frightening to look at – he had rather prominent, stern features.'[14] As for the other children, 'They were all girls except for little Digby, who was so little no one hardly bothered with him. And the girls were just considered as girls, and in those days that's all they were. Nobody paid any attention to them. They were not very important. It was rather a dysfunctional family I always felt.'

Neave's diary presents a warmer picture of Sheffield. On 11 July, they went to the Eton–Harrow cricket match together, which Eton won handsomely by an innings and 16 runs. 'After breakfast

Mummy took some photographs of Dad and I. We went by the 10.00 to Paddington and then took the underground to St John's Wood. We got to Lord's about 11.10, when play had just started. We had quite good seats in Stand G. Harrow were all out for 230 by about 12.45 and by the lunch interval were 59 for 0 [having been forced to follow on]. We went to a tent at the back of the grandstand for lunch ... Sandwiches, cider cup, strawberries and cream, cake and iced coffee ... After lunch we walked about and watched the match. We met on the field a friend of Daddy's ...'

In the summer holidays that followed, father and son pursued a Betjemanesque routine, playing golf and tennis together, making family visits to friends and relations in their Home Counties residences. One day, Sheffield took him off to Woodwalton Fen in Cambridgeshire, to check on the progress of a population of rare Large Copper butterflies that had been introduced a few years before. The diary entries are light and natural, with no hint of tensions or conflict. They contrast with the references to childhood that appear in the diaries Neave kept towards the end of his life, which do not suggest cloudless happiness or any great affection for the patriarchs of the family. His paternal grandfather was 'a selfish shit'.[15] As for the rest, 'they were a sad quarrelsome family. No one was happy. I suffered from them in my time.'[16]

Beyond the security and comfort of Eton and Bishop's House, the world was swept by confusion and conflict. The early 1930s were a tumultuous time at home and abroad. Britain was sunk in an economic depression that brought misery and despair, not just to the industrial North but to the mellow towns and villages of the Home Counties. In Europe, it was clear that the recent war had settled nothing and old hatreds burned as fiercely as ever. Late in 1932, a speech by Stanley Baldwin raised the spectre of a new war in which 'the bomber will always get through.'

It was in this baleful atmosphere that Airey Neave made his first visit to Germany, in 1933, at the age of seventeen. The trip would be a turning point, jolting him into political awareness and fixing him on a moral bearing that he would follow for the rest of his life.

Later, he would refer to the experience often, presenting it as an awakening: to the dangers of totalitarianism and the fragility of civilisation.

His parents had decided he would benefit from a spell in Berlin to improve his grasp of German.[17] Eton, like most British schools, took an academic rather than a practical approach to language teaching, with the result that, according to Jo Grimond, 'no boy who had spent hundreds of hours ... of classes could carry on the simplest conversation in French.'[18] He arrived in late summer to lodge with a family who lived at Nikolassee, a lakeside suburb west of Berlin. Hitler had been appointed Chancellor on 30 January that year and the Nazis were tightening their grip on German society.

Neave attended classes at the local school with one of the sons, who was a member of the Hitler Youth. 'At the entry of the teacher each morning we were expected to give the Hitler salute, but as a foreigner I was excused,' he remembered many years later. 'I was an unconventional pupil and at first an object of derision. I sat at the back of the class. My hair was much longer than that of the German boys and I wore a decadent yellow tie with black spots.'[19]

Neave soon learned that it did not do to mock Germany's new masters. Dietrich, the elder son of the family, who was at university in Berlin, was not a party member and admired the young guest's independent spirit but warned him that it could be dangerous. One day, waiting for the train at Nikolassee, Neave sniggered at the sight of a 'fat, brown-booted storm-trooper'. He recalled that Dietrich 'hastily manoeuvred me out of sight. I can remember the bloodshot pig-eyes of the storm-trooper glaring towards us.'[20]

The climax of the visit came when Neave went with Dietrich to a rally one warm evening in the first week of September in the centre of Berlin. Neave had signed up as a temporary member of a sports club in Charlottenburg to which Dietrich belonged, and although no great athlete, he was good enough to get into the relay team. When the Nazis announced a Festival of Sport in the capital, the club was advised to take part. It began with a classic piece of totalitarian theatre. At ten o'clock a vast procession of sports organisations set off from the Lustgarten, in the centre of the city, and marched to a rally near the Brandenburg Gate. These were the early days of Nazism and, although the signs of repression were everywhere, in Berlin there were still many who did not disguise their scepticism. Among some of the athletes, participation in the festival was 'seen as something of a joke'.

The sportsmen wore civilian suits and 'marched off with light hearts'. However, when they were joined by a band in Nazi uniform, 'our mood changed. I felt as if I was being drawn into a vortex. The young men beside me who, minutes before, had been joking, started singing. Suddenly the Festival of Sport had become religious and the marchers expectant.' His friend was as susceptible to the mood as everybody else, because when Airey broke step with the others, 'There was an angry shout from Dietrich, "Can't you march in step?"'[21]

With bands blaring and banners flying, they tramped past the Brandenburg Gate, which 'floodlit, and adorned with Nazi pennants ... looked like the gateway to some theatrical Valhalla.' The left- and right-hand marcher in each rank held a flaming torch. In the flickering light, the faces of the silent crowds lining the streets 'glowed ... with excitement and pride'. As they neared the rostrum where the speeches would begin, the band struck up the 'Horst Wessel Lied'. To Neave, the half-hour speech that followed from Reichssportführer von Tschammer was tedious. But then he looked round at his companions. 'They were intellectuals, university students, writers and artists. To my amazement, they were listening to this bull-necked Prussian in his brown uniform with fixed attention.' When von Tschammer at last stopped speaking, 'the huge crowd sang "Deutschland, Deutschland Über Alles" as the banners swayed in the breeze. The fervour of the women was breathtaking.'[22]

This was an extraordinary experience for a seventeen-year-old boy raised in a code of understatement and emotional restraint. The account he left of it was written in 1978 – that is, forty-five years after the event. Time and hindsight surely led Neave to lend a certain sophistication to the thoughts and reactions of his teenage self. Yet there is no doubt that exposure to the sights and sounds and passions of Nazism touched him and filled him with foreboding. It had given him an insight into the nature of Hitler's rule that turned out to be more astute than that of many of his elders, who still regarded Hitler as a temporary phenomenon, or as someone who was subject to the normal laws of diplomacy and power politics.

Neave returned to Eton with a new maturity. He was convinced that war with Germany was inevitable. According to some accounts, he won a prize for an essay warning of the danger posed to peace by the rise of Hitler, but no trace of it remains in the school archives.[23] His new interest in Germany was demonstrated in a paper he delivered to the Essay Society in 1933 on Walter Rathenau, the German liberal statesman murdered by ultra-nationalists eleven years before.

In the summer of 1934, he wrote an essay called 'The case against pacifism', in which he took a fatalistic view of Europe's future and lamented the 'illogical theories of selfish, muddle-headed … people who are trying to alter the vices of civilisation by talking about them and doing nothing'.[24] The 'horrible fact' was 'that man is still a very quarrelsome animal.' The tendency was currently on display in Germany, where 'nationalism … is both inevitable and dangerous because it always foments and bursts out when a nation is aggrieved and oppressed.' It was 'very unfortunate that a nation should be in such a condition but that is all the more reason for strengthening our defences by land, air and sea.'

Neave believed that war was 'regrettable but inevitable' and that the pacifist mood then current would evaporate when the first bombs dropped. 'No one really doubts that the Oxford Union [which the year before had voted 'in no circumstances to fight for its King and Country'] would go with the others when the time came.' While he believed that 'there are few people in this country who would not fight for England … I hope there are none who will fight for France.' Six years later he would do just that.

The essay appeared in a magazine called *Sixpenny: Stories and Poems by Etonians*. It had been started by Robin Maugham, nephew of the famous author, Somerset, and by the second issue Neave's initials appear as a co-editor. The two had similar backgrounds. Maugham came from an Establishment family and his father was a high court judge. Their temperaments and their school careers, though, were quite different. Maugham's autobiography reveals another side of Eton whose existence could never be guessed from Neave's diary. Maugham was bisexual and had a long liaison with a precocious boy he calls 'Drew'. Bullying, sexual predation and misery feature strongly in this account. At the same time, he acknowledges his debt to some inspirational teachers and concludes that much of his unhappiness was due to the house he had been assigned to.

Which house you belonged to was important, indeed crucial, to the experience of Eton. It was where you slept and ate, and the teacher in charge of it disciplined you, directed your education and acted in loco parentis. In Maugham's mind, Neave's house, presided over by John Foster Crace, was a haven of civilisation. It was only in upper school that boys could visit houses other than their own. Maugham was introduced to Crace's by Michael Isaacs, whose family were friends of his parents. Isaacs was Jewish, the son of the Marquess of Reading. He became Neave's lifelong friend. Maugham wrote glowingly of the coterie that he soon joined: 'Marcus Rueff, Patrick Gibson, Ben Astley, David Parsons, and Airey Neave. They talked about Suetonius and Mozart, Michael Arlen and Adler, and though they were all good at games they never discussed them.' He concluded wistfully, 'I am certain that if I had been in Mr Crace's house I would not have been persecuted. On the contrary, I would have enjoyed each term and my outlook would have been wider.'[25]

They were indeed a colourful and adventurous crew. Rueff was a talented musician who, while serving in the Rifles, was mortally wounded in a German ambush at Derna in Libya in April 1941. Patrick Gibson was captured in the same action, then later escaped, walking five hundred miles over the Apennines and crossing German lines to rejoin the Allies. He went on to serve in the Special Operations Executive, waging war in occupied territory. David Parsons would become better known as the actor David Tree, the handsome lead in thirteen British films. He lost a hand in a training accident and also joined SOE.[26]

Politically, Maugham and Neave took different paths. Maugham reacted to the rise of Fascism by becoming a socialist. When war came, he declined a commission in the Hussars and joined up as a trooper in an armoured regiment, serving in the Western Desert. What they shared was bravery, patriotism and a sense of duty. Maugham was credited with risking his life repeatedly to pull as many as forty men from stricken tanks. They also shared an association with the world of intelligence and espionage. After being rendered unfit for active service by a severe head wound sustained in the summer of 1942, Maugham became an intelligence officer and went on to play an important part in founding the Middle East Centre for Arab Studies, initially based in Jerusalem, a training centre for British spies and diplomats. After the war, he became a successful writer, best known for his novella *The Servant*, which was made into a film starring Dirk Bogarde and James Fox, with a screenplay by Harold Pinter. He struggled with a drink problem and his sexuality. Despite their contrasting outlooks and personalities, Neave and Maugham remained in touch and Robin stood as godfather to Airey's youngest boy, William.

Neave left school in the summer of 1934, bound for Oxford, twenty miles further up the Thames, where he had a place at Merton to read jurisprudence. His schooldays had seen only modest success. In the words of Michael Isaacs, 'I cannot say that Airey stood out among his contemporaries as likely to make any considerable impact upon public life. He was an agreeable and amusing companion, diligent in his work and quite tough physically.'[27] Eton may have provided little in the way of practical learning. It did, however, inculcate a certain way of looking at and dealing with the world, summed up by Jo Grimond, who had left a few years previously: 'Boys were taught that what they did there mattered. They were taught that responsibility rested with them and could not be sloughed off. They were taught to behave as members of a community and to have regard to the wider communities of their country and their fellow men.'[28]

Oxford was tinged with the same hostility to militarism and dread of another conflict that coloured the country at large. Among undergraduates, socialist and pacifist sympathies were unremarkable, even conventional. Neave remained impervious to the prevailing climate. The great RAF war hero and philanthropist Leonard Cheshire, who arrived at Merton two years after Airey, later claimed that, on arriving at Oxford, Airey had 'bought and read the full works of Clausewitz, and when being asked why, answered that since war was coming it was only sensible to learn as much as possible about the art of waging it.'[29]

This seriousness sat alongside a determination to have fun. As the constraints of school and home fell away, Neave threw himself into what Oxford offered in the way of hedonism, drinking, dining and making friends, while not paying overmuch attention to his law studies. 'I did little academic work for three years and then was obliged to work feverishly at the law in order to get a degree,' he recalled fifteen years after his departure.[30]

With Isaacs, he revived a defunct political dining club, The Chatham, but it foundered after a few meetings. More durable were the Myrmidons, a Merton institution to which he was elected in the summer of 1935. The club was self-consciously exclusive, named after a warlike classical tribe, and entry was by invitation only. Its members dressed up in tailcoats with purple gold and silver facings and sat down to dinners at which the drink was more important than the food. Former members included Lord Randolph Churchill and Max Beerbohm. Compared to his Eton contemporaries, the Myrmidons of 1935 appear rather undistinguished, and none apart from Neave seems to have made a mark in later life. Their antics were an affront to the prevailing egalitarian mood. The group photographs taken before the dinners show them standing defiantly in Edwardian rig, as if daring the world to challenge them. For all their studied outrageousness, it was hardly Sodom and Gomorrah.

The club's antics were part of a pattern of indulgence. Like 'many of the upper class', they 'liked the sound of broken glass'. Neave recalled a 'champagne party on top of my College tower when empty bottles came raining down to the grave peril of those below'.[31]

In his recollection, the authorities showed 'great forbearance and even kindliness' to this behaviour. The college archives, however, tell a different story. An entry in the Warden and Tutors Minute Book for 11 March 1936 records that Neave was one of a group of seven undergraduates gated for four weeks and fined three pounds each for 'disorderly and scandalous conduct on the chapel tower, in that some bottles were ... thrown from the tower by some members of the party'.[32]

On another occasion, he was fined for hosting a 'noisy lunch party'. Leonard Cheshire, whose own university career was boisterous, remarked that Airey 'would often do things that looked a little wild', though 'always in a rather nice way and never unkindly'. While this was a trait that 'undoubtedly endeared him to his school and university friends it possibly had a different effect on his father who one has the impression did not always give him the encouragement which inwardly he needed.'[33]

It seems that as time passed, the companionship of the early years had faded, and father and son drifted apart. Sheffield Neave had almost no role in his grandchildren's upbringing. Cheshire believed that his father's disapproval profoundly affected Neave's formation and that 'at an early age he learned to conceal his inner disappointments.'

Neave stayed in touch with Cheshire throughout the rest of his life. In the post-war years, he and Diana were friends with Cheshire and his second wife, Sue Ryder, and supported their charities. This insight from a sensitive and spiritual man is important. Despite his privileges and abilities, there would be many disappointments in Neave's life, and his way of dealing with them is essential to an understanding of his character.

But undergraduate life also brought satisfactions. His artistic streak found an outlet in the Merton Floats, the college drama group. In 1936, he served as secretary as well as acting the part of Smitty in a one-act play by Eugene O'Neill, *In the Zone*, and Pope Julius II in Max Beerbohm's *'Savonarola' Brown*.[34] A vague sense of duty and seriousness stirred from time to time and he joined the Oxford Union. In his third year, he shared digs with Michael Isaacs and they went to debates together. According to Isaacs, they 'occasionally made vocal contributions, none of which ... had any marked impact upon the proceedings.'[35] Neave remembered making three speeches at the Union, one of which was an inconsequential discussion of the merits of a motion debated the week before.[36]

The Union was a less impressive forum than its members liked to imagine. The tone was facetious and it was to some extent an arena for showing off. Nonetheless, it was a testing ground for young men, and later women, with political ambitions. In Neave's time at Oxford, two men who loomed large in his later life, Edward Heath* and Hugh Fraser,† held the presidency. Margaret Thatcher joined when at Somerville less than a decade later, but as a woman could not seek office. Neave's interest was casual, and raucous attendance at a debate seems to have been as much for entertainment as enlightenment. If he felt any political ambitions stirring at this time, they were not strong enough to propel him into the rough and tumble of Oxford politics.

In his later writings, Neave portrayed himself and his companions as odd fish, swimming against a tide of *bien pensant* leftism and pacifism. 'My failure to understand the merits of the fashionable intellectual notions of Socialism was regarded as a sign of mental deficiency by the dons,' he wrote. The mood of the times was defensive and self-deluding, for 'This was an Oxford where a few brave spirits still tried to emulate the joyful irresponsibility of the 'twenties. In the 'thirties the shadows lengthened and the voice of Adolf Hitler threatened across the waters but it had little effect upon my undergraduate world.'[37]

This outlook was seized on by the Nazis as evidence of terminal decadence among the youth of Britain, who would have no

---

* Edward Heath (1916–2005), educated Chatham House School and Balliol College, Oxford; Conservative MP for Old Bexley and Sidcup, 1950–83; Leader of the Conservative Party, 1965–75; Prime Minister, June 1970–March 1974.

† Hugh Fraser (1918–84), educated Ampleforth and Balliol College, Oxford; Conservative MP for Stafford and Stone, 1945–84.

stomach for another big war. It was, of course, a great mistake. Leonard Cheshire, who despite spending the summer of 1936 in Potsdam living with a militaristic family – an experience he thoroughly enjoyed – took virtually no interest in politics. 'I don't remember anything about Oswald Mosley and the Blackshirts,' he told his biographer Andrew Boyle after the war. 'I'm sure politics meant nothing.'[38] Yet this seemingly flippant, pleasure-seeking man about town joined the University Air Squadron as the landscape darkened, and went on to be one of the great figures of the British war.

After Neave went down, the young men and women he encountered in London were not very different: 'Few cared about Hitler and even less about his ambassador von Ribbentrop. Debutantes "came out" and went their way. It was fashionable to be almost inarticulate on any serious subject.'[39] Neave enjoyed the defiant sybaritism as much as anyone, but in one respect he was stubbornly himself. At the start of his second year he joined the Territorial Army. In everyone else's view, it was an eccentric thing to do: 'a sort of archaic sport as ineffective as a game of croquet on a vicarage lawn and far more tiresome'.[40] In December 1935, the *London Gazette* announced his elevation from 'Cadet Lance-Corporal, Eton College Contingent, Junior Division OTC' to second lieutenant in the Oxfordshire and Buckinghamshire Light Infantry. Neave wrote about his pre-war Territorial experiences in a tone of light satire over which an element of the ludicrous hovers. He described a large-scale exercise played out on the Wiltshire downs one summer: 'The sun beat down upon my Platoon as we hid from the enemy behind the chalk hills and listened expectantly for the sound of blank cartridges. I lay on my back beside a wooden Lewis gun. God was in his heaven and the crickets chatted merrily in the dry grass.'[41]

The entomologist's son picked out a 'Small Copper, a Fritillary and even a Clouded Yellow'. The idyll was shattered by the arrival of a First World War vintage brigadier with eyeglasses that glinted menacingly and a bullying manner, who was refereeing the war games. 'He began to speak, working himself slowly into a cold, terrifying anger at the conduct of my platoon. A position had been chosen that could be seen for miles around. He had seen the men in the chalk-pit with his own eyes from his imaginary headquarters ... He declared that he had never seen such ridiculous positions. As for my platoon sergeant in the chalk-pit, his left flank was entirely unprotected ...' Neave got to his feet. 'There was an imaginary platoon on his left flank, sir,' he said boldly. Even in the emptiness of Salisbury Plain, he claimed, 'you could have heard a pin drop. My Colonel, white in the face, stared at the ground. The Brigadier gulped.' The brass hat tried to bluster, 'but the spell was broken. Congratulations rained on me in the Mess and the old songs were sung far into the night.' Neave had triumphed with a classic bit of Eton cheek. It was immensely satisfying, but hardly a preparation for war.

He left Oxford in the summer of 1937 with a 'gentleman's degree' (third class), a result that can have done little for his relationship with his father. In London he joined an old-fashioned firm of City solicitors, where he dressed in bowler hat and dark suit and learned his trade processing the legal leftovers. He was set on being a barrister and obtained a pupillage at chambers in Farrar's Building in the Temple. By then his pessimism about the future of Europe was proving all too justified. On 12 March 1938, Hitler ordered the German army into Austria and the following day the country was declared part of the German Reich. Shortly afterwards, Neave transferred out of his Territorial regiment, the Ox and Bucks Light Infantry, and into the 22nd (Essex) Anti-Aircraft Battalion, a unit of the Royal Engineers. The move was presumably because its proximity to London would make it easier to meet his military commitments. At the same time, his interest in politics was growing. He joined the Castlereagh, a dining club which met in St James's about once a fortnight while the House was sitting, to hear the candid and off-the-record views of a Tory politician. Michael Isaacs remembered a dinner in July 1939 when the guest of honour was Anthony Eden, who had resigned as Foreign Secretary the previous year over Prime Minister Chamberlain's handling of relations with Italy. He had since become a major in the Territorials. 'He came on after drilling his [men] and spoke eloquently to us about the grim immediate outlook. We all realised that it was only a question of time …'[42]

2

Blooded

In May 1940, Airey Neave got his first real taste of war. The experience was bitter and depressing. The defence of Calais repeated some familiar tropes of British military history. It showed the country's politicians and generals at their worst and the troops they directed at their stoical best. The four days of fighting affected Neave profoundly. Almost everything he worked at thereafter was in some way shaped by what he saw and felt in the port's burning streets and shell-spattered ramparts.

Neave spent the Phoney War in mundane roles that underlined the truth that, much as he exalted the soldier's calling, a lot of military life was simply tedious. By transferring out of the infantry to a Royal Engineers anti-aircraft unit, he had removed the possibility of commanding front-line troops in battle. In the autumn of 1938, at the time of the Munich crisis, for reasons that are unclear, he switched to the Royal Artillery, and was assigned again to an anti-aircraft unit. Instead of firing guns, they operated searchlights. Their job was to dazzle dive-bombers and low-flying aircraft and to illuminate targets for the ack-ack gunners. It was not for this that he had studied Clausewitz. As he admitted ruefully, it was hardly 'a shining form of warfare'.[1]

The first six months of hostilities were spent in a field in Essex preparing for an invasion that never came. After a training stint in Hereford, he set off in February 1940 to Boulogne to join the British Expeditionary Force (BEF), in charge of an advance party. The searchlight men ranked low in military esteem. A remark by a Guards officer that their equipment was 'quite Christmassy' rankled. Yet although he might have preferred a more dashing outfit, Neave liked his comrades, and his accounts of his service with them are affectionate and respectful. By the time he reached Calais he was a troop commander with the 2nd Searchlight Battery of the 1st Searchlight Regiment (RA), in charge of about eighty men. They included 'a high proportion of older men with First World War experience. Most were industrial workers with a few clerks and professional men … All were vocal and democratic.'[2]

They 'did not see themselves as front-line soldiers', and with good reason. When they arrived in France they were virtually untrained in infantry tactics and were armed with rifles that most of them had never fired. Their other weapons were some old-fashioned Lewis machine guns and a few Bren guns for use against aircraft. As defence against the German armour that spearheaded the Blitzkrieg, they had the Boys anti-tank rifle. It fired slim, .55 calibre rounds at a rate of ten a minute that could penetrate a light tank at 100 yards but were little use against the Panzer IIIs in the divisions bearing down on the BEF. In any case, no one in the unit was qualified to operate it.

Nonetheless, what they lacked in regimental elan 'they made up in willingness to fight'. Again and again in the four days of the siege they showed extraordinary guts. Unlike the previous generation of upper-class British men who had served in the war, Neave and his contemporaries had had few dealings with people outside their social level who were not servants or tradesmen. The army had given him his first intimate exposure to how other Britons thought and behaved. It taught him that patriotism, courage and gallantry were not the preserve of the privileged.

Even after months of anticipation, the end of the Phoney War came as a shock. On 10 May 1940, the German forces that had massed along the borders of the Netherlands, Belgium and Luxembourg plunged west. The main thrust came where the least preparation had been made to meet it – through the Ardennes. In three days, forces spearheaded by the Panzer divisions of Heinz

Guderian cleared the forest and crossed the Meuse. On 13 May, aided by pulverising attacks by the Luftwaffe, they broke the French defences at Sedan. The armoured columns moved at a speed that surprised the Germans themselves, sweeping round behind the Allied armies arrayed around the Belgian border. On 19 May, the three divisions of Guderian's XIX Corps were in Amiens, less than fifty miles from the Channel. The following day they reached Abbeville, at the mouth of the Somme, driving home a wedge that divided the Allied armies in the Pas de Calais and Belgium from the French forces to the south.

Utterly sure of his instincts and confident in his tactics, troops and tanks, Guderian was set on a move that, had it succeeded, might have brought Britain's war to an end. His goal was the Channel ports, and in particular Dunkirk, which, once taken, would leave the BEF stranded and facing annihilation or surrender. Various factors combined to prevent him from maintaining the headlong pace. Not least was the caution of his superiors at Army High Command HQ, shared by Hitler himself, who feared the speed of the advance would expose XIX Corps to a devastating flank attack.

The Germans need not have worried. The Allied commanders were reluctant to credit the strength and extent of the breakthrough. The eventual move to counter it, a Franco-British drive south into the enemy flank around Arras on 21 May, achieved some initial success before being beaten off. However, it was to have important consequences. The action further reduced the appetite for risk in Berlin. Guderian was ordered to halt, dashing his hopes of a lightning victory.

On the day before the Allied counter-attack, the 2nd Searchlight Battery (2nd SL) was in Arras. That morning they received orders to move to Calais, seventy miles to the north-west. As they left, there was little sense of alarm in the British garrison. They drove off down long straight roads past Vimy Ridge and the flat fields that only twenty-two years before had been a vast killing zone. Neave travelled in the front seat of an old khaki-painted Austin Seven alongside his driver, Gunner Cooper. Cooper was large and eager to see action, frustrated at being diverted away from the defence of Arras to what looked like another spell of tedious duty. Neave was inclined to agree. He had heard that there were Germans around but he and his comrades did not believe 'that [they] had broken through ... We were confident that, at most, a few armoured cars, a few motor-cyclists or a few light tanks were threatening the Allied lines of communication.'[3] In fact, the countryside to the east and west was filling up with Panzers.

They spent the night under the plane trees of the market square in the mediaeval town of Ardres, ten miles south of Calais, and arrived the following morning at their destination, a village called Coulogne on the south-eastern approach to the port. Neave set up his HQ in the Mairie. No bombs fell that night and he wrote later that on going to bed he 'refused to believe that our role in Calais would be other than anti-aircraft defence'. But then he was 'twenty-four, unmilitary, with opinions of my own'.

Neave was being a little hard on himself. He had tried his best at soldiering, the theory as well as the practice. His failure to predict what was about to unfold was unsurprising. He and everyone else deployed in the defence of Calais were the victims of the extraordinary complacency of those in overall charge of operations, an attitude that was matched by an incompetence and vacillation that was surprising even to those familiar with the British military's capacity for deadly muddle. Years later, he made a detailed study of the episode using official papers and the accounts of participants. There will always be debate about what effect the siege of Calais had on the shape of the Battle of France. What has never been in doubt is that the direction of the defence from on high was a disgrace.

The German victory in the west has come to seem a preordained inevitability. That was not how it appeared at the time. The forces were evenly balanced. In the all-important realm of armour, the French had better tanks than the Germans and they had more of them. The Germans, though, made the maximum use of their resources. They were better organised and had better communications, exemplified by the radio links between individual tanks and from ground to air which could concentrate forces relatively swiftly to maximum effect. Most of all, they had a winning attitude. They were attuned to victory. Medium-level commanders were encouraged to initiate action without waiting for orders, and their men were eager to fight. These benefits on their own did not ensure success. But luck was on the Germans' side, and their good fortune was compounded by the slow reactions and bad decisions of the Allied command. In Neave's sector of the battle, both were on constant display.

He arrived as the scramble began to prevent catastrophe. Following the capture of Abbeville on the 20th, reinforcements were ordered across the water to the Channel ports. The 20th Guards Brigade was sent to Boulogne. Calais was to be defended by the 30th Infantry Brigade. Firepower against the Panzers would be provided by the 3rd Royal Tank Regiment and a Royal Artillery anti-tank battery (229th). However, there would be no field artillery and the huge demands placed on the RAF meant that air cover was sparse. The meagre existing garrison, which consisted of a platoon of the Argyll and Sutherland Highlanders and some anti-aircraft batteries, was to be boosted by three infantry battalions of the newly formed 30th Infantry Brigade. The force was under the command of Brigadier Claude Nicholson, a thoughtful and determined forty-two-year-old, whose reputation among his peers was high.

This seemed like a healthy addition to the defences. However, as Neave judged in his post-war study, 'Nicholson faced an impossible task ... Many among the 3,000 British troops were untrained for battle. They had neither proper equipment, arms or ammunition ... [he] had no field artillery and very few tanks. His only additional support were 800 French soldiers and sailors and a handful of Dutch and Belgians.'[4] The first infantry battalion to embark was the Queen Victoria's Rifles, a territorial motorcycle combination unit, which arrived with the 3rd RTR and 229 RA Anti-Tank Battery aboard the SS *City of Canterbury* in the early afternoon of 22 May. Confusion and miscalculation meant that the QVR arrived without their machines, transport or three-inch mortars. The two-inch mortars were stowed, but with only smoke bombs for ammunition. Four of the RA battery's anti-tank guns were somehow left behind. Unloading the RTR's forty-eight light and medium tanks was maddeningly slow, and the inefficient way that equipment had been stowed on embarkation meant the fast-moving Cruiser IIIs were the last to come off. The armament – three-pounder cannon and Vickers machine guns – had been packed in mineral jelly, which had to be laboriously cleaned off before a shot could be fired. The other two regular infantry battalions – the 1st Battalion, the Rifle Brigade, and the 2nd Battalion, the King's Royal Rifle Corps (60th Rifles) – arrived the next day. They were highly trained, but the Rifle Brigade had only half its ammunition and transport. Even when allowances were made for the inevitable balls-ups inherent in a last-minute embarkation, it was, as a young tanker officer remarked subsequently to Neave, 'the most extraordinary way to go to war.'[5]

Nicholson was famously unflappable. However, Neave reckoned he 'must have been deeply troubled' by 'a stream of contradictory orders'. In the course of the siege, from across the Channel came instructions to send his tanks first this way, then the other. At various times he was told to prepare to withdraw, then to stand and fight. The desperation of the situation was obvious to London, and Nicholson 'asked repeatedly for artillery, ammunition and food: he had explained his situation and the enemy's.' In addition, he had been 'visited by two generals, an admiral and a naval commodore'.

Neave wondered, 'if they knew that they were so unfairly matched, why did they not send the reinforcements for which Nicholson pleaded?' The answer was that from hour to hour events slipped further and further beyond the Allies' control, so they were constantly reacting to situations that had already changed for the worse. As it finally became clear that the entire BEF was facing a choice between annihilation or evacuation, the fate of the Calais garrison became a secondary consideration. Instead, it was allotted a sacrificial role and the dubious honour of fighting to the death.

The halt order given to Guderian was rescinded late on the night of 21 May. He was to resume his advance on Boulogne and Calais, fifty miles to the north and west. During 22 May, the fresh winds of the storm brewing on the horizon began to be felt by Neave and his battery, ensconced around Coulogne. The village began to fill up with refugees, seeking to escape from a German advance coming from they knew not where.

On that day his chief, Lieutenant Colonel R. M. Goldney, who commanded 1st Searchlight Regiment, moved up from Lille to Ardres to take control of the air defences of Calais. Goldney ordered all searchlight detachments to concentrate on their troop headquarters – the Mairie at Coulogne in the case of Neave's outfit. He would now be in charge of sixty or seventy men, armed with rifles, two Bren guns and one Boys anti-tank rifle, to defend the villages which had become the outer ring of the port's defences. His men got to work digging trenches on the south and south-east approaches to the village and setting up roadblocks.

As the day wore on, the flow of refugees increased. Like many who endured the siege, Neave later came to believe that among them were a number of Fifth Columnists. By now the port was under attack from the Luftwaffe. The troops on the checkpoints blocked the refugees' path to Calais, where bombing had wrecked electricity and water supplies. At the docks, in the lulls between bombardments, they struggled to disembark reinforcements and unload supplies, then fill up the returning ships with casualties and non-fighting servicemen deemed by London to be 'useless mouths' with nothing to contribute to the struggle.

That night, Neave 'lay awake in my bedroom at the Mairie and heard the tramp of their feet as they were turned away to sleep in the fields. The red glow of the fires of Calais, started by the Luftwaffe, shone on the ceiling and there was the sharp crack of the anti-aircraft guns.'[6] At dawn he was woken to deal with an emergency. A column of men, women and children, half a mile long and led by a young priest, was confronting the guards at the checkpoint at the Pont de Coulogne, which crossed the Canal de Calais. He arrived to find the priest trying to persuade the crowd to disperse to the fields, but they were determined to reach the port and a boat to imagined safety, and there were ugly shouts of treachery. They 'seemed about to rush the roadblock,' Neave recalled. 'I drew my .38 Webley revolver of the First World War and asked for silence. "Don't shoot, don't shoot, mon lieutenant," said several anxious voices.' He managed to calm them down and persuade them to turn back to the countryside. It was the first episode in a dramatic day.

Though he did not know it, the Germans were closing in all round. The British garrison in Boulogne, twenty-two miles to the south, was already under siege by Guderian's 2nd Panzer Division. A 1st Panzer Division battle group, under Oberst Walter Krüger, was only eighteen miles away from Calais. For the moment, Guderian was uninterested in Calais and still dead set on gaining Dunkirk. The troops were tired and operating on stretched lines. Their orders were to press forward and secure crossings over the Aa river to the east of Calais. They were to enter the port only if it was thought that it could be taken by surprise and a major battle avoided. That morning Guderian did not have control of the 10th Panzer Division, which had been held in reserve during the Allied counter-attack at Arras. At 10 o'clock it was restored to him. The decision was now taken to move them forward fast. They were given Calais as their next objective.

In the meantime Battle Group Krüger was advancing to the south of Calais, intent on capturing the bridgeheads that would allow Guderian's forces to close on Dunkirk. To do so, they had to get across the Canal de Calais. As they moved forward in the early afternoon of Thursday 23 May, the defenders of Calais and the Germans clashed for the first time. As the Panzers moved between the hamlet of Hames-Boucres and the village of Guînes, they met with 3RTR tanks commanded by Colonel Ronald Keller, who against his better judgement was responding to an order from the BEF HQ to proceed to St-Omer. In the action that followed, up to a dozen British tanks were lost – about a quarter of the total strength.

They were forced to withdraw and the Germans pushed on to Les Attaques on the Canal de Calais, a few miles south of Coulogne. The news of their arrival reached the commander of the 'C' Troop of the 1st Searchlight Battery, 2nd Lieutenant R. J. Barr, whose headquarters were at Ferme Vendroux, just to the north of the German line of march. Barr rounded up fifty men and a lorry and set off across the canal to prevent the Germans crossing at Les Attaques. His force was beefed up by reinforcements from 2nd Searchlight Battery from

Coulogne. Panzers began moving over the canal bridge at 2 p.m., to be met by fire from the Brens, rifles and Boys guns of Barr's improvised force. The hot resistance lasted for three hours, but eventually the defenders were surrounded and forced to surrender.

While this was going on, Krüger's infantry advanced on Orphanage Farm, less than a mile to the north of Coulogne, where the 1st Searchlight Regiment commander, Colonel Goldney, had set up his HQ. Goldney prepared to defend it with the padre, the medical officer and a handful of men, despatching a small force to hold a ridge on the southern approach to the farm against the attackers. When making his dispositions, Neave had posted Bren gunners on the south-eastern side of Coulogne, below the ridge held on the other side by Goldney's advance guard. When the Germans arrived, they opened up on the farm's defenders with 'very heavy rifle and automatic fire'. Sited in the lee of the ridge, Neave's men were unable to see the fray but nonetheless opened up in the direction of the fighting, 'narrowly missing' their comrades.[7] The result was that a despatch rider 'roared over the fields' from Goldney's farmhouse HQ 'with a well-deserved "rocket" from the Colonel and the Brens were moved forward.'

This was not a good start to Neave's fighting career and things were not about to improve. He had stationed himself at a barricade at the entrance to the village, constructed from the local undertaker's hearse and a couple of carts. Refugees were still arriving, pleading to be allowed into Calais, among them a family of Austrian Jews. While he was trying to dissuade them, a mortar bomb crashed into the roof of the Mairie, showering them with broken tiles. It was followed by several others. Above the mayhem, a small Fieseler Storch reconnaissance aircraft droned unconcernedly across the clear blue sky. Neave 'fired at it wildly' but without effect.[8] The barrage lasted a quarter of an hour, tearing up paving stones and starting fires. When it stopped, a young girl lay dead on the roadside. Neave watched a soldier pull her tartan skirt gently over her knees. His despatch rider was dead beside him on the pavement. He 'took his papers and looked down at him. He had been a cheerful man. He still had a smile that even a mortar bomb could not efface.'

Neave's account of these events is emotionally restrained and all the more effective for being so. The spare narrative gives a strong sense of what war is really like. Neave had learned in a few hours that it was formless. It was about confusion, frantic improvisation, sudden eruptions of indiscriminate violence and the body of an innocent girl in a village street. In the late afternoon, the defenders began to fall back against the Panzer onslaught. When tanks came up, the men on the ridge were forced back to Orphanage Farm, which then came under a sustained barrage from the Panzers' recently arrived artillery. At 7 p.m., after five hours of fighting, Goldney abandoned his HQ and ordered everyone to fall back on Calais.

Neave sent his men off by lorry, but for the moment he would not be joining them. He had been given an important task to complete before he could leave Coulogne. Together with a 'Sergeant Maginis' and a sapper equipped with some gun cotton, he was ordered to destroy the 'Cuckoo', the code name for an experimental sound-location device which the Searchlights had brought with them. On no account was it to fall into enemy hands. It was sitting on a trailer in the middle of the village and for five tense minutes the sapper fiddled with the explosive, trying to blow up the apparatus. The situation was resolved when two large French tankers full of aviation spirit came thundering down the road, with German infantry close behind. The drivers abandoned the trucks and gamely set them ablaze. The fire spread to the Cuckoo, which 'providentially' exploded, and Neave and his comrades were able to escape under cover of a thick cloud of black smoke.[9]

For a second time that day, events had not played out in the way Neave would have liked. Who knows what would have happened had the tankers not appeared? Nonetheless, in his post-war account, Neave gave the episode a positive spin. Quoting the 1st Panzer Division war diary, he reports that after the hot reception they received, it was decided that Calais was too strongly defended for them to attempt an improvised attack and they were ordered to push on to Gravelines and Dunkirk, leaving the capture of the port to 10th Panzer Division. From the German point of view, he wrote, 'a great chance was lost. Guderian's First Panzer Division had been hampered on its left flank as it advanced to Dunkirk, by British tanks and searchlights. If Calais had fallen to this division on the afternoon of the 23rd, Guderian would surely have sent his Tenth Panzer Division straight to Dunkirk and captured it before the defences were organised. The German records show that it was Goldney's stand at Orphanage Farm which made him change his plans.'[10]

Neave was in this sense an optimist. He had the happy ability to glimpse within the fog of apparent debacle 'providential' outcomes. It was a fortunate attitude that would sustain him in the many setbacks that assailed him in the months ahead and a key component in the resilience and determination to persist in unpromising circumstances that carried him through not only the war but much of the rest of his life.

After the scrambled departure from Coulogne, Neave set off to Calais by foot, arriving at the Porte de Marck, on the eastern ramparts of the city, at 10 p.m., 'shaken by the bombing … and my narrow escape.'[11] The geography of Calais was complicated. Calais-Nord was the dock area, a collection of basins and interlocking canals connected by bridges and overlooked by a massive sixteenth-century citadel. The southern half was Calais-St-Pierre, the modern centre dominated by the huge and florid Hôtel de Ville. The whole ensemble was protected by an enceinte, a defensive enclosure of walls and bastions designed by the great military engineer Vauban on Louis XIV's orders and added to over the centuries. It was pierced in several places by railway lines leading to the docks, but these fortifications now had to do service as a bulwark against the latest German invasion.

On the three-mile trudge from his outpost, Neave managed to pick up some members of his troop. He was 'nervous and footsore' but 'tried to appear unbowed'. The sector was held by the Rifle Brigade, the Green Jackets, whose renown derived from countless brave exploits in centuries of continental and imperial wars. Neave and his Searchlight comrades were now under the orders of Major

John Taylor, commanding 'A' Company. He spent the night lying on top of the ramparts, facing eastward, rifle in hand, while shells whined overhead to crash into the docks behind him, where intermittent efforts were being made to unload the Green Jackets' transport.

The fate of the defenders lay in the hands of London. Whitehall's ignorance of the true picture, though, produced a succession of hasty and short-lived decisions. Late the previous evening, the War Office decided that, having sent reinforcements to Calais, they were now going to pull them out. The situation in the Channel ports was untenable. Down the road in Boulogne, the 20th Guards Brigade, who had been holding out against a siege by Guderian's panzers, were already being disembarked, leaving French troops to hold on for another twenty-four hours. The War Office had apparently concluded that the situation in Calais was equally hopeless and that the highly trained troops of Nicholson's brigade should be extracted while there was still time. At 3 o'clock that morning, he received an order: 'Evacuation decided in principle. When you have finished unloading your two M.T. [Motor Transport] ships commence embarkation of all personnel except fighting personnel who remain to cover final evacuation.' It was not long before Nicholson was issued with completely contradictory instructions.

Neave watched the dawn rise over Dunkirk, whose vital importance, if terminal catastrophe was to be averted, was becoming ever clearer. He had been unable to sleep, 'so strong was the sense of danger'.[12] On the roads leading into Calais, the tanks, carriers, trucks and mobile artillery of the 10th Panzer Division were rumbling forward and the siege of Calais proper was about to begin.

Nicholson planned a layered defence, starting at an outer perimeter from which the troops could make successive withdrawals into the town. There was a huge area to defend. The walls of the enceinte stretched for eight miles. He had no artillery and a depleted tank force. Yet morale among the troops was good and had improved further as word spread that they would soon be on their way back across the Channel. At dawn, the first blows of the German assault fell on the QVR, holding forward positions on the south and south-west of the town. They were forced to fall back to the enceinte, which by midday had become the main defensive line.

During the morning, Neave was ordered to move his men from the eastern ramparts and wait in the sand dunes half a mile to the north, where hundreds of non-combatant troops were sheltered. It was an unsettling time. They were in the battle but not of it. 'Calais had become a city of doom and I was not in the least anxious to remain,' he wrote candidly afterwards.[13] He was tired and nervous. For something to do, he walked down to the Gare Maritime, where the railway met the port, in time to see one of the transport ships leaving harbour. The scene stayed with him. There were twenty dead bodies on the platform, victims of the night's shelling, and 'the sad corpses, covered in grey blankets, had begun to stink.' It was a clear day and he could see the white cliffs of Dover, so near but yet so far. Throughout the afternoon, German infantry, supported by tanks, attacked on all three sides of the perimeter, while shells rained down on the harbour area. The defenders fought with a ferocity that won the Germans' reluctant admiration. By the early evening, they had only managed to break into the southern side of the town in a few places, at a cost of heavy losses of equipment, men and tanks.

In the early afternoon, Neave got his chance to join the fray. Green Jacket officers called for volunteers from the crowd of unemployed soldiers sitting among the dunes. He rounded up fifty from the Searchlights and they formed up at the Gare Maritime, before heading south along the dock road to get their orders at the Hôtel de Ville. It was a proud moment for men designated 'non-fighting soldiers'. Marching off under the gaze of the Green Jackets, 'not a man faltered. It would never have done to be seen to be afraid even though the shells were coming in fast over the harbour.'[14] In the shadow of the gigantic clock tower of the Hôtel de Ville, Neave was told that he and his men were to reinforce 'B' Company of the 60th Rifles, who were holding a position by the western ramparts of the enceinte, which was under heavy attack from tanks and troops pushing in along the Route de Boulogne. They were led there by a staff officer through the deserted shopping streets to the Boulevard

Léon Gambetta, which ran east–west across the centre of Calais-St-Pierre. The enemy tanks and machine guns had a clear field of fire down the boulevard, so Neave's group moved west in the hot afternoon sun along a narrow parallel street. At some point it seems they could get no closer, and Neave led his men into a side street and left them in a doorway while he 'moved gingerly into the boulevard itself'.

Ahead lay the Pont Jourdan, which crossed a railway line coming in from the south. It was held by the 60th and it was there he would have to go to get his next orders. It was the greatest test of his courage that he had faced until now and he was not sure how he would fare. 'A steady hail of tracer bullets and some tank shells came flying over the hump of the … railway bridge,' he wrote later. 'They bounced off the paving stones in all directions as I clung for life to the walls of houses on the south side of the boulevard and crept towards the bridge. This was my first experience of street fighting and I was acutely frightened. It was difficult to understand how others could remain so collected under fire. Throughout the battle, the noise was so great that if you were more than ten yards away it was impossible to understand what was said to you.'[15]

Eventually, he reached the cover of the railway embankment that ran either side of the bridge, where he found Major Poole, the 'B' Company commander. Poole was a veteran of the last war, had been wounded, taken prisoner and escaped. Despite his great experience, Neave heard the anxiety in his voice. 'I am afraid they may break through,' he told him. 'Get your people in the houses on either side of the bridge and fire from the windows. You must fight like bloody hell.'

This account comes from Neave's book *The Flames of Calais*, which appeared in 1972. It intersperses his personal story, told with much detail and verbatim dialogue like the above, with the full story of the episode at every level, from decision-making in London and Guderian's headquarters to platoon actions. The broader narrative is well supported by official documentation and participants' accounts. But it is worth asking how accurate was his recollection of his own part in the story, thirty-two years after the event. There is no mention that he was working from a diary or semi-contemporaneous notes. Nonetheless, his account has the ring of authenticity. The recollections of combatants who were taken prisoner often have a fine-grained quality and an immediacy that is not so often present in other post-factum testimony. When removed from the battlefield and plunged into the tedium of captivity, he had plenty of time to obsess over events while the memory was still fresh. If the temptation for self-justifying adjustments to the narrative was strong, Neave appears to have resisted it. At no point in the story does he attempt to present himself as anything other than a tiny actor in the great events, often confused, frightened and ineffective, but always desperately concerned to do the right thing.

The right thing now was to obey Major Poole's instruction and fight like hell. He returned to the Boulevard Léon Gambetta, with bullets ricocheting around him, and found his men, now joined by two sergeants, crouched in the shelter of an ivy-covered wall. They were armed with only two Brens and some rifles. He ordered the sergeants to take up positions in the windows of the first floor of houses on either side of the street, from where they could fire on the German positions half a mile away on the Route de Boulogne. There followed a surreal episode of the sort that occurs with surprising frequency in the middle of battles. A door opened and a group of civilians scuttled past carrying the corpse of an old woman. There were other civilians about. The *patron* of a café near the bridge, proudly wearing his Croix de Guerre, spurned the mortal danger he was in to remain open, handing out cognac to anyone within reach and exhorting the defenders with a defiant slogan from the last war: '*On les aura!*' (We'll have 'em!)

There was danger behind as well as in front. A single rifle shot behind was followed by a shout of 'Fifth column!' After the battle was over, there would be many stories of mysterious gunmen appearing out of nowhere, some in German uniform, sniping at the defenders. They would reinforce the impression growing among many of the British troops that the French made unreliable allies. 'B' Company were deployed ahead on the far side of the railway bridge around an improvised road-block and facing down the Route de Boulogne. The Searchlights Bren teams reached their first-floor positions, smashed the windows and began to lay down supporting fire. Their eagerness and inexperience soon brought shouts of protest from the 60th on the far side of the bridge. Crouched in a doorway, Neave 'could hear hoarse shouts: "F---ing well look where you're shooting!"'[16]

In a lull in the fighting, he dodged across the boulevard to the corner of the Rue Edgar Quinet, a side street next to the bridge. From here he could see that the company's position was critical and the weight of enemy fire seemed certain to break the defenders soon if they did not drop back. The situation seemed to improve a little when, at 4 p.m., one of the British cruiser tanks arrived at the railway bridge and fired two or three rounds towards the attackers. The German response was furious: 'Tank shells and machine-gun bullets came thick and fast for twenty minutes. Ricochets off the walls and flying glass made my situation in the Rue Edgar Quinet ... rather exposed ... It was now without a sign of life, save for a young girl's white face at a cellar grating. The wall which sheltered me had ragged gaps where mortar bombs had flung bricks into the street. I began to look for a safer position.'

He could see nothing but clouds of smoke and dust, and the enemy felt horribly close. The Searchlight men were firing through the lace curtains, bravely but inexpertly, endangering defenders as much as attackers. One of the Brens began to fire fitfully, then jammed. He was acutely conscious of his lack of training and his impotence, able only to observe and offer encouragement. The sun beat down and the air throbbed with the heat from burning buildings. His thirst became unbearable. He had to get something to drink. He decided to make a dash for the café. He waited for a lull in the firing and was about to run when he 'felt a sharp, bruising pain in my left side. I collapsed to the pavement, my rifle clattering.' He tried to get up and found that he could still walk.

He staggered across to his original destination, the café on the corner, and took shelter in the side street, gratefully accepting a large cognac from the proprietor. A bespectacled medical orderly appeared, opened Neave's battledress and examined the wound. He pronounced him lucky – the bullet had passed half an inch from his heart. The orderly's cheerfulness and inclination to 'talk professionally about the condition of the wound' grated on Neave's nerves. His great fear was 'that the Germans would break through in the next few minutes, that I should be left behind and captured'. He swore at the medic and ordered him to take him to the next street. There they were joined by a Frenchman and between them they walked him away.

There was no sign of a regimental aid post (RAP), and he knew the nearest hospital was a mile away. He was calmed by the arrival of a scout car carrying a young officer of the 60th, Michael Sinclair, who like him was captured and ended up in Colditz, where he was shot dead while trying to escape in 1944. Sinclair 'smilingly drew my attention to a van flying the Red Cross'. The improvised ambulance, 'smelling strongly of stale vegetables', carried him at high speed back into the centre to the Pont Georges Cinq, the central of three spans that connected Calais-St-Pierre to Calais-Nord. They halted by a group of soldiers seeking directions to the 60th's RAP, but no one knew its whereabouts and an argument broke out as to which of the three hospitals in town he should be taken to.

Lying in the back, listening to the confused voices, Neave 'was suffering more from anger than pain'. He was still tortured by the thought that he might be captured. 'My chief interest,' he admitted frankly, 'was in evacuation by sea to England.' Eventually it was decided to take him to the Hôpital Militaire, a former convent only a few hundred yards away in the Rue Leveux, under the eastern wall of the Citadel. He was unloaded under the supervision of the 60th's medical officer, Lieutenant A. F. Stallard, who after examination told him he had received a 'penetrating flank wound' that would require an operation. He was 'carried, protesting, into the dark interior of the hospital where grinning French surgeons in white caps, and smoking Gauloise cigarettes, awaited me'.

Beyond the ramparts of Calais, great strategic events had conspired to cancel all hope of evacuation. Throughout the day, the realisation had penetrated the heads of those directing events in London that the BEF was facing extinction. Unless it could be saved, Britain's continuation in the war was seriously in doubt. Calais now assumed a new and different importance. It had become a key element in the struggle to bring the BEF home through the port of Dunkirk, thirty miles to the north-east. Their job was to drag the 10th Panzer Division into a fight to the last ditch, man and bullet, in order to delay it moving north and adding its weight to the enemy forces closing on the 200,000 beleaguered British troops.

Although the British did not know it, the threat of an armoured onslaught had temporarily subsided. That morning, Guderian had been ordered to halt his other Panzer divisions on a line on the river Aa, just to the east of Calais. Hitler had decided to give his exhausted soldiers a brief respite before moving against the French armies to the south. The British were beaten and he was prepared to allow Hermann Goering the chance to make good on his promise that the Luftwaffe would finish them off.

A further great decision settled the Calais garrison's fate. Lord Gort, the BEF's commander, came to the conclusion that the idea of attacking south to join up with the French army on the Somme was a fantasy. On the 25th, on his own initiative, he took what Neave described as 'the most vital decision of the entire campaign'[17] and ordered his army to fall back to the north and Dunkirk and prepare for evacuation. It was also one of the fateful decisions of the war. Had he prevaricated, the BEF would have been lost and with it perhaps any realistic hope that Britain could stay in the war and establish the conditions for eventual victory. But in order for the BEF to be saved, the Calais garrison had to be sacrificed. It became the tethered goat to distract the Panzers from the greater prize ahead.

The drastic change in thinking was signalled in orders which arrived late on the night of the 24th, crushing hope of an evacuation and telling Nicholson that he must fight on 'for the sake of Allied solidarity'. This was a reference to the furious reaction of the French to the news that Calais, like Boulogne, was about to be abandoned, scuppering their plans to establish a bridgehead that could be supplied by sea and keep resistance alive in the north-east. The theme was repeated the following day in a message to Nicholson from Anthony Eden, which arrived at 2 p.m., stating 'Defence of Calais to the utmost is of highest importance to our country as symbolising our continued co-operation with France. The eyes of the empire are upon the defence of Calais and HM Government are confident you and your gallant regiments will perform an exploit worthy of the British name.'

That day saw the launching of the evacuation plan, Operation Dynamo. There would be no further reference to Allied solidarity, and the signal drafted in London that night by Churchill, Anthony Eden and the Chief of the General Staff, Edmund Ironside, was stark. It read: 'Every hour you continue to exist is of greatest help to BEF. Government has therefore decided you must continue to fight. Have greatest possible admiration for your splendid stand.'

Nicholson needed no exhortations to keep fighting. That morning, the attackers broke into Calais-St-Pierre and at 8 a.m. the swastika was flying from the Hôtel de Ville. Three hours later, the Germans sent the town mayor, André Gershell, to Nicholson at his headquarters in the Citadel to demand his surrender. His reply was that 'If the Germans want Calais they will have to fight for it.'[18] A German officer led a second deputation in the afternoon, which was similarly rebuffed.

Neave spent the night of the 24/25th recovering from his operation in a ward in the cellars of the Hôpital Militaire. In the next bed lay a young Hurricane pilot who knew he was dying. He 'could still speak and begged me to keep talking to him'.[19] As it grew light, 'his body shuddered and his mouth fell open. The orderly saluted and, for a few minutes, the ward was very quiet.' He passed the rest of the day there, with the sounds of the fight piercing the thick walls and the occasional shell bursting in the vicinity, one of which showered his bed with broken glass. Outside, the defenders were being forced back street by street. Much of the town was choked with smoke and fire. In the early evening, the town was shaken by a prolonged artillery bombardment. Above the crackle of burning houses, Neave heard the 'groans and cries' of the wounded as they were brought down to the cellars.

At 9.30 in the morning, Stuka dive-bombers descended on the town, and an hour later enemy troops began crossing the bridges to Calais-Nord. The bombs shook the hospital and in the basement 'the smell of wounds and fear was overpowering.' Just before 10 a.m., a bomb landed in front of the hospital, blowing in the main doors. Fear seized Neave. He was 'terrified that with the next direct hit the wounded would be buried alive'. When the Stukas finally departed, he left his bed and found he could walk unaided. He decided to head for the Gare Maritime and find transport. He fixed on the hope that 'it might still be possible to evacuate the wounded by sea. Anything was better for them than entombment in the ruins of the Hôpital Militaire.'[20] He seems to have discussed the idea with an unnamed fellow patient, a corporal who volunteered to go with him. Dressed in what he could find – shirt, battledress trousers and steel helmet – he left the shelter. The hospital garden was a shambles of uprooted trees, with shattered masonry and glass lying around the graves dug for five riflemen who had died of their wounds in the cellar. The French military doctor commanding the hospital listened to his plan with amazement, telling him, 'You are crazy, mon lieutenant. You do not know what is happening in the town.' Neave repeated that the men would only be taken prisoner if they remained and insisted on his belief that it was still possible to get hospital ships in the harbour. 'You are absolutely determined to sacrifice your life?' the doctor asked. 'I was not interested in anything of the kind,' Neave recalled. 'I was irrationally confident that I could get through.'

The two injured men picked their way through the shattered and burning streets, Neave doubled up from the wound in his side and his companion limping. Calais-Nord was deserted after the dive-bombing, but as they passed the old fisherman's quarter called the Courgain which abuts the Gare Maritime, 'without warning, shells whistled and burst near us … The corporal vanished in the blinding flash and dust.' Neave fell to the ground unhurt and crawled to the side of the street where, miraculously, an old Frenchman offered him a bottle of cognac from a cellar window.[21] He drank from it and staggered on until he reached the Pont

Vétillard swing bridge which led to the Gare Maritime, where he could see British troops of the QVR in front of the station.

His 'apparition caused a sensation'. However, the reception he got was cold. The rumours of spies and German agents were now treated as established fact and his identity card was inspected several times. His demand that transport should be sent to collect the wounded from the hospital cellar 'was thought to be peculiar. Obviously I was either a fifth columnist or delirious.' Neave's pleas were ignored and he was packed off to another cellar, beneath the Gare Maritime, to join rows of wounded. The stay was short. The area came under intense mortar fire and he was soon moved to a tunnel under Bastion 1 of the enceinte, which had been transformed into a regimental aid post.

At 4 p.m. the Citadel where Nicholson made his final stand fell. Shortly before, the Rifle Brigade fought their last gallant action around the Gare Maritime, with some units fighting literally to the last round. Lying on his cot, Neave heard 'the hoarse shouts of German under-officers and the noise of rifles being flung on the floor of the tunnel. Through the doorway came field-grey figures waving revolvers.'[22] His war as a fighting soldier was over. His direct engagement with the enemy had amounted to a few futile shots, fired at a spotter plane.

3

'In the Bag'

The adrenaline that had carried Neave through his 'suicidal' stagger to the docks soon dissolved. His injury was serious and he had no choice but to accept defeat. He lay on his stretcher in the pungent gloom of the cellar ward, listening to the groans of his comrades, depressed, and fearful of what might happen next. In the morning, the Germans moved them to a makeshift field hospital in the Calais-St-Pierre covered market.[1] There was nothing to do but brood and endlessly go over the details of the battle. The siege of Calais had taught many brutal lessons. Neave's schooldays and TA experiences had made him sceptical of authority and disinclined to give those who wielded it unquestioning respect. The debacle could only reinforce that attitude. The heartache felt by Churchill and Eden over the decision to sacrifice the garrison was genuine. Nonetheless, their grasp of the situation had been tenuous and their reactions clumsy and slow.

Neave looked and sounded like an Establishment stalwart, but his judgements were often robust when he delivered his verdict on events. 'Churchill was often wrong about Calais,' he wrote years later,[2] citing as an example an intemperate memo the prime minister sent to his military assistant, General Ismay, on 24 May complaining of what he saw as the lack of enterprise in the defenders and the BEF in breaking the German siege. Churchill in time admitted the injustice of his remarks, but for Neave it was evidence of 'the terrifying ignorance of those conducting this campaign from

Whitehall'.[3] If anything, the performance of the army chiefs had been worse. Calais was a 'melancholy story of ... hesitation and bad staff work', exemplified by the shambles of departure. The manner in which the QVR had been rushed to war was 'shameful'. Their embarkation recalled the black comedy that suffused the adventures of Evelyn Waugh's hero Guy Crouchback 'in which farce and tragedy are intimately combined'. The same went for the tank units, whose 'orders were depressingly obscure and they had no idea what to expect on arrival at Calais.'

On the other hand, among those fighting on the ground there were more than enough examples of bravery and devotion to duty, carried out in a spirit of humanity and cheerfulness, to preserve the reputation of the British Army and sustain Neave's belief in the nobility of the profession of arms. His admiration for Claude Nicholson – his spirit of defiance and loyal attempts to execute the confused orders arriving from across the Channel – bordered on hero worship. His devotion to his memory was intensified by the tragic nature of Nicholson's end – dying in Rotenburg Castle, as a prisoner of war, in June 1943, at the age of forty-four.[4]

The defenders of Calais had much to feel proud about. They had accepted a hopeless situation without complaint and had fought with great effectiveness and determination. Once again, upper-class men were learning that gallantry was not the preserve of the privileged. Neave recalled how, at a corner of the Rue Edison, Captain Claude Bower of the 60th Rifles had defended a barricade of vehicles and sandbags for hours until he fell, mortally wounded. The street was lashed by machine-gun fire, which made it seemingly impossible for stretcher-bearers to bring him in. Then 'Rifleman Matthews drove in a truck across the open street. He backed it into position to rescue Bower, but he was already dead. Matthews removed several others badly wounded, and got away unscathed. Those who witnessed this wonderful achievement never forgot it.'[5]

Six years before, in his school essay making the case against pacifism, Neave had expressed the hope that no Briton would fight for France. Now he and a host of his countrymen had done just that, giving their lives and liberty in defence of a French town. The same could not be said of many of the French troops. Hundreds sheltered in cellars while the battle raged. There was some redemption, though, in the performance of a hard core of patriots, who fought almost to the last man on the ramparts in defence of Bastion 11, determined to preserve 'the honour of France'. Neave chose to see these men as the true representatives of their nation. He would come to rely on their sort – and their female counterparts – when organising escape and evasion networks on his return to the war.

With capture, Neave had his first encounter with Germans since his 1933 visit to Berlin. The soldiers who guarded him and the medical orderlies who tended his wound seemed civilised enough. But as he recuperated and thought about the future, 'It was the Nazis I dreaded, not the front-line troops who behaved well to the wounded.'[6] He claimed to have remembered the First World escape stories he read as a schoolboy and that his 'thoughts turned quickly to the chances of avoiding the inevitable journey to a prison camp'. At this early stage, when German control had not yet set hard, escape was easier to pull off and less hazardous than it soon became. Some of the defenders did manage to get away. A group of forty-seven men who had taken shelter under a pier in the port were picked up under fire by the Royal Navy yacht *Gulzar* in the early hours of 27 May.[7] A young Searchlights officer, Lieutenant W. H. Dothie, after leading a dogged resistance from the village of Marck, east of Calais, was finally captured, but escaped from a prisoner-of-war column and eventually made his way back to England after an epic journey by foot, bicycle and boat.[8]

The impulse to escape, and his adventures trying to do so, are a central part of Airey Neave's story and identity, and he wrote about them extensively. However, the account was delivered in fits and starts, over a long period and in different forms. Thirteen years after he broke out of Colditz, he published *They Have Their Exits*, which became a bestseller. He returned to the subject again in 1969, with *Saturday at MI9*. The first book skates over the period between capture in Calais and arrival at his first proper prisoner-of-war camp, Oflag IX-A/H, in the castle of Spangenberg, deep in central

Germany. In the second, though, he faces the episode squarely, owing to the low spirits and doubtful nerve he suffered in the months after Calais. Neave felt sharply the ignominy, not only of the debacle, but of his own insignificant role in the defence, and his recollections are tinged with a faint sense of shame. It was compounded by a feeling that he had not moved quickly enough to try and get away.

Initially, he was too weak to escape. While still recovering in a ward with four other officers in Calais, he was approached by a young French officer, Pierre d'Harcourt, working as a Red Cross orderly, who suggested substituting the live Neave for one of the dead patients who were regularly taken off for burial, but the plan came to nothing.[9] Neave had 'neither the nerve nor the physical strength to make the attempt', but as his health improved he found that his morale remained low and his resolve weak. In June, he was moved with other wounded to Lille, where the Faculté Catholique had been turned into a POW hospital. The lorry carrying them broke down in the town of Bailleul, twenty miles short of their destination, presenting him with a golden opportunity. While the lorry was being repaired, 'I wandered unguarded through the streets with other wounded survivors of Calais,' he wrote. 'We were welcomed at every door, food and wine was pressed on us, and many offered to hide us from the Germans.' Lille would become a centre of resistance in Northern France and, had he accepted, there would have been a high chance of success. Instead, 'At sunset, as the crowds waved and threw flowers in the main square ... I suffered myself, to my shame, to be driven off to hospital in Lille.'

Why such meek acceptance? Writing in 1969, he declared that 'though my thoughts had already turned to escape and its organisation, the weeks in hospital seemed to deprive me of all initiative.' He also suggested that lack of 'military training in such matters' had played a part in his vacillation. He was man enough to admit that 'this was not a heroic episode in my life.' He went on to propose that his inaction had in a way been providential, for 'had it not happened, I might never have escaped from Colditz to England and gained the experience which enabled me to plan the escape of others.' Once again, amid the dark clouds, Neave could see the silver lining.

In the improvised hospital in the Faculté Catholique, a 'sombre, red-brick affair with stone floors and a smell of wounds and disinfectant', he met a man who would later become his partner in the great enterprise to get Allied servicemen out of occupied Europe.[10] When they were reunited in London, he recalled how he had last seen him: a 'pale and strained [figure], playing cards in one of the wards. I remembered his high forehead and bright eyes as he sat on his bed dressed in a tattered shirt and trousers.' Captain Jimmy Langley of the Coldstream Guards fitted Neave's romantic ideal of the British warrior. He was slim, intelligent and apparently without fear, and had been captured at Dunkirk.

The Coldstream's orders were to hold up the Germans while the evacuation was under way. Langley was a platoon commander with '3' Company, 2nd Battalion. The company was led, with what feels today like lunatic determination, by Major Angus McCorquodale, who gave orders for any officer who showed an inclination to retire to be shot. Langley described later how a captain commanding a unit on the company's right came over to announce that he was planning to withdraw. The Germans were massing for an armoured assault on a bridgehead they were holding and his men were too exhausted to resist.[11] McCorquodale ordered him to 'stay put and fight it out'. The officer replied that his orders from the commanding officer were to retire as and when he saw fit. McCorquodale was having none of it. 'You see that big poplar tree on the road with the white mile stone beside it?' he told him. 'The moment you or any of your men go back beyond that tree we will shoot you.' The captain departed and McCorquodale picked up a rifle and ordered Langley to get one himself. 'When I returned with mine he said "Sights at 250. You will shoot to kill the moment he passes that tree …" We had not long to wait before the captain appeared, followed by two men. They stood for a long time by the tree and then the captain walked on. Both our rifles went off simultaneously: he dropped out of sight and the two men ran back.' This ruthlessness matched the determination with which the company did its duty. Langley was a marksman and accounted for many Germans before losing his arm to a shell. McCorquodale died at his post.

Langley did not let his injury delay his departure. While in Lille, he managed to contact local resisters who got him out of the hospital and took him to Paris. From there he crossed the demarcation line into the Unoccupied Zone. In spring 1941, the Vichy Armistice Commission passed him unfit for any further military service and he was escorted over the Spanish frontier to freedom. Neave and Langley teamed up again when serving in the secret escape and evasion organisation MI9. Though their backgrounds were similar, their characters were not, and their wars as fighting soldiers had taken very different forms.

There was a further contrast in the way they viewed their escapes. Langley claimed to dislike the fact that his return to fight another day 'would be a matter of some congratulation' and 'regarded as an epic of courage and endurance'. He protested that 'running away hardly came into the category of bravery … travelling by train and hiding in hotels did not call for much endurance.'[12]

For Neave, escape became his claim to fame, the thing he was most remembered for. He fostered its memory carefully through his books, and thirty years after the event was still giving regular talks to schools and clubs about his adventures. Writing in 1975, after a tour of army bases in Northern Ireland, he could not resist commenting that conditions in 'one or two are worse than Colditz'.[13] As well as his most memorable achievement, escape was also a turning point in his wartime life – the moment when he pulled off a private and bloodless victory over the Germans, restoring his self-respect and making up for his disappointing performance on the conventional battlefield.

The yearning to break free would become a 'fever' that mounted the longer he was behind bars.[14] But the further he got from France, the harder escape became. While he was still in Lille, a young Frenchwoman who brought flowers and food to the wounded offered to help him and two others – an early example of the courage and patriotism shown by so many of the female resisters he encountered. When senior officers in the hospital heard about the plan, they were 'lectured severely on the reprisals which might be visited on other wounded'.

It was too late anyway. In late July or early August, he was on the move again, on a 'grim march through Belgium', before embarking on a coal barge which chugged up the Scheldt and into the Waal, reaching the Rhine and the German frontier at Emmerich. Along with his belief in providence, Neave had an eye for the karmic readjustments that life sometimes delivers. He was pleased to note that his journey as a prisoner took him under the bridge at Nijmegen that he would cross four years later as a victor and see 'the dead Germans on the sidewalks as we made all speed for Arnhem'.

Oflag – meaning 'officers' camp' – IX-A/H was housed in a schloss overlooking Spangenberg, a small town in the heart of central Germany, 220 miles as the crow flies from the Dutch border, and further still from the French and Swiss frontiers. The castle, a Disneyish concoction with moat and drawbridge, had arched doorways and a clock tower which reminded him of school. The social hierarchy among the prisoners was also built on equally familiar lines, for there were 'strict codes of behaviour designed for us by our senior officers, and social cliques appeared from the very first day.'

Nearly all prisoners' memoirs speak of the desolation that descends when the journey is over, the destination is reached and the gates clang shut behind them. Neave's portrayal of the 'double tragedy' of imprisonment was particularly eloquent: 'First, there is the loss of freedom. Then, since there is no particular crime to expiate, unless it be personal folly, a sense of injustice scars the spirit … The prisoner of war is to himself an object of pity. He feels he is forgotten by those who flung him, so he thinks, into an unequal contest. He broods over the causes of his capture, and to himself and his friends he soon becomes a bore, endlessly relating the story of his last stand.'[15]

Neave, like many others, seems to have experienced a period of numb acceptance, trying to find a rhythm of life to ease the tight confines of a new universe. He had always felt the urge to write and he tried to alleviate the boredom by starting a novel 'about the life after death of an eighteenth century peer' and a 'superficial' study of Shakespeare's sonnets.[16] Essays on 'eccentrics' and other subjects for the camp publication, produced on a 'jellygraph', a gelatin duplicator used to run off school magazines and the like, did not go down well. They were 'rapidly dismissed as unsuitable' and Neave ceased his literary efforts. The lesson was that it was 'dangerous to tamper with the literary views of the average British officer' and that 'any attempt at being funny' in print was 'doomed to failure and will very likely lead to ostracism'.[17]

In these first months in Spangenberg, the rather adolescent bolshiness that surfaced in his Oxford days was again to the fore. The mood did not last long. By December he started thinking seriously about escape. Since the camp had opened in October 1939 there had been several attempts by inmates. Flight Lieutenant Howard 'Hank' Wardle, a Canadian who joined the RAF shortly before the war, was shot down in his Fairey Battle bomber in April 1940 and was the only member of the three-man crew to survive. In August, just before Neave arrived, he was being taken with other prisoners to a gym outside the castle walls when he scaled a high barricade and slipped away.[18] He was captured after twenty-four hours and sent to Colditz, already established as a prison for troublemakers.

Flying Officers Keith Milne and Donald Middleton, two more Canadians serving with the RAF, managed to get through the gates disguised as painters, complete with buckets of whitewash and a ladder. They too were soon recaptured and ended up in Colditz. If these exploits sounded light-hearted, there was a price to pay. According to Pat Reid, who later escaped from Colditz with Wardle, all three 'suffered badly at the hands of their captors, being severely kicked and battered with rifle-butts'.[19]

Such efforts were initially seen by the senior British officers in the camp as a threat to good order, inviting reprisals on the rest of the prisoners. Neave wrote that the pioneer escapers were 'often unpopular … They were considered a disturbing influence in the orderly life of the camp where the pre-war British military and class system was applied from the day of arrival.'[20] He blamed the discouraging attitude on low morale, caused by Britain's poor performance in the war and the debilitating effect of the meagre rations. In the autumn of 1940, Red Cross parcels started to arrive. With that, 'health and spirits improved, and with it the attitude of senior officers, who no longer claimed that escape was hopeless.'

At some point, Neave was moved with others to a new camp in the woods beneath the castle. The rural setting was a relief after the cold walls of the schloss, and the laughter of children carried to the prisoners from a path that ran by the boundary. The winter of 1940 passed 'in discomfort, but without great suffering, unless it be of the soul'. The main complaint was food, or the lack of it. The man who in his Eton diary had noted almost every meal he ate was reduced to a diet of bread, soup and root vegetables, cheered only by the occasional scrap of meat or treat from a food parcel. At Christmas, everyone was given a tin of steak-and-kidney pudding. His stomach had shrunk and he could not finish it.[21]

Early in 1941, there was another move which took him yet further from a friendly frontier. In February, the camp was temporarily closed and all the inmates moved by train to Stalag XX-A, a large prison complex based on a chain of fortresses surrounding the Polish city of Thorn, modern-day Torun, on the banks of the Vistula. Neave says the evacuation was a reprisal for the alleged ill-treatment of German POWs in Canada. The atmosphere and the attitude of the guards had certainly darkened. The new arrivals were met at the station by tanks, searchlights and Field Police with Alsatian dogs. Neave and his fellow officers were housed in semi-darkness in 'damp, cold, vault-like rooms', which had once served as ammunition bunkers in one of the forts, built in the nineteenth century to defend Prussia's eastern borders. The prisoners were the flotsam of a string of British defeats. There were hundreds of survivors of the Norway debacle of May 1940 and many who had been captured at Dunkirk and St-Valery-en-Caux, where the 51st (Highland) Division were forced to surrender. In this ambience of failure Neave felt his resolve harden. 'From this terrible futility,' he wrote, 'I determined to free myself.'[22]

Prisoners had two basic ways of dealing with incarceration. They could accept their fate and choose a settled existence, waiting for the end of the war and using the unmeasurable days of captivity killing time as best they could or engaging in self-improvement projects for a future that might never arrive. Or they could devote themselves to breaking free. Fatalists vastly outnumbered would-be escapers. An RAF report on Stalag Luft VI, the camp for NCO airmen at Heydekrug in East Prussia, estimated the proportion of escape-minded prisoners at only 5 per cent.[23] One of the most determined 'escapologists' of the war, the American RAF fighter pilot William Ash, came to the same conclusion. 'There cannot have been a single POW ... who did not think about escaping,' he wrote.[24] In an average camp, about a third would be prepared to lend a helping hand to others' attempts, by acting as lookouts, for example, forging fake documents or improvising digging implements. However, 'maybe only 5 per cent were committed to getting outside the wire at all costs.' And for most of those, one attempt was usually enough, leaving a handful for whom escaping was 'a way of life'. Prisoners' stories devote much time to analysing the elements that pushed a man into one group and not the other. They remain hard to define. There was little obvious connection with background, class, political outlook, nationality or even character. Ardent escapers could be introverts or extraverts, intellectuals or hearties.

In the end it came down to an impulse – something that had to be done. Pat Reid, who first wrote the story of Colditz, portrayed it as a supremely intoxicating pursuit on a par with winning the Grand National at Aintree. 'I can think of no sport that is the peer of escape,' he wrote, 'where freedom, life, and loved ones are the price of victory, and death the possible though by no means inevitable price of failure.'[25] It was echoed by Ash, who described the urge as something almost beyond his control. 'Escaping is quite addictive,' he wrote, 'and, like all addictive drugs, extremely dangerous.'[26]

Others cited more elevated motives. Aidan Crawley was a pre-war journalist and intelligence officer who joined the RAF. He was shot down and taken prisoner in North Africa in 1941. He later wrote the official history of escape attempts by airmen, in which he judged that 'no one could blame those who decided escape was not worthwhile.'[27] However, Crawley believed 'the arguments in favour of trying ... were overwhelming.' It was a self-imposed duty, 'because the return of a prisoner had considerable military value'. At the very least, he might bring back valuable intelligence about enemy dispositions or the details of potentially useful underground networks. If he was an airman, he could go back into action and his very expensive training would not have gone to waste. This latter argument was often wielded by Neave when justifying the existence of MI9 in its frequent turf wars with other intelligence organisations.

A few weeks after arriving at Thorn, Neave hatched his first serious, thought-out and well-resourced escape plan. Stalag XXa was like a small penitentiary town, with outposts and suburbs and a labour force made up of NCO and 'other ranks' prisoners, who the Germans put to work building roads and infrastructure and clearing land for the ever-expanding complex. The practice was within the terms of the Geneva Conventions, though officers were exempted. However, what might at first have seemed to the officers a privilege came by many to be regarded as a curse. Work, however menial, was a distraction from the long empty hours of brooding.

The main compound for non-commissioned prisoners was about four miles from Neave's cell in the fort. Inside it, there was a wooden hut where a British dentist had his surgery. The Germans allowed British officers to visit every Thursday. It was Neave's good luck to suffer from inflamed gums, a result of poor diet and his run-down condition, which required regular treatment. The dentist's hut would be the springboard for his dive for freedom. On his trips back and forth he worked up a plan. Even though Germany and the Soviet Union were still at that time uneasy allies, he reckoned that if he managed to make it to the frontier at Brest-Litovsk, the Russians would treat him well and 'I should swiftly be ushered into the presence of the British ambassador [in Moscow], Sir Stafford Cripps.'[28] It was a fantastic proposition. It meant a journey, via Warsaw, of 300 miles over heavily occupied territory, with a very uncertain reception at the end of it.

As it turned out, breaking out of Thorn was the relatively easy part. But to succeed he still needed help. There was plenty on hand among the soldiers in the work camp. Their ingenuity and selflessness left a deep impression. Every day a party of about a dozen made the four-mile journey from the compound to the fort to carry out maintenance work. Among them were two men who had belonged to Neave's battery at Calais. Through the messages that they carried back and forth each day, he was able to establish a team of helpers in the work camp to put the operation into action. He planned a phased departure from Stalag XXa. The idea was that he would slip away during a trip to the dentist and get into the compound. There, protected by the inmates, he would lie low until the hue and cry following the discovery that he was missing had died down. Then he would walk out with one of the work parties and hide at the end of the shift. When the coast was clear, he would strike out eastwards, disguised as a workman – Polish or German, depending on who challenged him.

The scheme was bold and ambitious. It needed considerable organisation, precise timing and significant resources in the form of clothing, food, money and documentation. At least a dozen accomplices were needed for it to work. Protocol required that the Senior British Officer, Brigadier N. F. Somerset, was kept informed as the plan matured. Neave had decided that he did not want to travel alone. He was unable to persuade any of his room-mates, who 'regarded my plans with friendly derision and few could be found who would even discuss them seriously.' He asked Somerset if he could suggest a companion – one who, like him, spoke some German. Flying Officer Norman Forbes, a Hurricane pilot with 605 Squadron who had been shot down just south of Calais on 27 May 1940 while Neave was spending his first day in captivity, was an excellent candidate. He was a 'tall, slender man with fair hair', quick, determined and shrewd. He had also been brought up a Christian Scientist and 'had faith in the success of our plan'.

By the second week in April everything was in place. Using barter and persuasion, he had assembled an impressive escape kit. His workman's coat and painter's trousers he obtained from a British officer who had 'decided to abandon escaping to read for a degree in Law'. He was one of many who took advantage of the system, operated under the Red Cross, which offered correspondence courses resulting in valid professional qualifications. Neave procured some reichsmarks by selling Player's cigarettes (tobacco was usually available to prisoners and a universal currency) to a Polish glazier. Rations in the shape of tinned sardines and condensed milk and chocolate came from the food parcels. All were smuggled out of the fort and down to the work camp.

Why had Neave chosen discomfort and danger over acceptance and making the most of a bad situation? Lying on his bunk bed at night as the hours to the escape bid ticked away, he struggled to explain it to himself. 'I desired only to be free from the terrible monotony of the fort and once outside under the stars I cared little what happened to me,' he wrote. 'I dreamed of nights sheltering in the shade of some romantic forest alone in the world. I felt that once outside the camp I should be happy if I were only free for a while.'

On the morning of 16 April 1941, he and Forbes set off under guard for the dentist's hut, just outside the British prisoners' compound, four miles from the fort. Under their overcoats, badges had been removed from their battledress tunics so they could pass as 'other ranks'. Neave left a detailed description of the events of the morning, embellished with literary touches.[29] Looking through the waiting room for his turn in the chair, he could 'see small groups of British prisoners among the pine trees pushing carts of wood, and from the distance came the strains of "Roll Out the Barrel" as a working party set off into the forest ... A light breeze blew among the pines.' The account was written twelve years after the event and it might be asked how he could remember so much. Some moments in our lives embed themselves in our memories, leaving the indelible trace of a smell, a voice, a colour. For Neave, this was surely one of them. His first escape was a landmark of his existence, the point when he at last seized control of his own destiny, in the process scoring a small but immensely pleasing victory over the enemy.

Everything went swimmingly. After his session in the chair, he made way for Forbes. In the waiting room he told the guard he wanted to use the 'Abort' and was allowed to go unescorted to the latrine next door. Inside, he stowed his overcoat and retrieved some lengths of wood hidden in the ceiling by his helpers to be used as props in the next phase of the escape. He was soon joined by Forbes and, at a signal from a sergeant who was keeping watch outside, they stepped out, carrying the timber, ostensibly just two ordinary soldiers engaged in some errand. It was a short walk to the main gate of the compound, where the sentry's attention was distracted by a corporal detailed to engage him in chat, and they passed through, mingling with the other POWs. At the door of a long hut housing warrant officers, Company Sergeant Major Thornborough of the Green Howards, immaculately turned out in spruce uniform and shining boots, grinned and shook their hands. They were left to rest for a bit until Thornborough returned, telling them there was a sight waiting that was not to be missed.

Picking up brushes and buckets so as to look like orderlies off on a fatigue, they followed him across the parade ground. Their escape had been discovered and the guards were angry and indignant. 'Around us a crowd of British soldiers were laughing and shouting sallies at the Germans,' he wrote. 'Furious Germans stamped around … Down the steps of the Kommandantur [administrative head-quarters] came agitated German officers gesticulating at the crest-fallen sentries.' They were joined by Field Police with dogs, who set off on the hunt in the opposite direction to where their quarry had gone to earth. The satisfaction was enormous. For the first time since the start of the war, Neave had put one over on the Germans. They spent the next three days hidden in the warrant officers' hut. There was one scare when they had to hide under their cots while the Germans conducted a search. Neave wondered why they now suspected they might still be in the camp. Thornborough had warned him there were 'one or two stool pigeons in the camp'. It was an early lesson that in the escape business it was wise to say the minimum and trust nobody, a policy that Neave's critics would later say he followed closely in his political life.

At six o'clock on the morning of 19 April, after a cup of ersatz coffee, he and Forbes left the camp in the middle of a party of 150 men. They spent the day at a farm, where they were put to work in a barn stuffing mattress covers with straw. During the afternoon, on a signal that the coast was clear, they climbed into the loft and burrowed into the hay. Earlier, their helpers had smuggled in two extra men on the ration lorry. When the guards counted the work party out they matched the number who had marched in. It was the final touch in a superb performance by the NCOs and men, and Neave never forgot these 'staunch and kindly people'. They 'ran greater risks of punishment than we did, but not one spoke of the consequences … During my stay there had been no feeling of class or rank among us, only a mutual desire to defy the Germans.'

When night fell, they climbed down from the hayloft and went to the back door of the barn, where one of the helpers had loosened the wire holding it shut. They stepped out into the starlit night and, for the first time in two years, breathed the air as free men. For the next four days, dressed in their rough clothes, they trudged east-wards. Since devising his original plan, he and Forbes had hatched an alternative. There was a German aerodrome at Graudenz, north of Warsaw. The Poles in the camp had provided enough informa-tion about it to sketch a map. Forbes was a pilot. Perhaps they could steal an aeroplane and fly to neutral Sweden. It had been tried before by two RAF inmates of Thorn, who had got as far as climbing into an aircraft disguised as Luftwaffe aircrew before being rumbled because they could not understand the instructions from the control tower.[30]

The trek started well, matching the fantasies he had entertained while day-dreaming on his bunk. It was 'like walking on air'. The language is telling, a further sign of the quasi-mystical importance Neave gave to the act of escaping. Relating the story of this first attempt, he stated that 'no one who has not known the pain of imprisonment understands the meaning of Liberty.'[31] The capital letter is his. For Neave this was more than a simple act of duty or defiance. It had an almost religious significance. 'The real escaper,' he wrote, 'is more than a man equipped with compass, maps, papers, disguise and a plan. He has an inner confidence, a serenity of spirit which make him a Pilgrim.'

After a few hours, the intoxication of freedom began to wear off. His sack of rations – tins of sardines and condensed milk and Red Cross parcel chocolate – cut into his shoulder, he was soaked in sweat and his feet swelled up painfully inside his army boots. In the morning it rained for hours. The countryside, carved through by the wide, muddy Vistula and dotted with small farms and orchards, was filled with ominous landmarks. They were following the river to Warsaw, taking the same route that the Germans had followed twenty months before, and the scars of the fighting were fresh. There were graveyards where Polish army helmets sat on white crosses, charred buildings and a smashed-up chapel with half a crucifix hanging over the doorway. Almost every farmhouse, no matter how small and mean, had new owners. The Poles had been turned out of their homes and German settlers put in. The pair were anxious to avoid all human encounters, but it was impossible not to feel the presence of the new masters.

Late that first morning, they were passed by a 'a four-wheeled open carriage ... driven by a German farmer in a flat cap, smoking a short cigar.' He turned back to examine them and 'his arrogant, fleshy face ... bore an expression of savage contempt ... and he fingered the stock of his long whip.' Neave had been exposed to Germans frequently in his short life, as a schoolboy visitor, as a patient in the care of the military and as a captive. Until now, these experiences had suggested that, despite the repellent philosophy of the new order, the population had its fair share of decent human beings. On this journey, the Germans seemed wholly bad.

A little later, skirting a farm, they met a Polish man who recognised that they were fugitives. He wished them good luck in English but warned them to move on quickly as the German farmer was 'very bad'. As they left they spotted him, 'thick-set with an evil-tempered red face like the man who had driven past us. He too carried a long black whip and smoked a short cigar. We hurried away from him down a slippery path into the valley and heard him shouting to the Pole as if to a dog.'

The cruelty of the German occupation made an ineradicable impression on Neave and these memories bubbled to the surface when, four years later at the Nuremberg War Crimes Tribunal, he served the indictment on the Gauleiter overlord of conquered Poland, Hans Frank. At the same time, he was profoundly moved by the stoicism of the Poles and the sacrificial generosity they were prepared to offer to those they identified as friends. Again, it was something he never forgot. Long afterwards, in the face of Foreign Office opposition, he campaigned doggedly for a memorial to the thousands of Poles murdered by their Soviet oppressors in 1940.

At dusk on their second day of freedom, they were too exhausted to face another night in the open. They approached a whitewashed house and knocked. The door was opened by a young Polish woman, who summoned her father, a farmer who had somehow avoided eviction. He made them welcome and gave Neave a pair of corduroy trousers to replace the thin, torn ones he arrived in. Their only drawback was that they lacked fly buttons. There was shy giggling as the girls of the house removed the buttons from the old trousers and sewed them onto the new pair.

But after this interlude the smiling stopped. Neave sensed that 'the room was heavy with their fear … I knew that the girls were watching for a glimpse of field-grey … at the window.' There was a crash of heavy boots and a loud knock and he and Forbes scuttled to the kitchen. The visitor was a young Polish man who held an urgent conversation with the farmer. Even though Neave knew not a word of the language, there was no mistaking the tone of disquiet. He wrote later that 'a great feeling of guilt ran through me as I witnessed their terror. Was it to destroy these simple lives that I escaped? Was it not better to endure the bitter frustrations of the Fort … all the degradation of being a prisoner? What did it matter whether I escaped or not if others were to die?'

This dilemma would confront every man who managed to get away from a German camp. As the war progressed, they were increasingly sited in Poland. Many – perhaps most – attempts required the assistance of Poles. Polish workers smuggled escape materials into camps and provided vital intelligence. Polish families gave food and shelter. All risked death by doing so and many paid the price. Most of the helpers were 'ordinary' people. Their fundamental motivation was decency and humanity. The question of whether these humble heroes and heroines should be put in mortal danger by the imperatives of the escapees was one that even the most thoughtful were never able to resolve. In the end, they could only comfort themselves with the thought that the assistance was freely given, in full knowledge of the deadly consequences.

Neave and Forbes were spared further agonising when the Polish farmer told them to sleep in the barn, asking them to be gone before dawn. The visitor had warned him that the local German settlers were looking out for them. The next afternoon they reached the large town of Wloclawek on the banks of the Vistula, about a hundred miles north-west of Warsaw. It was the day after Hitler's birthday and swastikas and bunting fluttered over the streets. As they slunk along, Neave saw an old man with the Star of David 'painted in yellow on his back' walking slowly along the pavement. At the same time, a small detachment of SS men came marching by. They were singing, 'their arrogant young faces scorning all around them'. Poles and Germans alike raised their hands obediently in the Nazi salute and Neave and Forbes quickly followed suit. The old man failed to see the Germans in time and 'a fair young thug stepped from the ranks and struck him on the head. His hat spun in the wind and rolled across the road.' The SS man pushed him off the pavement and he stumbled in the gutter and lay there moaning. No one dared to go to his aid.

They spent the night in a forest, serenaded by the grunting of wild boar. The following day, the third after their escape, progress was slow and painful. Neave's feet were a mass of blisters and his legs were rubbed raw. They tried to sleep in a dip in a ploughed field, shivering in the intense cold. At daybreak they set off again, determined to get to Warsaw that night. It seemed feasible. They passed through the town of Ilow, only thirty miles from their destination. Somewhere beyond it – the rough maps they had did not say precisely where – there was an administrative frontier marking the start of the Polish Territory established by the

Molotov–Ribbentrop pact as a buffer zone between the Russian-occupied zone and the lands given to German settlers.

Exhaustion made them reckless. When they arrived at an apparently unmanned white-painted border post and guardhouse they walked straight through it. But as they made for a patch of forest on the other side, they saw a pair of German sentries watching them in silence. The sentries picked up their rifles and walked slowly towards them. They were too tired to run. Forbes, who had the better German, did the talking. The Germans were 'stupid and fresh-faced', but they did not buy their story that they were on their way to visit their sick mother in a nearby town. When they were unable to produce papers, they were led back to the guardhouse and into a small office. There, 'a hard-faced man' in uniform with 'crazy blood-shot eyes' sat at a table with a heavy leather whip hanging from the wall beside him. He yelled at them to stand to attention, then Forbes was taken outside and Neave's grilling began.

He tried to stick to his story – that he was an ethnic German from Bromberg, the German name for a nearby district – but he had no hope of sustaining it. 'In my terrible fatigue, my brain refused to function clearly,' he wrote. 'I forgot my German and spoke to him haltingly.' The German just laughed and 'brandished the whip in my face'. He blundered on, hoping to buy time for Forbes to make a break. He himself 'no longer cared that I was caught again or even if this brutal official were to flog me to death.' There was no point in carrying on. He pulled out the metal disc that all escapers carried, stamped with his name and number: 'Prisoner of War No. 1198.' It was an essential precaution. The proof of combatant status was protection against being classed as a spy or saboteur and despatched to the gallows or a firing squad rather than returned to captivity. But the disc failed to impress his interrogator. Forbes was brought back and another official joined in the questioning. They refused to believe their new story. They were 'not Englishmen, but Polish spies'. Then Neave heard words that would stay with him for the rest of his life: 'This is a matter for the Gestapo.'

* * *

They were marched back the way they had come, to Ilow. Neave noticed Forbes furtively shredding a piece of paper as they walked. He realised it was a copy of the plan of Graudenz aerodrome from where they had considered stealing a plane and flying to freedom. A 'great fear' seized him – where had he hidden his? They were driven from Ilow to Plock on the north side of the Vistula and into a modern building with a sign over the door announcing it was Gestapo headquarters. They were hauled before a man in plain clothes with 'blond hair and a pale, cruel face'. They emptied their pockets and the Gestapo man went through Neave's wallet. He unfolded a small piece of paper. It was the missing plan of the aerodrome. The pair's status as spies now seemed confirmed. Even to Neave's thinking, there seemed only one explanation for the map. Graudenz was to the north of Thorn, yet they had been stopped heading east on the road to Warsaw and the Soviet lines. The obvious conclusion was that they were intending to hand the plan over to the Russians, whose commitment to the Nazi–Soviet pact was doubtful.

For the next ten days he lived in a fever of anxiety, expecting at any moment to be marched out before a firing squad. There were at least two further interrogations. Forbes and he stuck to the same story. They had been intending to hijack an aircraft and head to Sweden, pointing out that the same method had been tried out before by some inmates of Thorn, a fact that their captors verified in front of them with a phone call. One Gestapo man seemed almost affable and 'anxious to appear a "gentleman".'[32] But in the long solitary hours in his cell 'the threat of execution seemed very real, and I felt defenceless and alone.'

Neave never tried to hide the terror he felt during his time in Gestapo custody. Religious sentiment plays almost no part in Neave's memoirs and diaries, but coming back from the final interrogation he recorded that he prayed. He 'lay upon my bed, too frightened even to move. With every noise outside the cell there shot through me an intense pang of fear.'[33] The Gestapo were 'evil and dangerous, and without humanity'. He felt 'almost a longing' to return to the custody of the German Army officers at Stalag XX-A.

But in another respect he was more reticent. What precisely happened in those ten days? In his writings, Neave never said he had been beaten or tortured – though the sight of the whip on the wall in his first encounter with the enemy after capture made it clear to him that this is what he could expect. Nor, later, did he say as much to his children. Nonetheless, they sensed that there was a part of the ordeal that he kept to himself, something that had profoundly marked him psychologically. His youngest son, William, believes the experience was 'hugely scarring ... I don't know whether he had nightmares because of it latterly, but I suspect he probably did.'[34]

Many years afterwards, in March 1979, Neave was sharing a taxi in London with Gerry Fitt, a Nationalist MP from Belfast with whom he had become friends during his time as shadow Northern Ireland Secretary. They discussed the Bennett Report into police interrogation methods of terrorist suspects, which had just been published and which concluded that abuses had occurred. According to Peter Taylor, the BBC TV journalist and historian of the Troubles, Neave 'told Fitt that if and when he became Ulster Secretary he would institute a full inquiry into the allegations. He said he had been tortured by the Gestapo and it had left its mark.'[35] He did not get the chance to make good on his promise, for the following day he was dead.

The morning after the interrogation, Neave awoke expecting that it would be his last. Instead, the guard told him he and Forbes were going back to Stalag XXa. He seized his clothes and boots 'in wild delight, and dressed as if it were the first day of the school holidays'.[36] The stay at Thorn was short. At 3 o'clock one morning, he was woken and taken to join a small group of British officers, among them Norman Forbes, gathered on the drawbridge. The others he recognised as veterans of other failed escapes. When he asked where they were going, he was told, 'To the Bad Boys' Camp at Colditz.'

Airey aged about seven months with his mother Dorothy.

As a smart little seven-year-old schoolboy.

Airey with his siblings, Averil, Rosamund, Digby and Viola (seated on floor).

The sound of broken glass: Merton College dining club the Myrmidons in 1937. Airey Neave is front row, second from right.

The Sacrifice:
British troops
march into
captivity after their
heroic stand.

AN shortly after
arriving at
Spangenberg.

Colditz Castle.

Resisters and escapers: left to right, Francis Blanchain, Mario Prassinos, Hugh Woollatt, AN and Louis Nouveau in the flat on the Quai Rive Neuve, Marseilles, in the spring of 1942.

Jimmy Langley in 1944.

AN with Albert-Marie Guérisse ('Pat O'Leary') after the war.

The happiest day of his life. AN and Diana marry after a whirlwind courtship, 29 December 1942.

'Monday' – Michael Creswell on a shooting holiday during his stint as a diplomat in pre-war Germany.

Traitor: Harold Cole in one of his many incarnations.

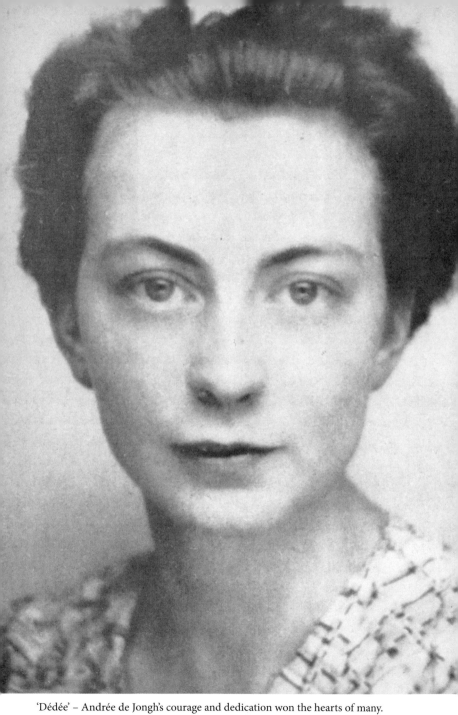

'Dédée' – Andrée de Jongh's courage and dedication won the hearts of many.

4

The Escaping Club

The first thing that struck Neave as he arrived at the castle at the end of May 1941 was the 'gay, Elizabethan' high spirits of the prisoners. They 'sauntered proudly beneath the turrets … British, French, Belgians, Dutch, Poles and Serbs.'[1] It was reminiscent of Crace's house at Eton, 'a salon filled with wit and self-confidence'. They were the cream of the escapologists, graduates of camps all over Hitler's empire. They would have a hard time exercising their talents in Colditz. The castle was the ancient seat of Augustus the Strong of Saxony. The thick mediaeval walls, ninety feet high, stood on a plug of rock with sheer escarpments on three sides. It was a physical definition of a fortress, and as difficult to get out of as it was to get into.

None of this deterred the prisoners. Every officer in the castle 'had but a single thought – to escape', and there was none of the fatalistic acceptance that had prevailed at Spangenberg and Thorn. Despite the unpromising geology, numerous tunnelling projects were under way, multinational affairs conducted by 'boards of directors'. By the end of July, there were about fifty British and Commonwealth officers among more than five hundred prisoners. The French made up the largest contingent (approximately 250), followed by the Poles, with 150. The place was abuzz with escape-related subsidiary industries. Every object that had a potential use was exploited: ancient lead piping could be melted down to make fake German uniform buttons and a dentist's drill was handy for cutting keys.

By the time Neave arrived, a team of twelve British officers and a Pole had been working for months on a tunnel. On 29 May, they made their bid. The tunnel led from beneath the floor of the canteen to beyond the eastern exterior wall. They believed they had an ally in a guard whose allegiance they thought they had secured with money, cigarettes and chocolate. He promised to arrange to be on sentry duty at the point beyond the wall where they planned to break surface. Their faith was misplaced. From the start, he had been reporting their progress to his superiors. Just as they thought freedom beckoned, the escapees were hauled out of the tunnel and off to a spell of solitary confinement – the standard punishment being four weeks.

This failure reinforced Neave's belief that tunnels were a waste of time. He nonetheless joined a Polish-led team who had sunk a shaft beneath the sickbay and for several months did his share of digging, working exhausting four-hour shifts, twice a week. It was a sort of therapy. 'Such activities strengthen the spirit of the prisoner of war,' he wrote. 'They occupy his mind and body and avoid the tedium which may lead to madness. This renders all escape operations worth while, however remote and harebrained the scheme.' He admitted there was another reason for signing up: 'because I still had a sense of being at school, I did not wish to be left out of the second eleven.'

The reference to school was telling. The prisoners' escape impulse was matched by a 'common desire to infuriate the Germans'. It was the same spirit that had animated the rags and mobbings of his Eton days. Like unruly schoolboys, the prisoners were determined whenever possible to undermine authority by mockery, some of it brilliantly subversive. Neave once told Norman Tebbit* a story that he did not include in his memoirs. Following a sentence of solitary

---

* Norman Tebbit (1931–), educated Edmonton Grammar School; Conservative MP for Chingford, 1970–92 (Epping 1970–74); successively Secretary of State for Employment, 1981–83, Trade and Industry, 1983–85, Chancellor of the Duchy of Lancaster, 1985–87; Chairman of the Conservative Party, 1985–87; created Lord Tebbit of Chingford, 1992.

confinement, he was lying in his cell, one of several along a corridor. One end of the passage was blocked off; at the other was an iron gate with a guard on the far side. '[Neave] was woken in the early hours of the morning by the sound of the cell door being unlocked,' said Tebbit.[2] 'There stood a prisoner from the cell next door – a Canadian who happened to be a locksmith in civilian life.' The pair chatted for a while. Before calling it a night, they could not resist the opportunity to wind up the guards. 'They wrote little messages saying, "Please wake me at 6.30. I would like scrambled eggs and bacon for breakfast," and stuck them on their doors.'

Neave was coming to believe that deception was a better way of outwitting the Germans than digging. The gap in the Germans' defences was mental not physical and in particular, their reverence for authority. He started to think that it might be possible to deceive the guards 'by a bold attempt to leave by the front gate in German uniform'.[3] By now the prisoners knew their captors' routines intimately. The comings and goings of the garrison were of particular interest. It was noted that anyone entering the castle's inner courtyard picked up a brass disc at the guardhouse, which they then showed to the sentry on the gate. A workman had been persuaded to hand over one of these discs in return for tobacco, and it was added to the communal store of escape aids. Neave hoped it would be his passport to freedom.

This time he would act alone. Even the escape-happy inmates of Colditz seemed to regard the scheme as fanciful. It involved concocting a fake German uniform and bluffing his way through the controls disguised as an NCO. There were at least four guard posts to negotiate. It was 400 miles to the Swiss border, but as he admitted, 'My plans hardly extended beyond the last gate of the castle,'[4] where he hoped to steal a bike and pedal to the frontier. Bit by bit, he assembled his military and civilian disguises. The latter consisted of an old RAF tunic, boiled up in a cauldron with the lead from indelible pencils and dyed blue, and Air Force trousers. The ensemble was topped off with a home-made Tyrolean-style homburg, made out of blanket material stiffened with glue. The uniform was even more improbable. A month's chocolate ration bought him a Polish tunic in khaki. There were no pencils of the right hue available to achieve an authentic German *Feldgrau*. He decided to use paint, which the Germans allowed to be sold in the canteen to create backdrops for the camp theatrical productions. An array of prisoners who had now retrained themselves as artisans provided fake insignia, a cardboard belt with silver paper buckle, a cap and a wooden bayonet and scabbard. The only authentic-looking item was a pair of Polish army jackboots.

Neave's disguise had no chance of succeeding in daylight. Even in darkness it was unlikely to fool anyone who gave him a cursory glance. His last escape attempt had been a physical and mental ordeal, and could easily have landed him in a concentration camp or in front of a firing squad. Yet despite this knowledge and the scepticism of Captain Pat Reid, the British contingent's escape officer, he pressed on. 'A hysterical impatience overcame me,' he wrote. 'My plans absorbed my whole life and influenced every thought and action.'

On a hot August evening in 1941, he was ready. At nine o'clock, he went with the others to the parade ground for the evening roll-call, his fake uniform hidden under a stifling British Army overcoat. With the order to dismiss, someone whisked away the coat and as the prisoners surged back to their quarters, he marched towards the main door of the courtyard. Producing the magic disc, he announced he had a message for Hauptmann (Captain) Paul Priem, the senior camp security officer. The guard let him through. Then it was on to the first archway. He claimed later that even in these nerve-racking moments the sensation of freedom was 'like a drug which brought an intense pleasure, an exquisite unburdening of the soul'.[5] If so, it was short-lived. Even before he reached the arch, there were shouts from the guardhouse behind. He turned back and saw the arc lights shining on his pathetic disguise. The tunic showed up 'a shade of pea-green'. The cap was the worst: 'It shone like a brilliant emerald in the glare.' He felt like 'a demon king under the spotlights in a Christmas pantomime', but nonetheless started to run.

A shout of 'Halt, or I fire!' stopped him. He raised his hands and was led away at rifle point for a night in the cells, with the threat that he would be shot for dishonouring the German uniform ringing in his ears. Next morning, he was brought before the camp commandant, Oberst (Colonel) Prawitz, who found the absurdity of the situation amusing. As he stood there, 'a sad joke in a burlesque uniform', Neave was ordered to salute, German fashion. The commandant was not satisfied and ordered him to do it again. He spent the rest of the morning under guard while passers-by examined him 'as if I were a newly captured animal'. There was a final humiliation. An elderly photographer was summoned from the town. He set up an antique camera and snapped him from different angles. Neave grew 'crimson with mortification' as he posed, 'perspiring beneath my dyed jacket ... I had reduced all escaping to a ridiculous farce, a music-hall turn.'[6]

The pictures are on display in the escape museum at modern-day Colditz. Far from looking mortified, Neave seems to be quite enjoying the joke, and the fake uniform is less amateurish than his self-flagellating account suggests. The Germans wrung one last laugh from the episode. That evening Priem, who, according to Pat Reid, 'possessed a rare quality among Germans – a sense of humour',[7] announced to the prisoners that 'Gefreiter [Lance Corporal] Neave is to be sent to the Russian front.' It was a good joke and the castle rocked with laughter. Neave's punishment was the usual – twenty-eight days in solitary. There was a backlog of miscreants. The castle's punishment cells were full and the town gaol had been pressed into service to accommodate the overflow. Even there, space was at a premium and it was several weeks before there was a vacancy.

In early October, he was marched from the inner courtyard where the prisoners were housed through a succession of guarded archways and onto the bridge across the castle moat. As they crossed the bridge, Neave's eye was caught by something that gave him fresh hope. A wicket gate in the bridge opened onto a pathway that ran down to the bed of the dry moat. There it crossed to the other bank, before disappearing by the side of a block housing married prison staff. It stood alongside the wall of the large park that adjoined the castle. If he could get onto the path, he would avoid the last guardhouse at the castle entrance. As far as he could see, there was no barbed-wire fencing on the far side of the moat. The only thing standing between an escaper and open country was the wall of the park. The prisoners were taken there for exercise twice a week and Neave knew the wall presented no serious obstacle.

He clung to this thought as he passed the next four weeks smoking cigarettes and the pipe he then affected, savouring Red Cross chocolate – a great luxury in wartime Germany – and reading novels. Like other prisoners, he found that a stretch in the cooler made quite a pleasant change from what he called the 'twitter' of the camp. He 'did not feel caged and helpless', as he had been when held for interrogation in Poland. In fact, he had 'almost forgotten the Gestapo. Now I thought only of escape.'[8]

Given the terror that he admitted feeling at that time, Neave had recovered his sangfroid remarkably quickly. Despite their bad-boy status, at Colditz prisoners 'were better treated than at Thorn'. The ambience tended to reinforce the idea that escaping was a kind of game, a gentlemanly extension of the field of conflict between honourable enemies. The prison food was grim – barley gruel with strips of hog hide or potatoes and turnip stews for lunch, and bread, spread with a little margarine and jam, for breakfast and supper. But the diet was supplemented by Red Cross parcels, shared by all, which came once or twice every three weeks. They weighed ten and a half pounds each and contained a selection of tinned meat, vegetables, cheese, butter, jam, egg and milk powder, tea or cocoa, sugar, cooking fat and, of course, chocolate.

Prisoners were woken at 7.30 and the first roll-call, or *Appell*, took place at 8.30, after breakfast. According to Pat Reid, thereafter they were 'free to carry on any lawful pursuit such as reading, studying, language lessons, music lessons, or exercise'. The Poles were great linguists and were happy to provide classes in a range of languages. In the afternoon, in the courtyard they played volleyball and 'stool-ball', a variant of the Eton wall game in which sides up to thirty strong fought for possession of a football. All methods were allowed and Reid regarded it as 'the roughest game I have ever played, putting games like rugby football in the shade'.[9] It was in the gaolers' interests to keep their charges busy, exhausted and reasonably contented. However, the calming effect of a relatively benign regime was constantly under attack by a larger imperative.

The inmates had their bad-boy status to maintain. One First World War escape yarn, written by Alfred 'Johnny' Evans, an RFC pilot, and devoured by schoolboys in the inter-war years, was called *The Escaping Club*. That, effectively, is what Colditz had become. To maintain your credentials, you had to keep on trying. Neave felt the impulse acutely. Among the motives driving him seems to have been the conviction that imprisonment had given him a chance to shine that had eluded him on the battlefield. His failed escape from Thorn was his most notable achievement to date. A successful one would not only bring him distinction, it could also be presented as a genuine contribution to the war effort: by boosting morale, tying up German resources in the inevitable hunt and potentially yielding important information about both prison conditions and enemy attitudes and dispositions.

In their anxiety to keep the inmates out of mischief, the Germans handed Neave his great opportunity. The camp had its own theatre, housed in a large room on the second floor of a block adjoining the guardhouse at the gate to the inner courtyard. There the prisoners put on regular concerts and variety shows. In December 1941, rehearsals began for a pantomime called *Ballet Nonsense*, dreamed up by Lieutenants Teddy Barton and Jimmy Yule. The production values were high and the enterprise was taken seriously. Given his literary enthusiasms and taste for amateur theatricals demonstrated in the Merton Floats, it was natural that Neave got involved. He contributed a sketch called 'The Mystery of Wombat College', a knockabout effort that smacked of Etonian humour. He wrote the part of Dr Calomel, the unpleasant headmaster, for himself.

While preparations for the panto continued, two ardent escapers had made an important discovery. Ferreting around in the rooms adjoining the theatre, Pat Reid and Hank Wardle, the Canadian RAF flier who had been sent to Colditz after a failed escape bid from Spangenberg, found a disused passageway that could be accessed from below the stage. The locked door at one end – easily picked by Wardle – led to an enclosed bridge leading to the attic of the gatehouse. As well as the guardroom on the ground, it housed an officers' mess on the first floor. The conduit had possibilities and it was Reid who came up with an idea as to how to exploit them. He proposed that two two-man teams, composed of one Briton and one Dutchman, dressed in German uniform, should aim to enter the guardhouse from the least expected direction and bluff their way through the successive castle gates.

As escape officer, it was Reid's decision who should get the chance. The protocol was that prisoners took their turn. However, despite the fact that he was not at the front of the queue, Reid chose Neave. Reid had been impressed by his 'dynamic determination'. All the other escape projects had been thwarted and Reid felt a success was vitally important. 'This young man was the man I wanted,' he remembered many years later. 'I chose him and pinned my faith on him and he proved it in the end.'[10] It was Reid's plan, but Neave claimed to have had a hand in the design. He wrote that 'it seemed to me that if two men in German officers' uniforms were to descend the stairs from the attic and emerge from the guard-house door through the passage which the door of the actual guard room opened, their appearance would not be questioned by the sentry outside. What more natural than that two officers, after visiting the mess above, should appear from the guard-room door [and start] walking towards the Kommandantur?' – the administrative offices that enclosed the outer courtyard.[11]

It was clear that the disguises would have to be a lot more convincing than had been used in Neave's previous dressing-up-box effort. Fortunately, an understanding forged between the British and sixty-odd Dutch inmates provided a solution. According to Reid, they were 'as obstinate as mules and as brave as lions'.[12] Most of them spoke good English and German. The two groups soon partnered up, with the Dutch using British escape supplies while they contributed their language skills and – crucially – the use of their uniforms. Netherlands army kit was a shade of greeny-blue which closely resembled German *Feldgrau*. Neave acquired a long overcoat, which the camp tailors remodelled to conform to Wehrmacht issue, complete with authentic-looking braid epaulettes, made from lino removed from the bathroom floor and painted silver. They also acquired neutral-looking trousers, jackets and coats that would pass for civilian outfits for the second part of their journey.

Neave's partner was Lieutenant Abraham Pierre Tony Luteyn, well-built, good-looking and amiable, but with a tungsten core of determination. Tony Luteyn, as he was usually known, was born in Batavia, in the Dutch East Indies, and was a cadet at the military academy in Breda, Holland, when the war broke out. He was one of a group of more than sixty members of the Royal Dutch East Indies Army who had refused the German offer of an amnesty if they signed a declaration that they would take no part in the war against them, and had chosen prison instead. He was a year younger than Neave and the ideal travelling companion. He was resourceful and had the stamina of mind and body necessary for the protracted crises and dilemmas of escaping. Above all, he spoke excellent German, far better than Neave's. From his own, modestly related account of the escape, it is clear that his superior grasp of the language was vital in alerting the pair to potential danger and talking them out of trouble, and that without him, the bid might easily have failed. The stresses of escaping could be enough to fracture even the most apparently durable friendship. Neave made no mention of the state of relations between himself and Norman Forbes during their escape. Of Luteyn he said that 'rebellious by temperament though I was, I found him easy to work with and we seldom argued with each other.'[13] This is a neutral-sounding endorsement and as we shall hear later, the relationship that resulted from their shared experience seems to have meant more to Luteyn than it did to Neave.

Once clear of Colditz, the pair intended to abandon their uniforms and dress as civilian 'guest workers', then head for the Swiss frontier by train, crossing via the German border town of Singen, 400 miles to the south-west. The route was proposed by the Dutch contingent, having already been proved by an officer of the Royal Netherlands Navy, Lieutenant Hans Larive, who had escaped from Oflag VI-A in Soest, Germany, in October 1940. He was caught at Singen but had learned from a talkative German the best place to cross into neutral Switzerland. On 15 August 1941, he and another Dutch naval officer, Francis Steinmetz, escaped from Colditz by hiding in a manhole under cover of a game of rugby during exercise in the Castle grounds. They reached Switzerland via Singen three days later and both made a 'home run' back to Britain, where they served on Motor Torpedo Boats. This feat, perhaps surprisingly, gets little mention in Neave's account, as do the escapes of the ten French and two other Dutch Colditz POWs who, by one means or another, made successful getaways before he achieved his own. This reticence might be taken as further evidence of the jealous pride that Neave took in his feat as the first *British* officer to escape and a reluctance to dilute it by reference to the exploits of others.

Luteyn had never met Neave, but once they were teamed up they started to spend time together. Luteyn would be disguised as a German captain, Neave as a lieutenant. Luteyn believed their body language should reflect the difference in rank. Neave struck him as rather 'nonchalant ... normally he walked with his hands in his pockets, like a lot of British officers.'[14] In order to 'to train him to be subordinate to me we walked for a week in the courtyard, up and down, him walking at my left-hand side ... when I turned he had to turn around me ... a well-dressed German lieutenant, walking with his captain.'

The original plan was for Neave and Luteyn to escape during a performance of *Ballet Nonsense*. During the noisy finale, they would climb through a trapdoor under the stage and shin down a knotted-sheet rope into the passage that led to the bridge to the guardhouse. After donning their uniforms, they would descend the stairs to the guardroom door and head for the moat bridge and the path that led to the park. In the event, the uniforms were not completed by the time the pantomime began its run. The prisoners passed a boozy Christmas, lit up by hooch distilled from currants and raisins, and on 5 January 1942, everything was in place. The weather was perfect. It was blowing a blizzard that would mask their disguises and deter the guards from over-zealous interpretation of their duties.

As he went down for the 9 p.m. roll-call, Neave had 'an overpowering sense that this was my last evening in the castle'.[15] After the order to dismiss, he and Luteyn went with Pat Reid and Hank Wardle to the darkened theatre and clambered beneath the stage. They loosened the floorboards and, one by one, slid down the sheet rope through a hole in the ceiling to the passage below. They crept to the door opening onto the bridge that connected to the guardhouse and, after an anxious ten minutes, Reid finally managed to pick the lock. The door swung open and they were in the attic. There were handshakes and 'good lucks' and Wardle and Reid padded away. Up the well of the stone spiral staircase drifted organ music playing on the guardroom radio. They took the steps confidently, past the light showing under the door of the officers' mess, to the ground floor. The guardroom door was half open, but no one gave them a glance. Then they stepped out into the freezing night air and the blinding white of the snowflakes swirling in the arc lights.

The sentry on the gate saluted promptly, but Neave sensed his eyes boring into their backs. They passed the first archway and the second sentry without incident. Two officers came up behind them, talking loudly, and in an effort to appear casual Neave clasped his arms behind him – until Luteyn told him not to be a bloody fool and to march with his hands by his side in proper Prussian fashion. Then they were through the clock tower, where the sentry gave another obedient salute. The moat bridge stretched ahead, and to the left, the wicket gate he had noted three months before. Down they went into the moat, stumbling and slipping on the snow. A soldier approached on the path. When he reached them, he stopped and stared.

'Why do you not salute?' snapped Luteyn.

The soldier gaped, then obeyed, and went on his way. They crossed to the far side of the moat and passed the married quarters. They groped through snow-laden shrubs to the high stone wall that bounded the park. Neave scrabbled to the top first and tried to pull Luteyn after him. The stones were caked in snow and ice and he kept slithering back. At last, he grabbed the Dutchman under the armpits and hoisted him up beside him. They sat for a few minutes filling their lungs with the freezing air. Then they dropped twelve feet to the frozen ground, landing heavily. Another minute passed. Neave was bruised, shaken and rather frightened. But there were no more obstacles and they were on their way.[16]

They shed their uniforms and got into their civilian outfits, completed by caps with earflaps, which were welcome in the intense cold. They had German money, chocolate bars, a compass and authentic-looking papers identifying them as Dutch electricians who had volunteered to work in the Reich, forged by a Dutch officer who worked in the Kommandantur and had access to an official typewriter and stamps. Their first objective was the small town of Leisnig, six miles away. On this adventure, trekking was to be kept to a minimum. They were going to take trains wherever possible. Their cover was plausible enough. Germany was swarming with workers from the conquered territories, drafted in to replace the men at the front. Their story was that they had been ordered to move from Leipzig – the nearest large town to Colditz – to Ulm, close to the Swiss border. They set off through the snow in their civvies for the train station, where they took an early workers' train to Leipzig.

At Leipzig station they learned there was no train south until 10.30 that evening. A dangerous day lay ahead. Their best protection was inconspicuousness, yet almost immediately Neave did something stupid. In the station waiting room, packed with dejected, down-at-heel passengers, he pulled out a large bar of Red Cross chocolate and started to eat. A young woman, with 'fierce, hysterical eyes, gazed at the chocolate as if she had seen a ghost.' In wartime Germany it was a fabulous luxury and no one had tasted it for months. As the nudging and muttering grew, Neave and Luteyn slunk out into the hostile streets.

Neave was disappointed that there were no signs of RAF bombing. As for the mood of the inhabitants, the young blonde women in short skirts, and the smart soldiers they gazed at with 'fiercely possessive blue eyes', seemed confident and hopeful. The older generation, though, looked 'shabby', 'hungry' and 'unhappy'. He 'could read memories in their worn faces and their hatred of Hitler's New Order'.[17] Whether these feelings occurred to him then or whether they surfaced later, they reveal a humane attitude towards the enemy. Unlike some of the wartime generation, Neave insisted on the distinction between Germans and Nazis. He was reluctant to demonise even the worst of them, trying hard to understand their motives before condemning, and in the case of Rudolf Hess, was ready to show them compassion.

Luteyn says that when they ducked into the shelter of a shabby cinema, Neave committed a second faux pas when he lit up an English cigarette whose distinctive Virginia tobacco 'you could smell for miles' and was told sharply by him to put it out. There Neave got his first real feeling of what had been going on beyond the prison walls during his eighteen months of incarceration. The newsreel showed footage from Libya – Rommel standing beside his staff car in the desert and Panzers churning through the sand. Then there was a close-up a captured British pilot. He was waving encouragement to his comrades still fighting in the air. In the castle, there had been a hidden radio on which they tuned into the BBC. Otherwise, all Neave knew of the progress of the war was from German propaganda. In his excitement, he grabbed the seat in front of him, to the annoyance of its occupant. 'I could have wept from joy,' he wrote. 'At least the war was not yet lost.'[18] The newsreel showed more good news. There were images of the Eastern Front, where the Germans were enduring their first struggle with General Winter. Soldiers dragged guns and vehicles through a blinding blizzard and frozen corpses littered the ground. The idea was presumably to impress the public with the troops' sufferings, in order to inspire them to greater sacrifices at home. It was clear, though, that the days of cheap and easy victories were over.

That night they boarded the train to Ulm. Their stories were holding up well. There was an alarming moment when a man in SS uniform invited them to share his compartment. Luteyn's German came to the rescue and before long the pair were chatting easily about the situation in Holland. According to Neave, when they arrived at Ulm station, they went to the booking office and Luteyn asked for two tickets to Singen. The girl behind the counter frowned. Neave's 'heart began to sink'. She asked for their papers and then told them to stay put. She was calling the railway police. They decided not to run but to bluff it out. The policeman who arrived took them to an office, where their papers were examined by a senior colleague. Luteyn's account differs somewhat from Neave's and he makes it clear that but for a stroke of luck, their bid for freedom might well have ended here. He says that he asked for a ticket to Tuttlingen, twenty miles short of Singen, which was less likely to be under close surveillance. This, however, aroused the female ticket office clerk's suspicions and resulted in them being marched off for interrogation by a police 'commissioner'. Things looked black until the officer examined Luteyn's (genuine) Dutch passport and noted that he had been born in Batavia. He told him: '"That's a nice hot country," and we started talking about Indonesia and how good it was.' The policeman nonetheless wanted to know why he had asked for a ticket to Tuttlingen when their papers only authorised them to go to Ulm. He replied: 'We are Dutchmen and we have never seen mountains.' They planned to spend the night there and return the following day. The officer replied that 'he had been young too. He would not report it but we were never to do it again.' With that they were sent off with an armed escort to the labour office in town which controlled the movement of foreign workers.

On the way, they both talked cheerfully to their minder, praising the beauty of the old town and trying to win his confidence. It seemed to work. He asked them about life in Holland and, when they got to their destination, left them at the front door, telling them they could make their own way to the appropriate office while he waited for them downstairs. The pair were 'hardly able to believe their good fortune'.[19] They roamed the building until they found some stairs that led to a coal cellar from where they escaped into the back streets of Ulm.

After buying a local map, they set off on foot for the town of Laupheim, where it seemed they could get a train for Stockach, about twelve miles from the Swiss frontier. By now, alarm bells must have been ringing everywhere and Stockach was as near to the border as they dared to go. They arrived at Laupheim at dusk and made for the station. There was no difficulty at the ticket counter and at 9 p.m. the little train pulled in to Stockach. From there Singen was, in theory at least, only a few hours' walk away. It was tantalisingly close, but the weather had conspired against them. The road rose 'steeply through the forests and great banks of snow were on either side of us,' he wrote. 'Even by two o'clock in the morning we still had many miles to go.' They trudged on and, at about 5 a.m., decided it was hopeless to try and cross the frontier that night, looking instead for somewhere to hide until the following evening. There were lights showing ahead on the road and figures emerged out of the darkness wheeling bicycles. They seemed harmless and they stopped to talk. They were woodcutters on their way to work. One asked the pair if they were Poles. Luteyn replied that they were. 'I don't believe it,' the questioner replied. 'Poles are not allowed out of their camp at five in the morning.' The oldest woodcutter then told one of the men to go and fetch the police.

Neave was always frank about the ease with which fatigue and discomfort could undermine his morale. After nine hours on the road he was instantly deflated by this setback. 'I was near to surrender,' he wrote. 'My feet seemed to be frozen in my boots ... I hardly cared that we had come so far only to be recaptured. I could only think of warm fires and beds.'[20] But it was soon clear that the woodcutters were frightened of them. They made no attempt to detain them, but just stood there 'irresolute and dumb'. An unspoken signal passed between Neave and Luteyn. Without a word, they set off simultaneously, floundering through the snow across a field and into a forest, running until they collapsed. When they recovered they searched for shelter. Luck was on their side. They came across a large wooden hut, found an open window and climbed in. One room had a bed, where they lay down together and, covered by an old blanket, slept without waking until the following afternoon.

They waited for nightfall, hearing once in the distance the barking of dogs. The hut was well equipped. They found spades with which they could dig themselves out of snowdrifts and white coats – left by bee-keepers, it seemed – which would make perfect camouflage against the snow that was again falling heavily. At five o'clock on the afternoon of 8 January 1942, they made their way through the forest, back to the road that led to Singen. West and south of the town there were woods, through which ran the road and railway line to Schaffhausen, just inside Switzerland. Freedom and safety were within their grasp.

They marched for a mile, with the spades on their shoulders and the white coats under their arms. Then, again, they saw bicycle lamps ahead. A voice shouted at them to halt. Out of the darkness came two boys in the uniform of the Hitler Youth. They were both carrying truncheons. Refreshed by his sleep, Neave 'felt no fear of them … I was determined they should not stop us.' In 'a hectoring fashion', the boys asked them their names and where they were going. Luteyn replied that they were Westphalians working in the neighbourhood. The Westphalian accent was supposed to be close to that of the Dutch. The teenagers seemed uncertain. Neave asked them what was wrong. One replied that they had been 'told to look for two British prisoners who have escaped and are thought to be trying to cross the frontier tonight'. The fugitives laughed. 'They won't get far,' said Luteyn. 'It's much too cold for prisoners.' The boys seemed suspicious, but they went on their way. Afterwards, Neave asked Luteyn what he had in mind if the boys had challenged them again. 'For me to kill one with my spade and you the other,' he replied. 'What did you intend to do?' Neave said, 'Exactly the same.'[21]

They walked through a blacked-out Singen and set off southwards through the woods, heading on a compass bearing to the frontier. At two in the morning, they reached the railway line to Schaffhausen. It was two miles north of the road that marked the German–Swiss border. They wrapped themselves in the white coats and slipped across the tracks, then moved carefully through the trees until they could see the lights of cars passing on the frontier road. Not far to the east was the glow of lanterns and the murmur of voices. It seemed to be a border-post. They settled down in a ditch and waited, watching a guard pace up and down only forty yards away. Beyond the road lay 'a smooth plain of snow surrounded by distant trees'. This few hundred yards of no-man's-land was all that now stood between them and freedom. They crouched there for an hour, finishing off the last of their chocolate and quenching their thirst with mouthfuls of snow. Clouds had covered the moon and a rising wind made the cold even more bitter. 'Do you agree to cross now?' Luteyn asked him. 'This is the moment,' he whispered back. They climbed out of the ditch and crawled towards the invisible frontier, 'ploughing on hands and knees through the deep snow. After what seemed an eternity we rose to our feet, and surged forward into Switzerland.'

It was 9 January 1942, and only eighty-four hours had passed since they walked out of Colditz.

5

Home Run

Half an hour later they arrived in the streets of a village. To Luteyn it 'looked like a painting ... lying asleep in the snow.'[1] They were still not certain that they were actually in Switzerland. As the church bell tolled a quarter past five, they heard the tread of heavy boots on the cobbles and darted into a doorway. A uniformed man was walking towards them. His long green overcoat and pointed hat suggested he was a Swiss frontier guard. There was nothing to do but chance it. They stepped out of the shadows and called out that they were British escaped prisoners. The guard lowered his rifle and smiled. The relief was overwhelming and 'with shouts of joy we flung ourselves upon him, shaking him by the hand and patting his back.' Then the three of them 'clasped each other's hands and danced in the snow, pirouetting and leaping first one way, then the other, so that the whole street echoed with our cheering.'[2]

When he wrote these words in 1953, Neave stated that the hours that followed were a time of supreme importance for him that he doubted would ever be surpassed. 'Never in my life, perhaps, will I ever know such a moment of triumph. Without weapons we had pitted our wits against the might of Nazism and cheated the Germans in all their self-conscious arrogance and cruelty.' Again, in 1969, he described his feat as 'the great emotional event of my life'.[3]

It profoundly shaped his political career and the public perception of who he was. The one thing that anyone who had ever heard of Airey Neave knew about him was that he had escaped from Colditz. Even in death, together with his association with Mrs Thatcher, it was presented as his main claim to fame. Indeed, she herself, when paying tribute to her old friend, remarked that people remembered him 'perhaps most of all for the fact that he got out of Colditz'.

As the first Briton to achieve a 'home run' from the Germans' flagship prison, he attained a celebrity that made up for the disappointments suffered in his conventional military career. In the words of Pat Reid, the castle's second-most distinguished alumnus, he was 'the dove we sent out of the ark'.[4] The question was, how was he going to make use of it? He would have plenty of time to ponder the problem in the months of inactivity that lay ahead. From the village of Ramsen they were taken to the nearby town of Schaffhausen. Switzerland was neutral and, though Allied escapers were assured a welcome, there were still formalities to be observed. They spent several days under 'hotel arrest', which involved sitting in the restaurant, drinking and eating to his heart's content, and chatting with the locals. He wrote a coded postcard to a Colditz inmate to pass the news of their success. He could not resist writing another to the commandant, showing girls in Swiss traditional costume, with a facetious message informing him that 'my friend and I have arrived safely for our holiday' after a pleasant journey. He delayed sending them in order not to spoil the chances of Lieutenants John Hyde-Thomson and H. Donkers, the second Anglo-Dutch escape pair selected by Reid. As it was, they made it out of the castle, only to be arrested at Ulm, where the authorities, having been fooled once, were on maximum alert.

Hotel life was starting to pall by the time Neave and Luteyn were told to pack. They were taken by train to Berne and delivered to their respective legations. This was the parting of the ways and they did not encounter each other again in Switzerland. Luteyn went initially to Curaçao, in the Netherlands West Indies, and ended up rejoining the Dutch forces in Australia. Neave's army record contains two letters from Luteyn seeking to get in touch with him. The second, dated October 1948 and addressed to the War Office, asks that 'as I have never heard anything from him since he left Switzerland in May 1942, I wonder if you could help me by sending me his present address so that I can start corresponding again?' Though Neave kept up with some of his wartime army comrades, as well as with his agents in the escape lines, Luteyn does not seem to have been among them. Intimate though the experience had been, neither had really got to know the other. When Luteyn was asked many years later what sort of man Neave was, he replied that it was 'hard to say'.[5] The fact was they had spoken little during their adventure. Luteyn regarded Neave's German as weak and that left only English, which for obvious reasons they could not use.

In Berne, Neave was put in the charge of the military attaché, Colonel Henry Cartwright, a veteran World War One escaper, and co-author of *Within Four Walls*, a book about his exploits which Neave had read and absorbed as a small boy.[6] Neave was kitted out in an 'awful green tweed suit' and sent for examination by Swiss doctors, one of whom, Dr Albert d'Erlach, was a Red Cross official who had examined him exactly a year before in Colditz.[7] In 1945, the War Office was still pursuing Neave for the cost of the consultation. There was nothing wrong with him, but he was ordered to rest for three weeks. He passed it in d'Erlach's chalet near Gerzensee. He was too preoccupied with all that had happened to read books. Sitting before the fire, looking out at the snow flakes drifting down, he 'felt a great restlessness. My success in reaching Switzerland was the summit of all my hopes. I had not turned my thoughts to the future in store for me … Nothing could ever equal that matchless moment in the streets of Ramsen. I waited, hoping that the end of my adventure would not bring disillusionment.'

But there was yet more hanging around. He was still under Swiss supervision and spent the next two months in the university town of Fribourg, where he stayed in a hotel under loose police supervision. There he lived a life of 'mild dissipation', drinking absinthe, hanging out with Polish officers who were interned in the neighbourhood and chasing girls. This activity carried more than the usual risks. Switzerland was an island of civilisation in a sea of Nazis and Fascists and their stooges. Enemy agents were everywhere, some of them, it was assumed, the convivial females hanging around on the student party circuit.

At last, he received word that he might soon be going home. On 15 April 1942, he was summoned to Berne to see Cartwright, who told him, 'We're sending you back first, Neave. MI9 have asked for you.' He added mysteriously, 'There is a reason, you know.'[8] He and another Army officer, Captain Hugh Woollatt, were to be sent across the Unoccupied Zone of southern France, controlled by the collaborationist Vichy regime, then across the Pyrenees to neutral Spain. He knew 'little or nothing of MI9. Nor could I understand why they should want me back.' Nonetheless, this was a welcome surprise. There were eight other British escapees cooling their heels in Switzerland. Woollatt had been waiting since September, when he had reached Switzerland after tunnelling out of Oflag V-B at Biberach, near the Swiss border.

Neave's ignorance of the organisation called MI9 was understandable. They were new boys in the complex world of military intelligence (for which the initials stood) and had struggled to win the blessing of the big players controlling the war effort and to secure a proper staff and budget to pursue their aims. By the spring of 1942, they were firmly in business but the outfit's existence had yet to become widely known among the prisoners it was primarily designed to help. MI9 officially came into being on 23 December 1939, under the command of Major Norman Crockatt, a handsome, urbane former regular infantry officer, who had won an MC in the previous war and brightened up the corridors of Whitehall by choosing to wear the tartan trews and bonnet of his regiment, the Royal Scots. According to Crockatt, the organisation existed to 'facilitate escapes of British prisoners of war, thereby getting back service personnel and containing additional enemy manpower on guard duties'. Secondly, it was to aid 'the return to the United Kingdom of those who succeeded in evading capture in enemy occupied territory'.[9] It was further engaged in 'collecting and distributing information', 'assisting in the denial of information to the enemy' and 'maintaining the morale of British POWs in enemy camps'.

The team around Crockatt was as diverse and unorthodox as the branch of warfare they were waging demanded. Among them was Christopher Clayton Hutton, an idiosyncratic but forceful character who had once challenged Houdini to escape from a packing case manufactured by his timber merchant uncle. Houdini, having bribed the workmen at the mill to use fake nails, won. 'Clutty' was put to work devising escape kits for issue to airmen. They included maps printed on silk handkerchiefs, miniature compasses, benzedrine pills and concentrated food tablets. He also designed uniforms and boots that could be converted to look like civilian attire. Tens of thousands of the kits were issued as standard to aircrew operating over occupied Europe following the fall of France.

Crockatt's mission was to cultivate a sense of 'escape-mindedness' in commanders and those they led. By the beginning of 1940, MI9 lecturers were trying to instil in soldiers, sailors and particularly airmen the notion that escape was not only feasible but a patriotic duty. As already noted, many of those who ended up 'in the bag' remained unconvinced by the argument that they could contribute to the war effort by making their captors' lives as difficult as possible. In the light of post-war analysis, there are reasons to believe they may have been right.

But war creates a climate in which the unorthodox, even the outlandish, gets a more respectful hearing than would ever be the case in peacetime. Crockatt was remarkably effective at inserting into official thinking the doctrine that escape efforts were to be systematically encouraged and supported. Of course, not everyone was convinced. MI9 would find that it was their brethren in the intelligence community who resisted their operations most fiercely. The world of the secret agencies was notorious for its bitchiness, feuding and atmosphere of mutual suspicion. For some at the top of the senior organisation, MI6, the activities of the newcomers had the potential to endanger their own operations. Crockatt and his team would have to tread carefully to come through the minefield of rivalries unscathed.

By the time Neave reached Switzerland, MI9 was beginning to involve itself in prisoner escapes. Cartwright, as well as being a military attaché, was the organisation's main man in the vital territory of Switzerland. According to the later account he left of this episode, Neave says that Cartwright told him, 'MI9 have sent orders for you and Hugh Woollatt to cross the Swiss frontier as soon as possible.'[10] If they were given a reason for their good fortune, Neave does not reveal it. In his case, perhaps, it was because the organisation was anxious to learn all it could about Colditz from the first Briton to have broken out of it.

Cartwright added that although 'we have sent one or two people through before ... you are still guinea pigs.' This seems to have been a reference to Lieutenant Michael Duncan and Captain Barry O'Sullivan, who had tunnelled out of Oflag V-B at Biberach on 13/14 September 1941 at the head of a column of about two dozen escapees that included Woollatt himself. Most were recaptured. Duncan and O'Sullivan travelled together across Bavaria, where they separated. According to the official historians of MI9, 'each knew, from smuggled large-scale maps, exactly where he wanted to go. They crossed into Switzerland in the Schaffhausen salient and were clearly aware of every twist and angle of it at the points they chose to cross; information that must have reached them from maps prepared under Crockatt's guidance and sent in by Clayton Hutton's ingenuity.'[11] Their plan may also have been helped by information reaching them from Johnny Evans, of *Escaping Club* fame. This was the route he had taken when he escaped in 1918, and he had returned to the area on walking tours in the 1930s, pausing to record the landscape in sketches.[12]

Once in Switzerland, Duncan and O'Sullivan were entrusted to Cartwright. He sent them over the border to be picked up by the 'Pat Line', an escape chain that had been operating since the fall of France. In the light of this, Cartwright's suggestion that he and Woollatt were 'guinea pigs' seems strange. One explanation could be that in view of the difficulties the network was then facing, the pair's experiences would prove whether or not the Pat Line was still reliable. The journey was not going to be easy. Since the armistice signed between the Germans and the French in June 1940, the country had been divided into an Occupied and an Unoccupied Zone. The 'demarcation line' between them ran roughly east to west across the middle of France, swinging south before the Atlantic, so that the Germans controlled the coastline as far as the Pyrenees. The Vichy government was technically neutral and supposed to control local affairs inside the Unoccupied Zone. Its attitude towards British servicemen who had evaded capture after Dunkirk was correct according to the Geneva Conventions. They were interned, mostly in three forts on or near the Mediterranean coast, in the Gard, at Marseilles and La Turbie, just inland from Monaco.* Conditions varied, reflecting the degree of enthusiasm for collaboration among those who operated it. At Marseilles, officers only had to turn up to roll-call on Monday morning, when they were issued with rations which they sold on the black market, using the proceeds to rent lodgings in the town. They were 'not quite prisoners, not quite free'.[13]

The status of escaped prisoners was more problematical and hazardous. It was illegal for aliens of military age to travel through Vichy territory unless they had diplomatic status. Any male caught trying to leapfrog to the Iberian peninsula was liable to be handed over to the Germans. The initial stages of the operation had a cloak-and-dagger quality that reminded Neave of the novels of E. Phillips Oppenheim, a bestselling inter-war thriller writer. The set-up felt melodramatic and amateurish. He was to head for Geneva, where a man reading a copy of the *Journal de Genève* would meet him at the station bookstall. The hotel where he then met up with Woollatt was also a brothel, with an aged procuress manning the front desk. More seriously, the cover story the pair had been given seemed ridiculously flimsy. They were travelling as Czech refugees, making for a reception centre near Marseilles. That neither of them spoke a word of the language and could not even pronounce the names on their forged identity cards did not seem to bother 'Robert', the slender Englishman in a pin-striped suit who organised their departure.

The Swiss authorities were in on the plan. Early on the morning of 17 April 1942, Neave and Woollatt were given a police escort to

---

* From January 1941, the camp at Fort St-Jean at Marseilles was closed and its internees moved to the other two.

a cemetery on the western edge of town, where they crouched down among the headstones to await sunrise.[14] Just before dawn, they vaulted the wall and negotiated a barbed-wire barrier on which Neave ripped a large hole in his trousers. Safely across, they headed for a crossroads with a signpost to Annemasse, the French border town just south of Geneva, where they had been told to wait for an elderly gentleman riding a bike, dressed in blue overalls and beret, with clogs on his feet and a clay pipe clenched upside down in his mouth. Even at this hour, the road was busy with men cycling to work, many of whom fitted the description. Eventually, one dismounted and introduced himself. 'Good morning, gentlemen,' he said. 'I am Louis Simon, formerly of the Ritz Hotel, London. Would you care to follow me to the frontier post?'[15] Such surreal moments were far from rare in the strange universe of escape and evasion.

From now on, Neave and Woollatt had little choice but to place their trust in each new figure who popped up to help. It required a considerable leap of faith. Neave's experience of the French had been contradictory. There was the memory of the defeatism shown by many French troops during the fighting at Calais, and the stories of collaboration and fifth columnists. Even in Colditz there had been a shameful episode when some French officers had demanded that the Jews among them be moved to separate quarters. Neave had spoken out vociferously against this betrayal.

The example shown by Louis Simon, and many other men and women like him, was an uplifting antidote to the contempt and bitterness that many British servicemen felt towards their former comrades as a result of their experiences in the Battle of France. Jimmy Langley was one of many evaders and escapers who found 'every sort of readiness to help … among the poorer sorts of people and every sort of reserve among most of the rich'.[16] Many of those who fed, clothed, sheltered and guided the fugitives were women. After Louis had shepherded them through the frontier post at Annemasse, they were handed over to a 'young, sad-faced French woman' called 'Mademoiselle Jeanne', who led them to the next safe house, a short distance away. As they waited in the kitchen,

Neave was struck by her 'mystic devotion and courage which placed her far above the desires of the world'.[17] This was an early encounter with one of the many extraordinary women he was to meet over the next few years. They were uncategorisable: some 'virginal and fanatical' like Jeanne; others warm and desirable like Andrée de Jongh, who would loom large in the time to come, to whom Neave, among many others, was passionately devoted. What they shared was a courage and resourcefulness that men of his upbringing did not readily associate with girls.

Before he escaped, women seem to have played little part in Neave's life, romantically or professionally. In his copious writings there is no mention of pre-war girlfriends, and the studied loucheness of his undergraduate days and early London bachelor life does not seem to have extended to floozies, though he does seem to have had one pre-war liaison, as will be seen later. Whatever his previous view of women, his experiences en route to London left him with a strong regard for female stoicism and resolve. This outlook shaped his approach to his work at MI9, and had its effect many years later on British politics and history.

A variety of helpers handed Neave and Woollatt down the line to the staging post at Marseilles, where they were to pause before crossing the Pyrenees. Alex, a flash young black-marketeer, could not have been more unlike the ascetic Jeanne, yet he was just as trustworthy and patriotic. He and another young resister, Pierre, escorted them on the overnight train west. Pierre's wife radiated fear when Neave and Woollatt turned up at their door, but she battled against her nerves and served them a meal before departure. Her behaviour won Neave's sympathy. Bravery came in many forms, and she was 'courageous in her weakness, seeking to struggle on for the sake of her husband'.[18]

After some anxious moments at Marseilles, they made contact with their next protector. Louis Nouveau and his circle were the exception to Langley's observation that a fugitive was unwise to expect help from the wealthy. Before the war he had been a stockbroker in the City of London and his friends were successful local businessmen, two of them of Greek origin and one married to a German communist.

The pair spent the next fortnight with Nouveau and his wife, Renée, in a modern flat on the Quai Rive Neuve overlooking the old port. Though he did not know it, they were in the hands of one of the major escape networks ferrying evaders who had avoided capture through occupied France and into Spain. It was now run by a man known as 'Pat O'Leary', who despite his Irish name was a former Belgian army doctor: hence the 'Pat Line'.

O'Leary had inherited the line, not founded it. It had been built up ad hoc by a small group of unassuming men who had been thrown together by the chaos of war and whose response to it had revealed the gleam of heroism beneath their modest exteriors. The story went back to Marseilles in the summer after the fall of France in 1940. An early arrival was the Reverend Donald Caskie, who had been the minister of the Scots Kirk in Paris, who decided that, in view of the fiery sermons he preached against the evils of Nazism, it was sensible to head south before the Germans reached town. He took over a seamen's mission at the port, which became an unofficial reception centre for British servicemen who by one means or another had fetched up on the Mediterranean shore.

He was soon in partnership with another Scotsman. Ian Garrow was a captain in the Highland Light Infantry serving as a transport officer with the 51st Highland Division. After the division surrendered at St-Valery-en-Caux on 12 June 1940, he and a group of his men set off westwards, hoping to make it back to Britain via the Channel Islands. After many adventures and several changes of plan, they were arrested near Cahors, in the Unoccupied Zone.[19] In October they were moved to Fort St-Jean in the old port at Marseilles.

Like Caskie, he had no experience of clandestine work, but they both turned out to be very good at it. Initially, Garrow was part of a team of British officers at the fort organising escapes. Rather than leave himself, he chose to stay behind and establish an efficient organisation to help others. Under the terms of his parole, he was able to move around reasonably freely. He made friends at the American consulate and among prominent local citizens, including Louis and Renée Nouveau. In June 1941, Garrow teamed up with

Albert-Marie Guérisse, a Belgian army doctor. Guérisse had been evacuated to England during Dunkirk and had joined the Royal Navy, serving on a converted merchantman carrying out clandestine work behind enemy lines for the Special Operations Executive. He had taken the cover name 'Patrick Albert O'Leary'. The first name was bestowed on him by SOE. The rest he borrowed from a French-Canadian friend he had met during a spell at school in England.[20]

In April 1941, Pat O'Leary had been arrested by the French during an operation to land agents and pick up evaders and escapers on a beach near the Spanish border. He was interned in St Hippolyte-du-Fort, north-west of Nîmes, where security was lax. He was soon in touch with Garrow, who organised his escape. He intended to get back to Britain and SOE, but Garrow was impressed by him and saw him as a lieutenant and possible successor. When Garrow was arrested in October 1941, O'Leary took over. The organisation he inherited was by that stage receiving financial help from MI9 in London and the services of MI6, under the cold eye of its Machiavellian deputy director, Claude Dansey. In 1941 he was 64 years old, with forty years in the spy world behind him. 'Z', as he was code-named, was vindictive, arrogant and contemptuous of those he deemed to fall short of his high professional standards – a broad category.

So far, MI6 had not had a good war. Their entire European network had been rolled up in November 1939, when German agents posing as conduits to a dissident group inside the Wehrmacht snatched two key British agents at the town of Venlo, on the Dutch-German border. With the creation of the Special Operations Executive, set up in July 1940 to carry out sabotage operations in occupied Europe and aid local resistance groups, the monopoly MI6 had previously had on undercover work in enemy territory was ended. Dansey deeply resented the encroachment into his domain and seemed to regard SOE as an enemy on a par with the Germans.

His attitude towards the other potential rival, MI9, was more nuanced. The relationship between MI6 and MI9 was imprecisely defined. In the words of the official historians, they were 'closely bound ... sometimes too close for comfort'.[21] However things looked on paper, in the end 'what Dansey wanted done was done, and what he wanted undone was undone.' What is more, 'he could have broken Crockatt, or anyone else in MI9, as easily as he blew his own nose.' Dansey moved in fast to exert control over the infant MI9. In the summer of 1940, he sent a young MI6 officer called Donald Darling to the Iberian peninsula to start re-establishing links between Britain and France, with which there was now no means of communication by land, sea, air or even radio.[22] Under his code name 'Sunday', Darling was soon in touch with Garrow in Marseilles and sending him money. Henceforth he would play a vital role supporting the escape networks in France and Belgium.

To the eyes of Neave and Woollatt, as they passed the days looking out at the spring sunshine sparkling on the waters of the Mediterranean from the comfort of the Nouveaus' flat, the Pat Line seemed efficient and reasonably secure. In fact, it was just recovering from the discovery that for months it had been completely compromised by the treachery of one of its most active members. For every story of selflessness that the Pat Line generated, Harold Cole provided a black counterpoint. The few pictures that exist of him show a nondescript figure with a long thin face, a high forehead and a square jutting chin. His hair was sandy and from time to time he wore a moustache. Despite his drab appearance, he was a master manipulator of both men and women. He was born in Marylebone in London in 1911 and, by the time war broke out, he was well known to the police, who held eleven warrants for his arrest. Cole had joined the Royal Engineers and was posted to France, where in the spring of 1940 he deserted after stealing an officer's uniform and chequebook.[23] He was arrested and imprisoned in Lille, but soon after the German attack in the west he broke out and moved in with a woman in the town, taking the name of her husband, who was off fighting for his country. When the war in France ended, Cole re-emerged in an unexpected role. He made contact with British troops stranded in the area and, using the French contacts he had made through his girlfriend, escorted them with local assistance to Paris and across the demarcation line to Marseilles. In the beginning at least, his motives seem to have been altruistic. News of Cole's good work filtered back to London and he soon won the approval of Claude Dansey. His name also began featuring in intelligence reports reaching Donald Darling in Lisbon. To 'Sunday', he seemed 'the antithesis of the Scarlet Pimpernel, in that he stood out as an Englishman in the very French surroundings in which he operated. Wearing plus fours and a pork pie hat, speaking rudimentary French with a cockney accent, it seemed incredible that he was not questioned and arrested by the Germans.'[24]

Darling reported his thoughts to London but 'learned to my surprise that Colonel Dansey [and MI9] thought he had a sporting chance of getting away with it for some time to come.' Nonetheless, Darling felt Cole was 'too good to be true'. He pestered London to run checks with the War Office and Scotland Yard. The silence that met his requests seemed 'tantamount to telling me to mind my own business'. Meanwhile in Marseilles, O'Leary was also growing suspicious. He had given Cole large sums of money to fund operations in Lille and he decided to check on how much of it had reached the intended beneficiaries. According to the story later recounted by Neave, in autumn 1941, while Cole was relaxing in Marseilles, O'Leary travelled to Lille and contacted a man called Duprez, who had given shelter to British airmen and was supposed to have been reimbursed for his costs.[25] Duprez denied getting any money from Cole and O'Leary brought him back with him to Marseilles to confront Cole.[26] When challenged, Cole denied the charge and insisted Duprez had been paid. After a fight, Cole escaped and returned to northern France, where he offered his services to German military intelligence, the Abwehr. O'Leary tried to warn the line's agents in the area. But according to the MI9 files, the information Cole handed over resulted in a wave of arrests, including that of his mistress.[27] From then on he was a full-time German agent. Neave reckoned that he 'cost the lives of fifty of the escape organisation's bravest helpers'.[28]

It was some time before the scale of his betrayal was pieced together and decisive action taken. In April 1942, just before Neave and Woollatt arrived in Marseilles, O'Leary crossed to Spain and was smuggled into Gibraltar for a summit meeting with Darling and Jimmy Langley of MI9. All addresses and cover names known to Cole were to be abandoned and anyone who encountered him was to shoot him on sight. As Neave pointed out, with communications with London relying on 'a shaky system of messages in toothpaste tubes brought by couriers over the Pyrenees', assembling vital information was extremely difficult. A radio link would have alerted everyone to the suspicions about Cole, but at this stage MI9's activities in the field were not given high priority by the Air Force, and without their help it was impossible to drop wireless operators and sets.

Fortunately for Neave and Woollatt, Cole's activities had not affected the Pat Line's Switzerland-to-Marseilles branch. After two weeks in the Nouveaus' flat, where they had to move about quietly to avoid raising the suspicions of the collaborationist occupants of the flat below, they were told to get ready to leave. An Anglo-French guide called Francis Blanchain took them by train to Toulouse. They stayed for a week while a party of other fugitives – Poles, Frenchmen, Brits and Australians – assembled. A slow train took them to Port Vendres, where they met their guide, a wiry little smuggler who was growing rich through passing people over the mountains. The trek took twenty-four exhausting hours.

On arrival in neutral Spain, there was none of the exhilaration that had gripped them in Switzerland. The regime was unwelcoming and escapees could, if captured, be thrown into gaol. A shifty-seeming local courier took them to the consulate at Barcelona and, on 1 May 1942, two immaculate Foreign Office types drove them in a Bentley to the British embassy in Madrid.

At the beginning of the war, Sir Samuel Hoare, the ambassador, had been anxious to do nothing that would jeopardise his mission's continued presence in neutral Spain. Donald Darling's activities had given him particular cause for concern. Since then, things had relaxed. On arrival, they were met by the first secretary, 'a big man with a welcoming handshake'. This was Michael Creswell, who as 'Monday' was a key player in MI9's Iberian operations and with whom Neave would soon be working. He led them to a large wooden building in the garden where twenty or thirty men were drinking beer and sherry. It was a stirring sight: 'They came from every Allied nation, all of them tough, hard and determined, all of them ready to fight.'[29] After his recent experiences, Neave felt he could hold his head up in such exalted company. The following day, the men boarded a bus and were driven south, bearing papers that identified them as a party of students. At La Línea the Spanish guards did not hide their disbelief but waved them through. In Madrid, he had met 'Monday'. Now, in Gibraltar, he came face to face with Donald Darling, 'Sunday', who interrogated him about his journey. Then he boarded a troopship for Gourock on the Clyde. His life as 'Saturday' was about to begin.

6

Room 900

If Neave was expecting a hero's welcome, he was soon disappointed. On arrival in London, he was subjected to a further interrogation by MI9 at an office in the Great Central Hotel in Marylebone. He remembered the dull and solid pile from his undergraduate days as a place to repair to after a night on the tiles, for a drink or a bath before taking the milk train back to Oxford. He was questioned by an earnest Intelligence Corps captain who recorded his experiences in War Office officialese. When he had finished, he showed Neave the result. The account was 'far less exciting than a report by the CID on their observation of a public convenience'.[1] To have his adventures reduced to a drab recitation of dates and places was annoying. He might not have been on the receiving end of a Gestapo rubber truncheon, but there was nothing in the testimony that could convey 'the sheer terror of being in their hands'. He pretended not to care. He was 'young and lucky' and alive.

He was impatient to visit his family, now at Mill Green Park, Ingatestone, Essex, which Sheffield had inherited in 1936 on the death of his father. This was more of a duty than a pleasure. He wanted 'to get the homecoming over and done with and then get back to London to make up for time lost'. As well as the fun to be had, he had promised some of his old Colditz comrades that he would call on their families with their news. But first, he was told, he could not leave before he had spoken to someone who was waiting for him downstairs. On his way to the rendezvous he ran into

Hugh Woollatt.[2] It was their last meeting. Woollatt was killed in Normandy in 1944.

The man waiting for him in the lobby was Jimmy Langley, who he had last seen in prison hospital in Lille. Neave knew nothing about his escape. Now here he was, neatly turned out in his Coldstream uniform, with one empty sleeve pinned to the tunic. Pleasure at the encounter was tempered by the news that he had been summoned to lunch with 'someone important'. Neave brightened up when he heard that the VIP was Langley's chief at MI9, Brigadier Norman Crockatt. He remembered his encounter back in Berne with Cartwright and the attaché's cryptic remark that MI9 'wanted me back'. He 'began to feel interested'. Lunch was in the masculine comfort of Rules in Covent Garden. After Neave had recounted a few stories of POW life, Crockatt came to the point. He outlined the work MI9 was doing. The escape-and-evasion picture was changing. Until the end of 1941, most evaders were still soldiers stranded after the fall of France. Since then, the tempo of the air war had picked up and the main task now was to recover aircrew who had been shot down. With the American Air Force about to go into action over Europe, the numbers would only go up. These men were highly and expensively trained warriors, whose return to action would advance the struggle.

To sustain the escape lines on the ground, the organisation had begun to train its own agents and to establish new routes to Spain. Crockatt mentioned the problems facing the Pat Line as a result of Cole's treachery. The Gestapo were on to it and it was not expected to last much longer. The men and women in the field needed money and communications. If Neave wanted to help them, Crockatt was offering him a berth working with Langley in MI9's secret escape section. Neave agreed immediately, telling him that 'it's the one job I should like to do. I have become used to the atmosphere of escape, and I would do anything to help the people over there.'[3]

This was a big decision to take without any time for reflection. Yet Neave never seems to have reconsidered his choice. From an early age he had been attracted to the idea of soldiering, joining the Territorials when uniforms were at their most unfashionable. Things had not turned out as he would have hoped. The one thing he had proved good at was escaping. He had the temperament for it. And undoubtedly he wanted to do what he could to repay those who had sacrificed their lives and liberty to help him get back home. But this was still a big step. By accepting Crockatt's offer, he was turning away from the sharp end of warfare and accepting what was probably going to be a largely desk-bound role. Hugh Woollatt was returning to his regiment, taking his place in the line again. Jimmy Langley would perhaps have preferred to do likewise, but he was minus an arm. Joining MI9 meant saying goodbye to Neave's dreams of martial glory. It was an understandable decision, but still a surprising one.

Why had Crockatt wanted him? In Neave's account, after accepting the offer he went on to say, 'I am very pleased, sir, that you think I am suitable.' Crockatt had replied sharply, 'Don't be modest. You are one of the very few who has had such experience – not only of escape from Germany but of the Resistance as well.' This was partly true. There were not many escapers at this point, but plenty of evaders who had made it back and knew far more about the workings of the Belgian and French resistance groups than Neave. And, if being an escaper was an important qualification, why choose Neave and not, say, Woollatt, who had also pulled off a dramatic home run? Espionage in Britain was often a family affair. Jimmy Langley's father had been in the secret service. The intelligence community preferred to recruit from among those they knew and felt comfortable with. If Neave had any family connections, he was too discreet to say so. The die was cast. Crockatt told Neave he would be assigned to the department called IS 9(d), based at Room 900 in the War Office in Whitehall, working alongside Langley. The 'IS' stood for Intelligence School, a meaningless designation at this point. Here Neave's example will be followed and the outfit will be known simply as 'Room 900'. His broad job description was to 'look after secret communications with occupied Europe and training of agents'. The post came with a promotion. He would start as a captain. It was all very gratifying. He left Rules savouring the prospect of 'another great adventure'.

But before that there was a fortnight's leave to enjoy. His father came to meet him at Ingatestone station. Neave 'walked up to him and we said nothing for a moment. It was not a time for words.'[4] The companionship recorded in the Eton diaries seems to have stiffened into something cool and formal. He had written to his parents several months after his capture, complaining about a bureaucratic glitch which had prevented him from being promoted to full lieutenant, something he was entitled to as a result of his TA service. His mother had taken up the cause vigorously, bombarding the authorities with letters, and Sheffield Neave had supported the campaign loyally. Nonetheless, the family maintain that for most of his life, relations between father and son were distant, if not hostile. One cause of the estrangement, they say, was his father's treatment of his mother. Dorothy suffered bad health and had been desperately ill while he was a POW. She had rallied a little just before his return but would die ten months later. How Sheffield Neave dealt with the situation is not documented. However, the family say he was not a faithful husband and that at this time he had already taken up with his assistant, Mary Hodges, who he married in 1946.

Back in the family home, Neave looked out at the meadows beyond the walls of the house, bathed in moonlight. 'There was not a sentry box in sight, no wire, no glint of steel. And yet they were with me always.' Each night, when he heard the chimes of Big Ben before the BBC news, he 'wondered what was happening in the camp'. He was home but his mood was melancholy, and the experience of incarceration had left him with a 'sense of persecution'. It was a natural response, a mild form of survivor guilt, and like any decent person who has been blessed by a deliverance, he could not help thinking about the plight of those left behind and the perils facing those who had helped him on his way.

With the new job, he could start to repay the debt. The pleasures of wartime London helped him recover his spirits. Jimmy Langley had been given a flat at 5 St James's Street, an elegant stucco-fronted building with tall sash windows next door to the wine merchants Berry Bros and Rudd, and he took rooms nearby: 'a flat ... fit for

Bertie Wooster with twentyish furniture'.[5] He spent freely on cigars, tobacco for his pipe and stylish shirts. He was a military man about town with a hush-hush job who, after many setbacks, was having a good war, as the MC – for which he was gazetted as soon as he completed his 'home run' – attested.

Yet he still functioned inside a faint fog of depression. He was out and about at the cocktail parties that abounded in wartime London, but he found that the 'heartless chatter ... became difficult to endure'.[6] Neave makes no mention of any women in his life prior to this time. However, his later diaries do reveal the existence of a pre-war girlfriend. On a trip to Geneva in October 1973, he had dinner with the UK's permanent representative to the UN there, Sir David 'Toby' Hildyard (an Eton contemporary), and his wife, 'my old girlfriend Millicent Baron'.[7] The Barons were Jewish, wealthy and well connected, and friends with the Rufus-Isaacs. It is probable that Airey had met Millicent through his friend Michael Isaacs. She was quite a catch. According to her daughter, 'My mother could have had the pick of the young men about town looking for an heiress to pay off death duties.'[8] Millicent ended up marrying Dickie Longmore, son of a senior RAF officer. Dickie, having followed his father into the service, was killed in action in 1943 while attacking a U-boat.

Despite the lively London social scene, Neave was lonely and often in low spirits and perhaps therefore particularly susceptible to falling in love. There is no doubt, though, that when it happened, it was the real thing. Neave's marriage was more than an emotional fusion. It was an alliance, a partnership that would sustain him until his dying day. The romance began at one of the unendurable cocktail parties. It was a July evening and he was 'standing in a corner talking to a red-haired girl, and laughed with her at simple things. I found in her the confidence I needed. The veil of depression was lifted – for the first time since I was a prisoner I was gay again.' They were 'soon in love'. According to William Neave, they met only three times before Airey proposed and Diana accepted. On 29 December 1942, they were married by the Bishop of Lichfield in St Mary the Virgin and St Chad's, next to the bride's family estate in

Staffordshire. It seemed then that everything that had happened to him – his escape, his return and his marriage – was ordained by God, for as the bishop gave his blessing, 'the sun came suddenly out of the clouds [and] its rays shone on the spot where we were standing in the chancel.'[9]

The red-haired girl was Diana Giffard. She was slim, lively and intelligent, with striking green eyes. She was three and a half years younger than him – just right – and her background fitted well with his own. She was the daughter of Thomas Giffard, who had married Angela Trollope, a kinswoman of the great Victorian novelist. The Giffards had been in Staffordshire since the Norman conquest. They lived at Chillington Hall, whose park had been landscaped by 'Capability' Brown. There was even a romantic link to Neave's own recent history. The family had given shelter to one of the most celebrated evaders of British history, Charles II. To complete the perfection of the match, Diana was in the same line of business as himself. She had started her war work as a nurse at an RAF hospital, but had soon been approached by the Foreign Office and entered the intelligence world, working as a liaison officer with the Polish government-in-exile in London.[10]

The move may have been the result of a family connection. Diana's aunt Sylvia Trollope worked for the intelligence services. According to Marigold Neave, she spent part of the war in Cairo doing 'something hush-hush'.[11] After their marriage, Sylvia arranged for the couple to take over her maisonette above a bakery at 39 Elizabeth Street, near Victoria Station. Agents would spend their last evening in friendly territory there, having a meal and a drink before being parachuted into occupied Europe. Others would celebrate their at least temporary deliverance, having been brought back from London when things got too hot, for a respite and to be debriefed

Diana and Airey started life together as equals, respecting each other's qualities and abilities. Henceforth they would be a team. Their secret occupations created a certain awkwardness at home and the normal chit-chat about events in the office at the end of the day was somewhat circumscribed. Neave used to like recounting how, shortly after his marriage, he ran into his new wife in a Whitehall corridor that was restricted to those with high security clearances. There followed 'one of those ludicrous "What are you doing here?" confrontations'.[12] There were less amusing manifestations. The family tell a story of how both returned home at the end of a difficult day in a deep depression, each having lost an agent to the Germans. Only much later did they discover that it was the same one. According to Hugh Tilney, a family friend, Diana's intelligence background 'gave her the ability – that others didn't have – to contradict Airey, to debate and often win in discussions with him. She was a big, powerful force for him.'[13]

On the morning of 26 May 1942, Neave reported for his first day of duty at Room 900. The small team there were involved in the most secret operational aspect of MI9. Much of the parent organisation's work concerned collecting intelligence about Allied prisoners of war, mostly gleaned from interrogating returnees. This was then used for systematic briefings across the three services on how to avoid capture, or else how to escape. The headquarters were in Beaconsfield, where from 1942 the staff worked harmoniously enough with their American counterparts, MIS-X.

Neave was alongside Langley at the sharp end of the operation, nurturing the networks through which escapers and evaders could get to freedom and back into the fight. Despite what Crockatt had said, he was not directly involved in supporting escape operations. Although Crockatt was Langley's immediate boss, he also answered to 'Z'. In the words of Donald Darling, he was 'very much under the watchful eye of Colonel Dansey', and made sure his strictures were observed.[14] Chief among them was that they were not to get involved in gathering intelligence, let alone in carrying out sabotage operations. That was the province of SOE, new in the game and, according to Langley, 'not popular'.

Neave arrived at a difficult time. The Pat Line was tottering and new conduits would have to be found. That would require resources, but at this stage escape and evasion was a low priority. The corner of the War Office they occupied proclaimed their status. Before their arrival, it had been used for making the tea. The chances of getting a sympathetic ear when it came to begging flights to drop agents or equipment seemed slight, especially given the competition from other secret intelligence agencies – like SOE – who claimed higher priority.

That first morning Neave was summoned to the presence of MI6's tricky deputy chief. Claude Dansey made him wait, scratching away with a steel-nibbed pen at some paperwork before breaking the long silence. 'Many congratulations,' he said. 'The best escape – so far.'[15] This gladdening opening was soon doused in a shower of cold water. Dansey began to talk of the dangers involved in the operations that Room 900 was running. He cited the precedent of Nurse Edith Cavell, the British nurse who was shot by the Germans in 1915 after being found to have hidden prisoners in her clinic in Brussels and helped them escape to neutral Holland. The implication was that Cavell was also gathering intelligence on behalf of SIS and that, by straying into the business of escape and evasion, she had compromised espionage operations.[16] Nurse Cavell was greatly revered in Belgium, as well as Britain, but to Dansey she was the epitome of amateur bungling, and her story not a stirring tale of heroism but a warning of what happened when secret organisations overlapped each other, endangering security and complicating operations. He was determined that the next generation of escape-and-evasion networks would not be allowed to jeopardise grander but unspecified designs.

It seemed that, in any case, Room 900's operations were unlikely to be on a scale that would cause problems. Dansey talked about training organisers, wireless sets, codes and couriers, but it seemed to Neave that they 'would not be allowed many of them'.[17] His first-day enthusiasm evaporated. The War Office seemed just as crazy as Colditz, though somehow less human. There was one last matter to address before lunch. He would need a code name and Langley asked him to pick one. On learning that Darling was 'Sunday' and Creswell in Madrid 'Monday', he decided to follow suit. Henceforth 'Saturday' would hide the identity of Captain Airey Neave.

Neave maintained that he and Langley were essentially a two-man band, though the IS9 files at the National Archives show another officer, Major Page, playing a large part in the management of Room 900. This reticence may be due to the fact that Page was attached to MI6 and when Neave wrote his post-war accounts he omitted the name for security reasons. At the Rules lunch, Langley had already given him the outlines of his specific brief. It was to build up an organisation in Belgium and Holland 'in case anything happens to Dédée'.[18] The obvious next question received an intriguing answer. 'Dédée' was Andrée de Jongh, a twenty-five-year-old Belgian woman who for the last ten months had been sending British evaders from Belgium, through France and across the Pyrenees. Her name had come up again in the meeting with 'Z', who had made it clear that he had doubts about her credentials.

Dédée would have no more passionate a supporter than Airey Neave, and the competition was fierce. Michael Creswell, the intelligence officer who as 'Monday' was MI9's man in Madrid, was thought to have been in love with her.[19] She was idolised by every young airman who struggled behind her up the rocky paths of the Pyrenees as she strode indefatigably onwards, chic and trim in her blue sailor's trousers. Neave reported that when, during interrogation, returnees spoke about her, 'their eyes filled with tears … she inspired not only respect, but also deep affection.'[20] The line she ran became known as 'Comète'. In his copious writings about Dédée, Neave gave her the credit for founding the organisation and there is no doubt that it was her energy and spirit which drove its work along.

When the Phoney War ended in May 1940, Andrée de Jongh was working in Malmedy as a commercial artist with the giant Sofina conglomerate. She answered a call for auxiliary nurses to tend the expected flood of wounded and returned to the family home, at 73 Avenue Émile Verhaeren in Brussels, where her father Frédéric, a primary school headmaster, was, without her knowledge, already involved in the underground. She nursed wounded soldiers and British prisoners of war and, by February 1941, had forged links with other resisters. In Dédée were combined a strong but gentle manner, astonishing bravery and neat good looks. It was a devastating mix, and in his subsequent telling of the Comète story, Neave gave her star billing, going as far as dedicating a book, *Little Cyclone*, to her exploits. It was not what she sought or wanted. When the war was over, Dédée slipped gratefully back into obscurity and spent much of the rest of her life nursing in Africa.

As he told it, in late August 1941, she had turned up out of the blue at the British consulate at Bilbao with three men in tow. She explained that one was a British evader from St-Valery-en-Caux and the others were Belgian officers who wanted to join the Allies, and they had just come over the mountains from France. She claimed with the help of friends to have set up a chain of safe houses and couriers who could ferry men from Brussels to the western Pyrenees. She was offering her organisation's services to the British if they wanted them. All she asked in return was for expenses to be covered. Dédée was told she would have to wait for a response from London. For one thing, the expenses were not negligible. It cost money to transport, feed and shelter 'parcels' – as the evaders were referred to – and the Basque guides wanted payment for their services. For another, who exactly was she? Was it possible that she was a German plant? That was certainly Dansey's first reaction when her arrival was reported to him, and he continued to make 'dark hints' about her reliability, until he was eventually silenced by the evidence of her magnificent record.

The Bilbao consulate was behind her from the start, as were Creswell and Darling. On 17 October, Creswell met her in Bilbao, after she had once again crossed the mountains, this time with two Scottish soldiers who had been hiding since escaping while en route to prison in the summer of 1940. He told her that the British government were 'vitally concerned' with recovering the crews of aircraft shot down over Holland, Belgium and France. MI9 agreed to pay the costs of getting the men across. Dédée insisted that the money should be a loan that would be repaid when the war was over. It was a way of reinforcing the line's independence. Darling signalled his approval of the new asset to Dansey in London in a message that also repeated his doubts about Harold Cole. He received a robust reply: 'Your summing up of the Cole and De Jongh situations is not appreciated and do not write further in this vein.'[21] Dédée was initially codenamed 'Postwoman', in keeping with the 'parcel' delivery service she operated. According to a note in the MI9 files, she rejected this, as she 'wished to be known as if she were a man' and it was duly changed to 'Postman'.[22] Some time later in 1942, the line would become semi-officially known as 'Comète', Comet in English, though who named it so and why is unknown.

By the time Neave took over responsibility for Dédée and Comet, its modus operandi was established. The line passed from Brussels to Paris, then to Bayonne and St-Jean-de-Luz, in the Spanish frontier sector of the Occupied Zone. The evaders – by now mostly airmen – were escorted by young men and women couriers. At each stopover they were sheltered in safe houses by quiet patriots whose commitment carried appalling risks. The chances of detection while travelling were high. The sight of well-nourished, fit young males in civilian dress was unusual in the middle of a total war, and few of the evaders had the language skills to sustain a cover story if they were challenged. Nonetheless, at the outset, Comet produced remarkable results. In the first three months that Neave was at MI9, Dédée and her Basque guide, a tall and immensely strong forty-four-year-old called Florentino Goïcoechea, escorted fifty-four men over the Pyrenees. They made for Bilbao or San Sebastián, where the consul would send a message to Creswell in Madrid. He then drove two hundred miles to meet her. Every week, he sent a report to Neave about Comet's activities.

Neave was fortunate to be working with two consummate professionals. Like Darling, Creswell was an intelligence officer who dipped in and out of diplomatic posts to cover his activities. He was warm, adventurous and a brilliant linguist. His family had been linked to Gibraltar for generations and he spoke flawless Spanish and French, as well as German. He knew the enemy well, having served in the Berlin embassy in the years before the war and got close to the Nazi hierarchy, shooting game in the mountains with Goering. He was an amateur aviator who flew several times over the Pyrenees and loved motor cars, thinking nothing of driving from London to Gibraltar on a whim.[23] His buccaneering approach was matched by a fine understanding of the game in play. For all her spirit and energy, Dédée would need every bit of help she could get.

The initial chaos following the fall of France offered multiple opportunities for British servicemen to evade or escape, and the risks for those who helped them were relatively small. By the end of 1940, German control had tightened over Belgium and occupied France and the Reich's multiple security organisations were active and efficient. Even as Dédée was making contact with the British in Bilbao, the Gestapo were knocking on the door of her father's house in Brussels asking questions about her. Three months later, in February 1942, it was the turn of the secret police of the Luftwaffe, who had a direct interest in shutting down an organisation that existed to ferry shot-down airmen back to their squadrons. Unable to lay hands on Dédée, they arrested her elder sister, Suzanne Wittek. Frédéric was away, just across the French border in Valenciennes, organising couriers. It was clear that Brussels was now too hot for either of them, and from then on father and daughter would operate from Paris.

The new chief in Brussels was Baron Jean Greindl, who belonged to a wealthy family that had made its money in the Congo. He was now a director of a Swedish Red Cross canteen in Brussels that fed and clothed the city's poor children, and provided a useful cover for Comet's activities. By summer 1942, the majority of its clients were airmen, mostly British but later with a heavy addition of Americans. The destruction of German cities was hotting up under the direction of Air Marshal Arthur Harris, and Bomber Command's losses were mounting. A surprising number of aircrew were able to struggle free from their stricken machines, brought down by flak and night-fighters as they came and went from their targets. In Holland and Belgium, many found refuge among country dwellers, who passed them on to local resistance networks, to be taken to Brussels and fed into the Comet line.

From there, small groups of three or four were taken by train to Paris, where Dédée and her team took over. She was helped by Jean-François Nothomb, another young Belgian, and Jeanine de Greef, whose mother Elvire was the linchpin of the operation in the south-west. Madame de Greef, also Belgian, was as remarkable in her way as Dédée. She was small and endlessly resourceful, hard-wired to resist fear and gifted with an uncanny ability to bluff. She and her husband, Fernand, had left Belgium after the German invasion, ending up in the town of Anglet, in the Pyrénées-Atlantiques department, ten miles from the Spanish border. Fernand was employed as an interpreter at the local German administrative headquarters and was well placed to gather information and documentation. They were helped by an Englishman, Albert Johnson, who had worked as a chauffeur in Brussels before the war and somehow ended up joining the de Greefs' circle at Anglet.

The Paris trio would escort their charges on the overnight train to Bayonne. From there they were in the hands of 'Tante Go', as Madame de Greef was known, who directed them to a safe house on the border, ready for the crossing. The psychological stress of the journey was now replaced by the physical ordeal of the climb. Neave painted a picture of how at nightfall they would set out from some remote farmhouse, led by Florentino Goïcoechea, a man of the mountains who, sustained by frequent pulls on a bottle of cognac, powered up the rocky tracks, deaf to entreaties to slow down. Further impetus was provided by Dédée, who, as the vice consul at Bilbao, Arthur Dean, described in a report to London, 'with her own haversack on her shoulders, literally drives the men through the eight hour struggle'.[24]

It was hard enough in summer, when the unavoidable barrier of the Bidassoa river was on its ribs, but in winter the journey was potentially lethal. The river became a frothing torrent and one Belgian courier, Count Antoine d'Ursel, Jean Greindl's successor in Brussels, was swept to his death in December 1943.

Neave's devotion to Dédée is not hard to understand. Who could not be moved by her character and qualities? In some ways they were an exalted manifestation of those that he would admire in Margaret Thatcher. Certainly, Dédée's example persuaded him that women were at least as valuable as men in the work of Room 900. In January 1944, when he was finding it difficult to identify candidates with the strength of character and qualities needed to operate as IS9 agents behind enemy lines, he contacted his colleague in the London-based Belgian Security Service, Captain Delloye, with a suggestion. 'It seems to me that we can make use of the opposite sex,' he wrote. 'Women make good guides.'[25] Soon women were being trained in parachuting, coding and all the other arts of the trade to the satisfaction of their male supervisors. 'She is in my opinion a very good type of guide and will be very useful as such,' was the verdict on one trainee. There was no one, though, to touch Dédée in Neave's esteem. She was a pioneer who had begun her adult life making her way in the very male world of Belgium's biggest business enterprise. She was quick-thinking, arriving at decisions and acting on them in a way that contrasted completely with the dithering female of stereotype. But for all that, she remained very much a woman.

Comet's successes brightened the summer of 1942. They were reinforced by some coups pulled off by the Pat Line. At the April 1942 meeting in Gibraltar between O'Leary, Darling and Langley, it had been agreed to try a more direct method of exfiltrating servicemen from the south than the arduous mountain route. Between July and October, O'Leary's team pulled off three well-executed seaborne operations. By now the escape line's activities had caught the attention of the Air Ministry, who began requesting help to get specific airmen back into the fray. The first concerned an RAF celebrity, Whitney Straight, an American by birth and a Grand Prix racing driver before the war, who flew fighters in the Battle of Britain. After being shot down near Le Havre on 31 July 1941, he made his way south but was captured within sight of the Spanish frontier. He gave a false name and claimed to be a soldier. According to Neave, 'Had his true identity become known, the chances of getting him back would have been remote.'[26] Room 900 was under pressure from the Air Ministry for action and in June O'Leary engineered his delivery, along with another thirty-four airmen, to a beach where a British trawler was waiting to take them to Gibraltar. There was another sea evacuation in September following a mass breakout from the internment camp at Fort de la Revère, near Nice, and one more a month later.

Though there was much good news that summer to boost the standing of Room 900, the winter brought a crop of disasters. In November, a concerted attack by German intelligence on the escape networks began. On the 18th, a trusted courier turned up at the home of the Maréchal family in Brussels with two men in civilian clothes, who he introduced as American airmen. Georges Maréchal, his English wife, Elsie, and their daughter, also Elsie, were all Comet members and had given shelter to fourteen Allied airmen.[27] Though the guide did not know it, the 'airmen' were Abwehr agents. The Maréchals were arrested and, according to Neave, ended up in the hands of the Gestapo. The 'bastards beat eighteen-year-old Elsie until she was covered in bruises'.[28] In two days, nearly a hundred people connected to Comet were in German hands.

The line was hopelessly compromised. In early January 1943, after her twenty-fourth trip from Paris to Bilbao, Dédée returned to Paris, where she persuaded her father that it was time to leave the country. They set off for Bayonne on the 13th, with two other helpers and three RAF aircrew. The Bidassoa was in flood and it was decided it would be too dangerous for Frédéric de Jongh to make the crossing. He was to stay with 'Tante Go' in her villa in Anglet and Dédée would return for him after delivering the airmen. The party struggled through a torrent of mud, up a stony track, to a remote house in the mountains near the village of Urrugne. It was the farm of Françoise Usandizaga, who lived there with her three children and had often fed and sheltered Dédée's parties before they began the trek across the frontier. Even Florentino felt the night was too wild to make an attempt. He left for his home, saying they would try again tomorrow. At noon on 15 January, according to Neave, they heard the sound of a car grinding up the track. Minutes later, German police were at the door.[29] Dédée, Françoise and the airmen were arrested. The evaders were taken off to a series of prisons, where they were subjected to brutal Gestapo interrogations. Françoise ended up in Ravensbrück, where she died on 12 April 1945. After a long calvary, Dédée spent the remainder of the war in

Ravensbrück and Mauthausen, but survived. Her father returned to Paris, where he was betrayed in June 1943 and executed with two other resisters on 28 March 1944.

Despite these blows, Comet staggered on. Within a fortnight of Dédée's departure, Johnson and Nothomb led another party over the Pyrenees. On the same day, far away in Brussels, Jean Greindl was arrested, tortured and sentenced to death. An accident of war pre-empted the execution when he was killed in an American bombing raid on Brussels-Evere aerodrome seven months later.

The Pat Line was collapsing too. In February 1943, Louis Nouveau was picked up, betrayed by French Gestapo agent Roger le Neveu, who passed himself off as a patriot. The number of his victims is unknown. His biggest scalp was Pat O'Leary himself, arrested in Toulouse on 2 March. Despite passing through the horrors of Buchenwald and Dachau, both Nouveau and O'Leary survived the war. Hundreds of others did not.

For all that the escape lines suffered that winter, the damage done to SOE by German counter-intelligence operations was even worse. In June 1942, the Abwehr captured an SOE agent equipped with a radio transmitter. Armed with the correct codes, they conducted a long dialogue with the unsuspecting organisation in London, in an exercise known as Operation North Pole. More than fifty Dutch agents were parachuted into Holland and into the arms of the waiting Germans. Forty-seven of them are thought to have been killed.

The men and women who operated the Pat and Comet lines suffered greatly for their heroism. From the outset, it was known that there would be no mercy from the Germans and even a spontaneous act of humanity towards their enemies could bring death. The MI9 files are full of grim messages that filtered back concerning the fate of humble helpers. Neither age nor sex gave any protection. 'Emile Fraipont, Celeste Fraipont and Lucie Vis, all from Liège, were condemned to death for having given hospitality to a British airman whose aircraft was shot down on Belgian soil,' reads one report passed on by Belgian security. 'Emile Fraipont was 70, his wife 68.'[30]

The resisters were fighting an unequal struggle and it was inevitable that what successes they had should come at a high price. They were facing an enemy that was lavishly funded and resourced and intelligently directed, and which acknowledged no constraints on its behaviour. The German secret and police services were clever and manipulative, operating from a standpoint of utter misanthropy and cynicism. They could draw on the scum of the countries they conquered – the criminals, misfits and sociopaths for whom German occupation had provided a playground for their malignity. Dédée and O'Leary and the hundreds who helped them understood the need for guile and ruthlessness. But their motives were noble and their functioning depended ultimately on trust and faith in human decency.

There were other factors that handicapped them, some self-inflicted. The Pat Line did not receive a radio and operator to link it to London until April 1942, relying instead on a slow and laborious system of couriers and '*messages personnels*' broadcast on the BBC. As Neave reflected, had a radio been provided, Cole's treachery might have been uncovered sooner. Dédée refused a radio operator on principle, fearing, with some justification, that Comet would then come under increasing control from London, which was less able than she to judge conditions on the ground. Neave did send an agent and transmitter to Belgium in February 1943, but a month later he was found dead in unexplained circumstances.

With all the dangers, Comet members sometimes showed a disregard for their own safety which could have fatal consequences. Their tragic recklessness was revealed in the Maréchal disaster. In Neave's account, Jean Greindl was alerted by young Elsie Maréchal to the arrival of the suspicious 'American' visitors. He told her to return home and 'stop these men from leaving at all costs. Interrogate them carefully.'[31] When she got to the house, the Germans were waiting. Having heard no more, Greindl sent another member of the team, twenty-five-year-old Victor Michiels, with instructions to watch the house but not to approach it unless he was certain there was no danger. He observed the house for half an hour, then knocked on the door, whereupon German Field

Police emerged from the shadows. When he ran off, they shot him dead.

The following day, one of the Paris team, Elvire Morelle, arrived by train in Brussels and, having received no warning of the disaster, went straight to the house, where she was arrested and hauled off to the Gestapo.[32] The losses angered Neave and Langley's overlords. Neave claimed that 'the very existence of Room 900 and its contacts with underground escape lines was threatened.'[33] They were 'subjected to violent criticism of the potential dangers of escape work to military information and sabotage' – that is, to MI6 and SOE operations. Crockatt, as head of MI9, defended them, arguing that without some degree of direction from London, the dangers to security would be even greater. He also pointed out that despite the casualties the lines had sustained, their efforts had resulted in the return of a large number of airmen to carry on the fight. Crockatt enlisted the help of the Air Ministry to press the point. With this intervention, survival was secured. By May 1943, even Dansey, 'destructive at first, and determined to put up the shutters at Room 900, was … appeased'.[34]

Despite Neave's indignation, the attitude of Dansey and others does not seem entirely unreasonable. Even when hindsight and the harsh demands of warfare are taken into account, some of Room 900's actions seem misjudged. Neave himself placed inordinate faith in a woman whose behaviour and manner set alarm bells clanging elsewhere. Mary Lindell appealed to his sense of the romantic. She was an Englishwoman in her mid-forties, married to the French Comte de Milleville and living in Paris when the war started. She was arrested by the Gestapo for helping escapers in 1941 and sent into solitary confinement at Fresnes prison, but was later released. In July 1942, she turned up in London, having reached there via Barcelona. She offered her services to Room 900, saying she was prepared to go back to start a new escape line.

To modern ears, Mary Lindell sounds like nothing but trouble. Neave's first impression of her was of 'fearlessness, independence and not a little arrogance'.[35] To that could be added wilfulness, egomania and obstinacy, and a recklessness that endangered not just herself but others. He noted admiringly that 'her contempt and disdain for the Germans was enormous.' But that was surely a serious disadvantage if she was pitting her wits and her life against them.[36] Lindell was to be the first woman agent Room 900 specially trained and Neave was put in charge of her. The decision to send her back seems extraordinarily rash. She told Neave that after receiving her nine-month prison sentence from the Germans in late 1940, she told the court martial that this was 'just sufficient time for me to have a baby with Adolf'.[37] After her release, she came to the notice of the German security services, who started hunting her and she was forced to go to ground. Nonetheless, her argument that if she stayed out of Paris she would be relatively safe was accepted. Not everyone was happy about it or her. Neave admitted that 'she did not endear herself to the Establishment in London by her outspoken behaviour.' Even he was concerned that her return 'might endanger her own life and those of others'.[38]

In the third week of October 1942, she was flown in a black-painted Lysander to a landing site in the countryside near the town of Ussel, sixty miles south-east of Limoges. Neave went with her to Tangmere, the fighter station in Sussex from where operations were launched in full moon periods. She left without a radio operator. She had fallen out with the one she had been assigned, Tom Groome, and remarkably, given how vital wireless communications were to their work, Room 900 had no one else trained and available at the time. It was decided to try and parachute one in later.

She was landed without incident and arrived safely at Ruffec, near Angoulême, from where she was planning to set up a new route to Spain, as there were believed to be a number of stranded Allied airmen in the area. Her efforts to find reliable guides failed. Some time towards the end of the year, she was knocked down by a car while riding a tandem and almost killed. This meant that she was recuperating in Lyons, hundreds of miles away, when her first customers called. On 18 December, two men arrived at Ruffec looking for help. Major Herbert 'Blondie' Hasler and Corporal Bill Sparks were survivors of Operation Frankton, an audacious commando raid on shipping at Bordeaux docks. In breach of security procedures, they had been told to head for the town, where they might find friends. By chance they turned up at the Hôtel de la Toque Blanche, a haunt of Mary Lindell's. She was still recovering from her injuries in Lyons but word reached her of their arrival. Despite her condition, she managed to arrange for her eldest son, Maurice, to escort them to Lyons. She went to see Cartwright in Switzerland to try and arrange for them to be moved there, but this would mean a delay to their return and London wanted the 'Cockleshell Heroes' back fast. Eventually, Lindell found a guide to take them to Spain. At the end of March, the pair arrived safely in Madrid, along with two RAF airmen. Her efforts had saved their lives. Under the Hitler 'commando order', if caught, they would undoubtedly have been shot like their comrades, six of whom were executed. But it had been more by luck than efficiency, and in November 1943 Lindell was arrested again, ending up in Ravensbrück, with no further successes to record.

Neave maintained that the old guard at MI9 were 'unfairly critical' of Mary's exploits in France, but 'being young', he 'was delighted with her unconventional ways'. They stayed friends in the years after the war.[39]

Lindell was one of two women agents handled by Neave. The other, Beatrix Terwindt, was a Dutch former KLM air hostess who volunteered for SOE. Room 900 had virtually no presence in Holland, over which Allied bombers were frequently shot down. When Neave came across 'Trix', he was impressed by her quiet determination and fluent French and English and decided that she was the ideal recruit to set up an escape line. SOE were willing to let her go, and on the night of 13/14 February 1943, she parachuted straight into the custody of German agents who, thanks to the success of Operation North Pole, knew all about her mission. Once again Neave had gone to see her off, helping her into her parachute harness before she climbed into a Halifax bomber at Tempsford, the special operations base in Bedfordshire. It would have been strange if he had not felt uneasy at the incongruity of a soldier in uniform sending women civilians to a destination that held every prospect of pain and death. There were occasions when the chance arose to share at least some of the perils. It had been suggested that Neave accompany Mary Lindell when she was flown to France, to make sure she was safely delivered. This would have been a breach of the standing rule that staff officers directing secret operations from London and who knew the names of agents should not risk capture by the enemy, but he and Langley did not like the idea of her going unescorted. In the end, the idea came to nothing as SOE decided to send another agent on the same flight and there were only two passenger seats in a Lysander. Years later, Neave wrote that he had 'no hesitation in recalling my deep sense of relief' when he heard the news.[40]

There was a further opportunity in early 1944, when Room 900 began overseeing the 'Shelburne' operations, a series of successful evacuations by sea from the Brittany coast. Between the end of January and the end of March 1944, one hundred and eleven men were rescued at night under the eyes of the Germans. The plan was overseen by Neave and Captain Pat Windham-Wright, who had joined MI9 in September 1943 after losing an arm and winning an MC earlier in the war. Windham-Wright went with the Royal Navy Motor Gun Boats that took the men off. Neave had proposed acting as escorting officer himself, but was turned down by Crockatt. After Langley was transferred to MI9 headquarters in September 1943, Neave was the senior man at Room 900 and simply knew too much to risk falling into enemy hands.

Much of Neave's post-Colditz career had passed in safety and comfort while those he directed were daily facing arrest, torture and death. In his early, office-bound days at MI9, he had reflected that 'it did not seem a soldier's life.' Behind this disquieting thought there was a bigger concern, one that loomed over Neave's entire time with the escape lines: the question of whether it was all worth it. Could the results achieved justify the appalling price in human suffering inflicted on the brave men and women who operated them?

One hundred and fifty-five members of Comet died resisting the Nazis. Forty-eight of them were women. Then there were the many who were imprisoned, tortured and abused but somehow survived, often to lead lives that were cut short as a result of their sufferings. The main justification for these sacrifices was that, terrible though the price was, the contribution to the war effort that resulted made it worth paying, and Neave advanced this argument repeatedly in his books. The value of a foot soldier, be he officer or other rank, was limited. The worth of an airman, however, was considerable. It cost £10,000 to train a pilot – enough, as 'Bomber' Harris pointed out, to put ten men through Oxford.

When fighting Room 900's corner against the sceptics in the intelligence establishment, Neave and Langley asserted that 'the saving of a bomber pilot's life could be as important as blowing up a bridge ... that much of the intelligence received from occupied territory had less relevance to the war than the recovery of a fully trained aircrew.'[41] If that was true, then the escape lines had indeed made a major contribution to the war effort. A total of 2,198 RAF evaders got back to England through their efforts. A similar number of American airmen were also rescued. How many RAF aircrew actually returned to operational flying is impossible to quantify. What is known is that by 1943 the Air Force training machine was at full speed, producing easily enough men to supply the needs of all commands. In the case of many of the Americans, on returning to Britain their operational war was over and they were not required to fly further combat missions.

Neave did not need to strain quite so hard to validate the work of the escape lines. The resisters had made their choice alone and none needed to be persuaded of their duty. They did what they did because they were driven to it by their courage and ideals. As he rightly said, 'They were the exceptional people ... natural leaders. They had in common the ideal of service to humanity.'[42] When the struggle was over, there would be no recriminations. To Neave, the survivors showed only gratitude for the support he had given them and a lasting affection.

7

From Normandy to Nuremberg

With the arrival of D-Day, Neave at last got his chance to leave his desk and the life of a military civil servant and take to the field. His writings give the impression that the landings were as much a liberation for him as they were for France. Nonetheless, it was not until 11 July 1944 that he finally set foot in Normandy. He was now a major and he was eager to get into action. However, he was forced to endure many anxious days hovering impatiently behind the front line, looking for an opportunity to bring off a series of rescue missions he had been planning since the previous autumn. It was clear that the invasion would change the nature of MI9's operations. It was preceded by a great shift in the direction of the air effort. Bomber Command and the US Army Air Forces were diverted from their long-term work of destroying the German war industry. They were now given the task of smashing up the enemy's transportation links to the invasion zone, with the aim of 'isolating the battlefield'. The French countryside filled up with burned-out bombers. Those who made it out of them alive were turning up in villages and towns, seeking help from underground organisations.

It was Neave who came up with an idea about how to protect them in such a swirling and unpredictable environment, and then to get them home. His great fear was that the Germans, knowing the war was lost, would abandon whatever restraints still bound them and murder any Allied airmen who fell into their hands. Rather than leaving them to stay put in safe houses in town or country, he proposed establishing camps in isolated forests where they could be sustained by local patriots, until the front lines pushed past them. Reports from agents in the field indicated there were hundreds of stranded aircrew who had come to grief in missions to attack railways, transport nodes and the Atlantic ports, scattered across the Northern half of France. There were more in the Low Countries who had been shot down on the way to or from Germany. Neave suggested setting up three camps: one in the Rennes area in Brittany; one in the east, in the forest of the Ardennes; and another southeast of Paris, close to Châteaudun. Months in advance, agents were sent in to liaise with local organisations and – equally important – to persuade the aviators that it was in their best interests to group together in hiding, when the natural boldness that came with choosing to fight in the air was spurring them to make a break for it.

The plan, code-named 'Sherwood', was initially considered 'imaginative but too risky'.[1] It was a complicated business to find and equip the camps and move the evaders to them, and it required resources. Furthermore, the Belgians, determined as always to maintain their independence, rebelled against being told what to do. Faced with their opposition, the Ardennes plan came to nothing. Then, to Neave's chagrin, the airmen who were gathered near Rennes decided not to wait to be rescued and broke camp to seek their own salvation. However, the operation to rescue 120 men living under the boughs of the Forêt de Fréteval, near Châteaudun, was a triumph that Neave would savour all his life.

The arrangements for the camp had been made by Jean de Blommaert, a twenty-nine-year-old Belgian aristocrat and veteran of Comet, who had escaped to Britain in 1943 after being 'burned'. In April 1944, he was parachuted into the area with Squadron Leader Lucien Boussa, who had previously commanded 350 Squadron of the RAF, which was manned by Belgians and equipped with Spitfires. In conjunction with the local resistance organisation and helped by farmers and tradesmen, they located camp sites and dropping zones. Late in May, airmen who had been hiding in Paris began to arrive by train at Châteaudun and were sheltered by local families.

On 6 June, the day of the invasion, the first group of thirty arrived in the forest. By the beginning of August there were 152 fugitives, living in tents and eating well, thanks to the generosity of the locals.

While the battle of Normandy raged, Neave was forced to wait impotently for the lines to move. Having left Room 900 in London in the hands of Donald Darling, he was formally a member of IS9 (Western European Area), which had evolved into a joint British-American formation, commanded by Langley and a US army lieutenant colonel. Neave spent some weeks hanging round the Bayeux headquarters and making trips to the front at Caen, still in German hands despite Monty's predictions of swift victory. Then, at the beginning of August, with the American success at St-Lô, the impasse was broken and the front began to move fast. General Patton's Third Army swept down to take Brittany, with Neave hotfoot behind. He 'packed his jeep, in high elation' and led the American sections of IS9 (WEA) southwards. The road to Avranches was choked with dead Germans, mules and horses and burned-out vehicles, victims of the merciless harrying of the Allied fighter-bombers. He was on a high: 'The exhilaration was unforgettable. The restraints of London and the beach-head were past and the smell of pursuit was in the air.'[2]

Arriving in Le Mans on 10 August, he was disconcerted to find that instead of pressing east towards Chartres, Vendôme and the camp in the Forêt de Fréteval, the Americans were now going to swing north to Alençon, to help close the Falaise Gap, where the death blow would be dealt to the German army. He had been counting on being able to call on their armour to support the rescue operation. It was difficult to know the dispositions and strength of the Germans in the area, and he had only half a dozen jeeps and a few automatic weapons to protect his party and the airmen if they ran into trouble. He drove to the Headquarters of XV Corps, north of Le Mans, to try and persuade the staff it was their duty to lend him an escort. After all, half the men in the forest were American. It was no use. He drove back to Le Mans 'greatly depressed', but on arrival had a remarkable piece of luck. In the courtyard of the Hôtel Moderne, where he had set up shop, was an array of armoured jeeps and, milling around them, dozens of British soldiers in maroon berets. It was a squadron of the Special Air Service, four officers and thirty-four men, under the command of Captain Anthony Greville-Bell, twenty-four years old, the son a Ceylon tea planter and already a veteran of the SAS. They had just finished their operations in Brittany and were awaiting orders. Greville-Bell, 'a dashing young man with a DSO, ideally suited to "private warfare"', listened enthusiastically to Neave's proposals and sent a signal to his chiefs. The following day he received permission to escort Neave and his team to the Forêt de Fréteval. Thus began an association between Neave and the SAS that continued through the rest of the hostilities, into the Cold War period, and lasted until the day he died. The regiment's ethos matched his own approach to warfare: unorthodox, questioning and inclined to prefer the tangential and subtle over the direct and frontal.

On 14 August, 'a fine, hot morning', he set off with the SAS at the head of a column of requisitioned buses and trucks on the sixty-mile journey to the forest. At the turn-off to the camp, they found de Blommaert and Boussa and a large crowd who greeted them with cheers. If felt like 'the departure for a seaside outing'. The airmen were lean, tanned and dressed in rough peasant clothes. Some were angry at the delay and about twenty had already departed. It was nonetheless a great moment for Neave. Sherwood had been his idea, and he had not only made it happen but been there at its execution, exposing himself at least in some degree to the risks faced by the men and women he directed. He recorded proudly that of those he helped rescue 'nearly all went back on flying operations.' For some of them, their liberation brought only a short respite. According to Neave, though he does not cite a source, thirty-eight of them were killed in action before the end of the war.

The following day, there appears to have been another sort of rescue operation, one that he never referred to in his writings. On 16 August, while hurrying back to rejoin headquarters, he arrived in Chartres. The city was in American hands, but there were still Germans about. He found the main square deserted, apart from three American tanks, their guns trained on the Cathedral, a Gothic jewel of European civilisation. According to the account given by Jean de Blommaert (who was with him) to Diana, shortly after Airey's death, a Texan sergeant told them that German troops were holed up in the clock tower and his captain had just returned with orders to blast them out. Neave approached the officer and asked him if he could really justify opening fire on an architectural treasure. He was told that his orders were 'to demolish rather than risk a single American life'.[3] Neave declared, 'I am in charge of Special Services in this sector and this is a special case. Wait five minutes before firing – no more. I'll go and look myself, and wave my handkerchief if all is clear.' Neave entered the cathedral unarmed, with de Blommaert behind him holding a rifle. He told him, 'Keep your distance, so we aren't a double target up this damned spiral staircase, and if you must shoot, try not to hit me.' The clock tower was empty. He waved his handkerchief to the Americans below and Chartres cathedral remained intact. Neave was normally not shy about advertising his exploits. This one he never mentioned in print. Another version claims that it was an American officer with XX Corps, Colonel Welborn Griffith Jr, who with his driver carried out a reconnaissance of the streets around the cathedral and declared it to be free of Germans, sparing it from bombardment. Neave seems to have arrived towards the evening, by which time Griffith had moved on (he was killed the same day), so it may be that there were two separate incidents when the cathedral was menaced and both men share the honour of saving it.

No one reading Neave's accounts of the days of that dangerous summer of 1944 would guess that he had just become a father for the first time. Marigold Elizabeth Cassandra Neave was born on 5 May, at Chillington Hall, her maternal grandparents' home in Staffordshire. Fatherhood seems to have done nothing to temper his eagerness to make up for lost time. After the Sherwood adventure, he hurried on to Paris, to check on the well-being of his agents. For many, like Jean-François Nothomb, the arrival of the French and American liberators in late August had come too late. He had been betrayed by Jacques Desoubrie, a Franco-Belgian Gestapo agent responsible for the capture of hundreds of evaders and helpers, including fifty of the Comet line. Nothomb had been arrested in January and sent off to a series of concentration camps, pursued by a death warrant that mercifully never caught up with him, and was eventually freed in April 1945. On the eve of the liberation, rumours had abounded of massacres and reprisals. Neave arrived to find Paris *en fête* and most of Room 900's helpers safe and well. He did, however, carry out another minor rescue operation. After setting up his headquarters in the Hotel Windsor, he came across an excited mob and intervened, 'rescuing two Germans from an angry crowd'.[4]

This small episode revealed a principle that governed his post-war attitude to the vanquished. While he was in favour of the sternest justice for the chief criminals of the Nazi regime, he had no taste for mass punishments of the defeated, or the imposition of punitive terms on the population that would only nourish a future conflict. In the case of Rudolf Hess, he became one of the chief advocates of compassion, campaigning in the early 1970s for his release from Spandau prison.

There was a pause in Brussels, where he was relieved to find more old Comet hands still alive. Then it was on to Holland, where the headlong Allied advance had come to a sudden halt and the debacle of Arnhem had brought an unwelcome opportunity for him to put his expertise to work. The failure of the airborne operation on 17 September to capture the bridge over the Lower Rhine had left several hundred troops from the British 1st Airborne Division and attached units cut off behind the German lines on the east bank, where they were being sheltered by the Dutch resistance. Neave arrived in the first week of October and set up headquarters on the outskirts of Nijmegen. He claims that while there he made a 'discovery which revolutionised the situation of the airborne survivors'.[5] The power station at Nijmegen was linked by a telephone line to transformer stations across the Rhine in enemy-held territory. He learned this from Dutch resistance workers on the liberated southern bank who were using it to stay in touch with their people on the other side, so the discovery was hardly his own. However, he seems to have seen its potential for organising a rescue operation. Many of the stranded troops were thought to be hiding around Ede (to where the phone link extended), twenty miles from Nijmegen.

Neave wrote that when he proposed a plan to his superiors, the 'cold feet department' were 'horror struck', believing the Germans must surely have tapped the line. However, the resistance continued to insist it was secure, and soon they were getting a nightly report from an anonymous British officer, later revealed to be Major Digby Tatham-Warter of the 2nd Battalion, the Parachute Regiment, who had been wounded at Arnhem and captured, before escaping from hospital, with information about the number and state of health of the evaders. They received further intelligence from agents Neave had sent to Holland to set up escape lines for Allied airmen long beforehand.

By now, Neave had been joined by a congenial brother-in-arms. Major Hugh Fraser had been seconded to IS9 (WEA) from the GHQ Liaison Regiment, a reconnaissance outfit also known as 'Phantom', which was charged with scouting the front lines. Fraser was a member of the Scottish warrior clan and the younger brother of Lord Lovat, whose exploits at the Dieppe Raid and commanding the family regiment, the Lovat Scouts, at D-Day had made him a legend. He was sardonic, relaxed, brave, modest and good fun.

The two got on well and respected each other, and they remained close friends until Neave's death. Fraser too became a target for Irish Republicans, who in 1975 planted outside his house in London a bomb which went off, killing his neighbour, Professor Gordon Hamilton Fairley, a pioneering cancer specialist. It is perhaps difficult to think of someone so emotionally restrained as Neave inspiring deep affection in another man of his class and outlook, but the bond between them was strong. In the opinion of the historian Antonia Fraser, Hugh's wife of twenty-one years, 'Hugh loved Airey.'[6] Another member of the team was less satisfactory. Captain Peter Baker had also arrived from Phantom, where he served with Fraser. He was exuberant and bold, qualities that Neave normally admired, but also a fantasist, chancer and glory-hunter. During the Forêt de Fréteval episode, Neave had already had to prevent him from casting off his uniform and heading to Paris in advance of the troops with the aim of scoring a sensational journalistic scoop for an American newspaper.

Any escape plans were dependent on the resourcefulness and bravery of a large network of Dutch resisters from across the social spectrum who sheltered and helped organise the disparate bands of survivors from the Arnhem operation. Among them were several senior Airborne officers, including Brigadiers Gerald Lathbury and John Hackett and Lieutenant Colonel David Dobie, who thanks to the Dutch underground were eventually reunited. Their initial appreciation of their situation had included a plan to stay put in order to carry out behind-the-lines operations in partnership with the resistance when the Allies made another attempt to cross the Rhine. The first thing to do was to establish contact with headquarters.

On 18 October, with the help of Dutch guides, Colonel Dobie arrived in Allied-held territory after an adventurous journey dodging the Germans and involving two river crossings. He was taken to General Sir Miles Dempsey, commander of the Second Army, who told him that the priority was to evacuate all stranded troops and to make a plan to 'get 'em out'. Dobie teamed up with Neave and others and rapid arrangements were made for a mass evacuation.

In the meantime, on the night of 11/12 October, Neave had sent Baker across the River Waal to enemy-held territory to liaise with the local underground and set up a formal escape route. Baker arrived at Tiel, sixteen miles west of Nijmegen, where he teamed up with Fekko Ebbens, who had a fruit farm near the town and who was prominent in the local underground. An American, Private First Class Ted Bachenheimer of the 82nd Airborne, whose German-Jewish family had fled to the US in 1934, had volunteered to join him and arrived a day or two later. Their task was to organise a chain of guides to bring the evaders and escapers down in small parties from their hiding places around Ede. It was made clear that the pair were to wear uniform at all times, to reduce the risk of being shot as spies.

No more was heard of them for six days. Then a Dutch messenger arrived with bad news. Baker and Bachenheimer had been captured and were believed to have been shot. Neave took the courier back to the crossing point with a request to return the following night with further information. When he reappeared the news was better. Baker and Bachenheimer had been arrested but might still be alive. It was not until after the war that the full story became known. On the night of 16 October, a German patrol turned up at the house of Fekko Ebbens, pretending they wanted somewhere to consult their map. It was a ruse. They appear to have been tipped off that the farm was a base for resistance activities by a Dutch collaborator. It was also suspected that the authorities had been alerted by the sight of Baker and Bachenheimer walking around in the neighbourhood in daylight in civilian clothes.

Baker left an account of the episode in which he maintained that he had been told by his hosts to change out of his uniform.[7] Whatever the truth, Ebbens's fate was sealed. He was arrested and, despite efforts by the underground to buy his freedom, was executed along with four other Dutch resisters a month later. Baker and Bachenheimer were able to show the Germans their uniforms and claim they were simply soldiers on the run and therefore entitled to protection as prisoners of war. The pair were sent off by train to Stalag XIB at Fallingbostel. En route, Bachenheimer managed to prise open a window and escape with three other prisoners. The group split up and the American struck out on his own. A body believed to be his was later found with two bullet wounds in the back of the head. How he met his end will never be known, but there is a likelihood that he was murdered after his Jewish origins became known or suspected.[8]

The disaster caused consternation at MI9 and much resentment among the Dutch resistance. An inquiry cleared Neave and Langley of responsibility. This episode, grim though it was, did not impede Baker's post-war career. Like Neave, Hugh Fraser and another IS9 (WEA) officer, Maurice Macmillan, he became a Conservative MP. However, his career ended disastrously when, after starting a publishing house which ran up huge debts, he was sent to prison for forging signatures on financial documents and expelled from the House of Commons. He died in 1966, aged forty-five, after strenuous failed attempts to clear his name.

With the arrests, the dangers surrounding the plan for a mass evacuation – now codenamed Pegasus – multiplied. Despite fears that the Germans had been alerted, it was decided to press on with the operation nonetheless. It went ahead on the night of 22/23 October. A crossing point, about 150 to 200 yards wide, had been chosen on a stretch of the Rhine near the town of Wageningen, on the occupied bank of the Rhine, and Randwijk, a village in Allied hands on the southern side. The operation would be launched from a deserted farmhouse which stood on the bank, a quarter of a mile from a dyke road which was out of sight of enemy territory. The men were to be shipped in assault boats supplied by a company of the Royal Canadian Engineers. A few days beforehand, they were moved by lorry and hidden in farmhouse outbuildings. An artillery barrage was laid on, miles from the launching point, to divert any Germans in the area. At the same time, a Bofors gun was to fire ten rounds of tracer every fifteen minutes, thus providing a point on the friendly bank for the escape parties to aim for. A force of thirty American paratroopers were to travel in the boats as armed escort. Once ashore, white tapes directed the escapees through the fields to another farmhouse, which acted as a reception centre and first-aid post.

At midnight the boats slid into the water. Neave and the team settled down to wait for the signal that the escape party was in place on the far bank – the letter 'V' flashed in Morse code on a red torch. When it came, it was 400 yards to the right of where they expected it. 'There were whispered orders and the Americans entered the boats which, with a splash of oars, began to move off,'[9] he wrote. There was a burst of fire from enemy territory. Had a German patrol stumbled across the operation? It was not difficult to imagine the bloodbath that would follow. But the silence rolled back and after twenty minutes the boats appeared out of the darkness. It was Neave's job to count the men ashore. There were 138 of them, mostly soldiers of the 1st Airborne Division, along with several Dutchmen fleeing the Gestapo.

Pegasus was a triumph, and Neave was justified in judging it 'a striking, indeed memorable performance'. His name would be associated with it thereafter, though like any complex operation of war, the plan was a joint effort involving, among others, Fraser, Dobie, Tatham-Warter and Lieutenant Colonel Robert Strayer of the US Army's 101st Airborne. British government propaganda made a feast of the coup, which was lauded in an article in the *News Chronicle* based on interviews with Brigadier Lathbury and other escapees as 'one of the greatest stories of the war'.[10]

Neave was in a hurry to carry out another operation before the winter rains made the rivers too tricky to navigate in small boats. Pegasus II would clearly be a more difficult proposition. The Germans would surely have worked out what had happened. Communications with the remnants of the 1st Airborne Division were conducted through 'Fabian', a Belgian officer serving with the SAS who was in direct radio contact with headquarters. Communication with Neave's own agents had to be relayed via London and was subject to a delay of twenty-four hours. A new crossing site was chosen and the planners managed to commandeer flat-bottomed boats fitted with silenced outboard motors to deal with the rain-swollen river. Neave set the preliminary date for 16 November to move a second group of 140 men, and the arrangements were passed to the fugitives.

The date slipped by a day and Neave began to have doubts about Pegasus II. It 'involved the possibility of serious casualties among men … who might be killed instead of spending the rest of the war in prison camps'. But everything was in place. The men were alerted and their hopes 'could not be dashed'. Neave was right to have hesitated. On the first night, no one came and the reception party was shelled by the Germans. The second night, voices were heard calling across the river and a boat was launched. It brought back three men in civilian clothes, two Dutchmen and Sergeant J. M. Mescall of the RAF. They were the only ones to arrive out of a party of 120 men, most of them from 1st Airborne. They had set out from north of Ede, about twenty miles from the river, on the previous evening. While crossing the Ede–Arnhem road they ran into a German patrol, who put up flares and opened fire. Several were killed. Seven escaped. The rest were taken prisoner.

Neave was 'deeply depressed' by the news. It was the end of any thoughts of further large-scale escapes. Like others involved in the operation, he would later lay some of the blame for its failure on the appearance of the newspaper article, whose contents could easily have been conveyed to the enemy via neutral capitals. In fact, the piece appeared *after* Pegasus II had already come to grief and contained nothing that would not have been obvious to the Germans.

He returned to London in December to take charge of Room 900. He still worked with 1S9 (WEA) in Nijmegen, and was able to arrange canoes and other craft for individual waterborne crossings at the mouth of the Waal. Thirty soldiers from 1st Airborne were ferried out of occupied territory before the Allies finally crossed the Rhine the following spring. He was also able to get supplies to one of his agents, Dick Kragt, who had been dropped into Holland in June 1943 and had been a coordinator for both Pegasus operations. Kragt also arranged the exodus in February 1945 of Brigadier John Hackett, the commander of the 4th Parachute Brigade, who had been severely wounded at Arnhem.

Neave did not return to Europe until April 1945. After the Germans withdrew from Arnhem, he, Hackett and Hugh Fraser walked across the famous bridge over the Rhine for which so many lives had been sacrificed and through the rubble of the town. He moved forward on the heels of the retreating Germans, and in Barneveld he was reunited with Kragt. The German forces in Holland surrendered on 5 May and Neave crossed their lines, to arrive in Amsterdam three days later: VE Day. He was there to check on the welfare of his agents, but 'the Dutch thronged the streets in a frenzy of welcome and rejoicing and it was hours before I could reach the addresses of our helpers.' On Crockatt's orders, he spent the rest of the summer in The Hague, overseeing the congenial work of recommending honours for the hundreds of men and women whose bravery had kept the escape lines open. Then, in August, he was given the opportunity of coming face to face with the perpetrators of the horror, destruction and bloodshed of the preceding years.

* * *

Neave's appointment to the British War Crimes Executive was merited on the grounds of his ability to read and speak German reasonably well, his Oxford degree which had given him a grounding in international law, and his pre-war experience as a barrister. It was a plum post that carried considerable kudos, as well as giving him a participatory role in one of the great dramas of the century. It also brought a further promotion, from major to lieutenant colonel, and from October he could add the ribbon of the DSO to that of the MC on his tunic, awarded for 'gallant and distinguished service in the field' – presumably his part in Pegasus I. His initial job was to help gather evidence against the twenty-four senior political and military leaders of the Third Reich who, after much debate, had been chosen to stand trial for war crimes at Nuremberg. The tribunal was controversial from the outset. There was no consensus on how to punish the Nazis. Churchill, Eden and others had initially been in favour of selecting fifty to a hundred senior figures and executing them without trial. This course was soon discredited by the argument that to do so would only ensure they died as martyrs. Some process was essential in order to publicly expose the horrors of Hitler's reign. The legal procedures at Nuremberg were rough at the edges. It could hardly be otherwise. Unprecedented crimes called for novel justice.

Neave was twenty-nine when he returned to Germany. In his short life, his association with the place had been complex and intense. It had started with his exposure as an adolescent in September 1933 to a Nazi rally in Berlin. In his writings, he often referred to the Germans he encountered in caricature terms. They were brutal and bullying or stupid and preposterous. Nonetheless, he professed to feel no animosity towards the German armed forces, declaring that having been 'fairly treated as a prisoner at Colditz … I understood the difference between the Nazi leaders who were to be tried at Nuremberg and the ordinary German soldier.'[11] Nor did he accept the new job 'in any spirit of personal revenge'. He had received enough satisfaction nearly four years before, when he crossed the Swiss frontier from Colditz. His detached outlook did not make him sympathetic to the attitude of some Allied jurists who were pained at the crudeness of the tribunal's legal machinery. Nor for a moment did he swallow the *tu quoque* claims of the defendants who bleated that what they were accused of was no worse than what the Allies had done to them. Putting the guilty to death did not trouble him, as long as their culpability was properly established. Throughout the proceedings he maintained an impressive detachment and sense of proportion, evidence of a rationality and coolness that marked his subsequent career in politics.

Before he arrived in Nuremberg, Neave was given a preliminary mission. At the end of August 1945 he went to Essen, home of the Krupp works which had forged the tools for much of Germany's war industry. He was charged with collecting evidence that linked the firm to the Nazi party, to the production of any weapon that was forbidden under international law or to the use of foreign slave labourers in Krupp enterprises. Essen had been on Bomber Command's target list from the beginning of the strategic air campaign and the town and surroundings had been flattened. As Neave remarked grimly, 'the RAF had done their job.'

Amazingly, the Krupp residence, the 200-room Villa Huegel which sat above the town, was still intact. It was a 'tasteless mausoleum' and 'looked like an early railway station'. Gustav Krupp, who had enthusiastically collaborated with Hitler and the German interwar rearmament programme, had been partially paralysed since 1941 and was deemed to be too ill to stand trial. The prosecutors tried to substitute in the indictment his son Alfried, who ran the company in his place, but the move was rejected by the judges. At the villa, Neave discovered nearly a ton of documents, which would form a large part of the prosecution case when Alfried was finally put on trial by an American tribunal two years later. Chilly, unrepentant and a convinced Nazi, he was convicted of crimes against humanity relating to Krupp's wholesale use of slave labour, including workers from Auschwitz. In July 1948, he was sentenced to twelve years in prison and the forfeiture of his property. Three years later, he was free and his inheritance restored to him.

As Neave interrogated the firm's directors and staff, he heard no word of regret over the fate of the tens of thousands of Poles,

Russians, Czechs, Hungarians, Romanians and Jews who had been beaten, starved and worked to exhaustion and death in Krupp enterprises. The astonishing speed of Alfried's return to grace and Krupp's revival were a source of wry wonderment in later years, but he told himself that he 'should have known that the burning passions of 1945 would soon subside'. Although it was not something he brooded about, he believed that history, if allowed, could repeat itself, and only a fool would not be always on the look-out for warning signs.

At the end of September, he was summoned to Nuremberg. The trials were due to start in November and he arrived with other members of the investigating team early one evening in the first week of October. The city had been chosen because it housed a large Palace of Justice which had somehow escaped bombardment, and for its symbolic value as the site of the great Hitler-worshipping rallies of the 1930s. The narrow streets and half-timbered houses, home of the Meistersingers and birthplace of Dürer, were in ruins. Corpses still lay under the mounds of rubble. The people he passed were pale and gaunt and wore clothes 'the same drab colour as if they had risen from the tomb'.[12] They looked at him with expressions of misery and hate. He was unmoved. 'It was Hitler who did this to you!' he shouted in German once in response to an accusing look.

At Nuremberg he would be working with the judges of the tribunal, whose president was a Briton, Geoffrey Lawrence. Neave's name had been proposed by the head of the British War Crimes Executive, Colonel Harry Phillimore. On 18 October, he was standing in the lobby of the Grand Hotel, where the senior staff had their headquarters, when a phalanx of men in dark suits approached. At the centre was an intimidating figure, a bronzed man with a neat moustache and smart clothes: the principal American judge, the former Attorney General of the United States, Francis Biddle. Surprisingly, Biddle seemed to know who he was and asked him if he was 'ready to serve the indictment'. This was news to Neave. He had yet to meet the British judges and no one had told him what his precise duties were. Biddle expressed surprise at Neave's youth, then proceeded to explain in a theatrical voice that under the tribunal's charter 'the defendants have a right to a fair trial and to counsel of their own choice. We have appointed you to advise them of their rights and select them German lawyers.'

This was a huge responsibility for someone whose legal experience to date had been confined to the lowest rungs of the British bar. Neave 'nodded as calmly as possible'. However, he felt as if he had suddenly been invited to sing at Covent Garden or deliver a lecture on higher mathematics. It was 'the most dangerous situation I had faced since Colditz'. He spent a restless night at his billet in the neighbouring village of Zirndorf. Then, on the afternoon of 19 October 1945, in his best uniform, Sam Browne gleaming, he set off with the American governor of the prison, Colonel Burton C. Andrus, to face the men who had plunged the world into war.

The defendants were held in Nuremberg prison, next to the courthouse. Its three storeys of cell wings were grouped around an atrium covered with wire netting to prevent prisoners jumping to their death. In Neave's writings, he is always alert to the connectivity of events. A sight, a landmark or an experience triggers off a recollection of a related incident. Often there is irony in the observation, or a sense of the wheel of fate coming full circle. So it was when he observed the wire netting. It brought to mind the fate of one of the agents he had trained, Captain Dominique-Edgard Potier, who was parachuted into Belgium in July 1943 to start up a new escape line for Allied aviators. After returning to England he was dropped into France for a second mission. He was captured at Reims and tortured by the Gestapo for several days. On 11 January 1944 he broke free from his guards and jumped from a third-floor window, dying hours later.

At a meeting at the Palace of Justice that morning, Neave's procedure had been decided. He would introduce himself to each defendant in turn, hand over a copy of the relevant indictment, list the prisoner's rights and announce he would return the following day to answer any questions. He was accompanied by a large party. With him were the American General Secretary of the Tribunal, Harold B. Willey; Major Wolfe Frank, a refugee from Germany who had joined the British Army and acted as expert translator; a chaplain, should the prisoner require spiritual sustenance; a psychiatrist, to record his reactions; and a strong security detail, led by Colonel Andrus.

The first encounter was with the most charismatic and complex of the prisoners, a man who inspired both mockery and a fascination heavily tinged with fear. As the cell door swung open, Neave got his first glimpse of Hermann Goering. The Reichsmarschall's eyes were 'small and greedy ... he had the look of a woman about him ... He appeared exquisitely corrupt and soft ... My first impression was of meeting a dissolute Roman emperor, game to the last.' His once-bloated form had deflated and his grey air force uniform hung off him. Neave handed him the indictment and told him his rights. Goering's response was a theatrical 'So it has come.' All afternoon Neave traipsed from cell to cell. Next came Hess, then Ribbentrop, Streicher, von Schirach, Frank, Funk and Frick, Kaltenbrunner and Ley. Last on the list was the German naval chief, Karl Doenitz.

Neave appears to have made a record of his first impressions soon after these visitations. It was another thirty-two years before he aired them in a book. He thought it best to wait until the 'dark passions of 1945 had cooled', and it was Diana who persuaded him, in the early 1970s, that the time was now right. His assessments of the men in the cells were a valuable contribution to understanding the character of the Nazis and Nazism. The pen pictures are shrewd, precise and not inhumane. He felt most sympathy for Hitler's deputy, Rudolf Hess, who in 1941 had flown himself to the estate of the Duke of Hamilton in an attempt to broker a peace with Britain. He was clearly mentally unbalanced. He wore an old grey tweed jacket and on his feet were the same Luftwaffe flying boots he had worn four years before, 'all that remained of his mad, courageous mission, which had brought him ridicule and disappointment'.[13]

Neave's greatest contempt was reserved for Hitler's Chief of Staff, Field Marshal Wilhelm Keitel, 'a weak man trying to be brave', who had got religion since incarceration. He had a particular reason for his animus towards Keitel. It was he who had signed the order authorising the execution without trial of the 'Cockleshell Heroes', the Royal Marine Commandos captured after the raid on Bordeaux. There had only been two survivors, the men helped to freedom by Neave's agent and protégée, Mary Lindell. When the task was completed, he reported to the judges, describing the reactions and demands of the defendants. It was quite a debut. Apart from defending a young soldier on a charge of accidentally shooting a woman as she rode along on her bicycle in France during the Phoney War, 'this was my first essay in advocacy before a court.'

The tribunal was unprecedented. There were difficulties and delays as it groped its way towards an approximation of justice. The proceedings stretched into the new year and it took ten months to conclude. The British prosecution team was led by Hartley Shawcross, Attorney General of the incoming Labour government, and Sir David Maxwell Fyfe, who served as Solicitor General under Churchill. Maxwell Fyfe was Edinburgh-born, the son of the headmaster of Aberdeen Grammar School, and a progressive Conservative who had been involved in making policy to meet the aspirations raised in the Beveridge Report for a fairer Britain. He entered parliament in 1935 and managed successful parallel careers as both politician and lawyer.

The 'short and lively Scot' made a deep impression on Neave. He admired his 'industry and skill' and the way he was able to strike fear into the Nazis. 'Their patronising smiles and bombast vanished before his questioning,' he wrote. Maxwell Fyfe's greatest moment came with his forensic evisceration of Goering over the case of the seventy-seven Allied airmen who tunnelled out of Stalag Luft III, at Sagan, south-east of Berlin, in March 1944. The feat became famous as the Great Escape. The breakout infuriated Hitler, who ordered all the captured prisoners to be shot, a breach of the Geneva Conventions. Until this stage in the trial, Goering had handled himself with increasing confidence. He had held up well under cross-examination by the American prosecutor, Justice Robert H. Jackson, and there seemed a chance that he might escape the noose.

Questioned by Maxwell Fyfe, Goering denied any knowledge of the 'Sagan' order. He claimed that he was on leave when it was issued and only learned later that fifty recaptured escapees had been shot. Maxwell Fyfe 'skilfully tested his alibi as if he were prosecuting a burglar at the Old Bailey'. Neave 'listened, fascinated, to this historic exchange ... cross-examination at its best'. Repeating his denials, Goering became 'alarmed and blustering'. He 'lost his self-control'. The sneaking respect felt by some for the Reichsmarschall's bravado evaporated. 'Goering had lost the battle,' wrote Neave. Maxwell Fyfe's 'cross-examination saved the face of the Allied prosecution' and 'marked Goering down for the death sentence'.[14]

The episode on which he had been skewered – the murder of escapee POWs – obviously had a special meaning for Neave, which Maxwell Fyfe acknowledged when they spoke in the lunch interval at the end of the opening session. Neave congratulated him, saying, 'You've got him.' Maxwell Fyfe 'smiled at me and said, "I know how you must feel."' The significance of his acquaintance with the advocate-politician went deeper than that. Here was someone to look up to, and in time perhaps to emulate.

The conduct of the Soviet legal team also left a deep impression, but of alarm and revulsion. They were clearly controlled directly from Moscow. The Soviet alternate judge on the bench, Colonel Alexander Fedorovich Volchkov, was said to be People's Commissar for Justice and a professor of international law. Neave suspected he was not a judge at all. Instead, it seemed more likely he was an intelligence officer serving with the NKVD. Neave makes clear in his book on the tribunal that as well as his courtroom functions he was still acting as an intelligence operative. He wrote that 'the intelligence services of the Western world, whose representatives at the trial included myself,' sent back reports on Moscow's man. Later, he came to believe that Volchkov was involved in the Katyn massacre of 10,000 Polish officers and intellectuals in 1940. Among the many atrocities of the war, this one held a particular significance for him – perhaps because of Diana's connection with the Poles.

When his day's work was done, Neave enjoyed the febrile social life that swirled around the tribunal. The town was full of soldiers, lawyers, secretaries and journalists. In the evenings the well connected gathered in the Marble Room of the Grand Hotel to gossip, flirt, dance and drink. Nuremberg lay in the American zone of occupation, a Land of Cockaigne through which flowed a river of booze. The Soviets, who had gone in no time from uneasy allies to the likely next enemies, were not seen much in the Marble Room and got drunk in the villas they shared with their women, singing, dancing and firing their revolvers. One night shots were heard outside the Grand Hotel. A Russian officer staggered into the lobby, collapsed and bled to death. In order to avoid embarrassment to the Soviet delegation, the band in the Marble Room was ordered to play on.

Neave entered into the spirit of rather desperate fun, including a drinking contest that was arranged among the principal participants in the trial. Each contestant had to gulp down as much as possible of the appropriate tipple. For the Americans it was bourbon, for the Russians vodka, for the French cognac and for the Brits whisky. The winner was Airey Neave.[15]

An undercurrent of anxiety and melancholy ran beneath the victors' surface euphoria. The shrewd eyes of Rebecca West, who was covering the trial for the *Daily Telegraph* and the *New Yorker* magazine, observed that they were 'gay for moments but were permanently depressed'. She was then fifty-three, a literary lioness whose love life had been as adventurous as her voyaging. H. G. Wells was an old flame. Francis Biddle became a new one. She and Neave hit it off immediately. Biddle may have been struck by Neave's youthful looks, but West 'took him for a man of forty, and rather worn at that'.[16] He impressed her in other ways. It seemed to her that he divided 'his attention between ideals of a sort that refused contentment, amusement at the world, and a puzzled interest in the persistent wickedness of man'. She noted a marked humility. A 'number of people who had had dealings with him during the war thought more highly of him than he did himself.' Above all, he grasped the significance of the event. In her view, he was 'as conscious as anybody there of the true meaning of the trial'.

On 1 October 1946, the sentences were delivered. Twelve defendants were condemned to death, seven imprisoned for terms from ten years to life, and three acquitted. The hangings took place on 16

October. Neave was not there to witness them. A fortnight before, he had flown back to England, wondering what role he would play in the new world that was taking shape and how he was going to provide for his wife and growing family.

8

The Long March

In the early afternoon of 1 July 1953, Airey Neave stood on the balcony of the Queen's Hotel, Abingdon, with Diana at his side, as supporters in the crowd below cheered the new MP. Like most of the important things in Neave's life, success had not come without effort. This was his third attempt to enter parliament. The struggle had not been made easier by the sight of lesser men breezing their way to Westminster – not least, his untrustworthy subordinate of IS9 days, Peter Baker, who had made it on his first try, in the 1950 general election.

Neave had also stood in the 1950 election, contesting the Labour stronghold of Thurrock, where he was, as expected, thrashed. In the election called in October the following year, he lost again to Labour in the more promising constituency of Ealing North, where he came within a whisker of success, only 120 votes behind the winner. He nonetheless decided to try his luck elsewhere. Within a few months of the election, a glittering prize beckoned. Sir Ralph Glyn, Conservative MP for the Abingdon division, was standing down. Neave presented himself with a clutch of other hopefuls and reached the shortlist of six. He was youngish (thirty-six), by now reasonably well established as a barrister in London and had a fine war record. On 18 March 1952, after a selection meeting at Didcot Conservative Club, he was selected as candidate.

It was another fourteen months before Sir Ralph was raised to the Lords, and the by-election to replace him was set for 30 June 1953, three weeks after the coronation of Queen Elizabeth II. He was facing manageable opposition. The main threat came from Labour, represented by Ted Castle, a pencil-moustachioed David Niven lookalike who was selected less than a fortnight before polling day. He had seen out the war as night editor of the *Daily Mirror* and was married to the formidable Barbara Castle, one of the few women in the House of Commons. She was a combative redhead and an acolyte of Labour's deputy leader, Aneurin Bevan, whose ferocious manner and radical agenda rattled the teacups of Middle England. Such associations were unlikely to endear Castle to undecided voters in what was a traditional Tory seat. Neave did his best to link his opponent to the Bevan camp and claimed that his credo included 'near-Communist ideas'.[1] Castle protested in vain that he 'never had any connection whatsoever with the Bevanite group'. His cause was not helped when 'Nye' appeared during the campaign to harangue a crowd of five hundred in a field.

The by-election came nineteen months into the Churchill premiership and was seen as an important test of the government's standing. The great man sent Neave a message of support, flaying the 'Socialists' – as the Tories invariably referred to their opponents – and trumpeting his administration's achievements. Churchill reminded voters that the Korean War was over, and far from being – as Labour charged – Cold Warmongers, 'hopes of peace are foremost in our minds.' At home they were keeping their promise to build 300,000 new homes a year and 'a new and bright spirit' was pervading the nation. Journalists descended on the constituency, including the *Daily Mirror*'s 'Cassandra' – the columnist William Connor. 'Abingdon is a maddeningly amorphous constituency that is very hard to get a grip on and has driven both the candidates red-eyed with the weariness of pursuit,' he wrote. 'There are 127 outlying villages. There are thousands of resolute Tories and an equal number of unshakeable Socialists. Their occupations range from growing turnips to making nuclear energy.'[2]

Naturally, Connor spoke highly of his colleague, describing Castle as 'lively, energetic, likeable'. But he also had positive words about Neave. He was 'compact, somewhat reserved, and with a military record that, if valour on the field was the same as political ability, would sweep him to Westminster.' He went on, 'Unfortunately the two qualities are not interchangeable.'

As Airey criss-crossed the division, Diana was almost always by his side, undaunted by the fact that she was only weeks away from the birth of their third child, William. Many years later, she told him that it had been 'a tremendous vote-catcher being pregnant'.[3] As it turned out, Abingdon was in effect gaining two members for the price of one. Over the years, Diana Neave would devote almost as much energy to the constituency as her husband did, and later perhaps more so when he was diverted by his Northern Ireland duties. Neave won by a comfortable margin of 5,860, increasing the Tory vote by 977. He now had a solid base on which to build a career in national politics and would represent the constituency until his death. It suited the Neaves very well, particularly Diana. Marigold can remember her mother 'being not at all keen on Ealing', and 'Thurrock equally she wasn't too excited about.'[4]

It covered nine hundred square miles, a vast area including five main towns, stretching from the suburbs of Oxford in the north to the outskirts of Swindon in the west, enclosing ancient market towns like Wantage and Faringdon and the mellow villages of the Vale of White Horse. It was well populated with traditional Tories of robust views. Though he was courteous and attentive to this layer of his support, such folk were not really the Neaves' type. One night they went to dine with a retired general, a stalwart of the local party in a neighbouring district, who 'did a good deal of drinking'. Afterwards Neave recorded in his diary his host's 'patronising' attitude to the local MP, and his surprise at the fact 'that Diana was *allowed* to make political speeches'. As he drove away from the general's manor house, he was 'glad it is not in my constituency'.[5]

More to their liking were the Oxford dons, literary figures and scientists among his constituents. They included the workforce of both the Atomic Energy Research Establishment at Harwell and the Royal Military College of Science at Shrivenham. Neave had received little formal scientific training, but his interest was deep and in time he taught himself enough to be able to understand the fundamentals of important contemporary technological developments. Their impact on politics and the economy would become his special subject and his primary area of parliamentary expertise.

Abingdon might be considered safe Tory territory, but he never took his tenure for granted. Despite comfortable majorities at every successive election, he fretted constantly over the soundness of every ward and village, badgering his agent, Leslie Brown, and local party chairwoman, Meredydd Saunders-Davies, a former intelligence officer, for information about the local mood and machinations. Neave's relationship with Brown was sometimes fractious but Meredydd, a true-blue spinster, stout and good-hearted, who lived with her sister Gwenfra, was a friend as well as a vital ally whose judgement he relied on heavily. His successive secretaries, Hannah Hulme and Joy Robilliard, provided another mainstay. They dealt stoically with a heavy workload, typing up and despatching the scores of daily letters to constituents, officials and ministers that in the pre-email age drove political activity, as well as dealing with his business interests.

For the next twenty-two years, the Neaves' life – for in many ways it was a single existence – was largely passed shuttling back and forth between London and the constituency. His appetite for work was insatiable, his engagement complete, and if interest and energy and a modicum of aptitude are the key ingredients of political success, then steady advancement seemed assured. With hindsight, the transition from soldier to MP appears natural, but there was nothing inevitable about the development. Neave wrote much about the forces that drove his wartime service. None of his books say anything about why he decided on a peacetime political career.

There was no real family tradition of political service and there were few early indications that he was set on a course for Westminster. The adolescent trip to Germany had stimulated an interest in 'abroad', but at university he took only a casual interest in the Oxford Union, traditional nursery of aspiring politicos, and never sought office. Despite his engagement with the wider world, there is not much evidence that he was particularly concerned with what went on at home. He left nothing behind that reveals his attitude towards the great question of what sort of Britain should emerge from the blood, sweat, toil and tears of war. There is no record of his thoughts about the Beveridge Report, which ushered in the welfare state, nor his reaction to the shock defeat of Winston Churchill in July 1945.

That he chose the Conservatives was unsurprising, but not inevitable. There were others with his background and wartime experience who decided that the future lay with Labour; men like Aidan Crawley, who took part in numerous escape attempts from Stalag Luft III. Crawley would prise staunchly Conservative Buckingham from the Tories with a massive swing in the 1945 election. Neave was not burdened with the attitudes towards those beneath him on the social ladder that afflicted some with a similar upbringing. The war had provided continuous proof that it was unwise to make assumptions about people on the basis of background. Nonetheless, he was no radical, inclined rather towards gradualism and continuity. He had a strong romantic streak, but it was circumscribed and qualified, only given full rein in time of war and in matters of the heart.

The decision to try for a career in politics seems to have been taken some time during his stint at Nuremberg. It was one he would regret many times, particularly in the early 1970s, by which time, after a brief junior ministerial career, he had spent a dozen years on the back benches with little reward or thanks and no hope of a reprieve in sight. In one of many diary entries expressing gloom and disillusionment, he dropped a hint about how the fateful move was made. On Monday 30 July 1973, he recorded that he 'had tea in the garden and reflected on what might have been'. He concluded that he had 'been far too shaken by the war to have gone to the Bar and politics', and he 'should have gone into a steady job like my father wanted', such as a post as a legal civil servant in the Parliamentary Counsel's office, but he was 'much too restless'. Instead, he was 'influenced by the Kilmuirs when they were at Nuremberg into fighting elections.' Lord Kilmuir was the title taken by David Maxwell Fyfe, whose performance at the tribunal had so impressed Neave. As well as being a star of the Bar, he was a

Conservative MP who went on to become Home Secretary and Lord Chancellor. His wife, born Sylvia Harrison (sister of Rex, the actor), ended up vice chairman of the Conservatives and was a prototype of the committed and energetic political confederate that Diana would become.

That summer day in Abingdon, the gamble he had taken was vindicated and a reasonably secure future assured. It was just as well. There were mouths to feed and school fees to be found. Marigold, born in 1944, was followed in November 1947 by Richard, always known by his middle name, Patrick. William arrived six weeks after the by-election. Providing for the family was not easy. Neave seems to have received no significant financial support from his father, and the Giffards' ancient lineage and broad acres did not mean that Diana was particularly well provided for. Apart from some later legacies that allowed them to buy two small houses that provided a rental income before being passed on to the boys, Neave had largely to live off what he could earn.

In 1943, while serving with MI9, he had found time to arrange admission to the Middle Temple, which entitled him to practise as a barrister. On leaving the War Crimes Commission, he found a place at 5 King's Bench Walk, the chambers of Frederick Lawton, a criminal advocate and QC who welcomed young talent. At Nuremberg, Neave had been a player in a great historical and jurid-ical event. The work on offer to a junior barrister in London in 1946, traipsing around the magistrates' courts and quarter sessions of Greater London, represented quite a comedown. The defendants in the dock at Nuremberg had been among the greatest criminals of all time. The men and women he now had to prosecute or defend were often guilty of little more than hopelessness and stupidity. The law at this level was desperately uninspiring. Neave was no Maxwell Fyfe and had neither the natural aptitude nor the drive to haul himself easily to the higher reaches. Even after entering parliament, he was still trudging off to Home Counties courtrooms to appear in dull cases. In September 1953, he was at Wallington, Surrey, prose-cuting five men who had stolen a car, smashed a shop window and made off with two television sets, then knocked over a policeman at the end of an 85 mph car chase, causing him to lose his leg. The following month he was in Essex, in a case involving underage drinkers.

Entering the Commons meant ending his active association with the military and the world that had shaped him and made his name. After returning from Germany in the autumn of 1946, he had elected to carry on in the Territorials. He chose to retain his nominal connection with the Royal Artillery but was seconded to the Intelligence Corps. He was posted to the latest incarnation of his old outfit, now officially No. 9 Intelligence School TA. By the beginning of 1950, he was second in command, and when in March the incumbent stood down due to ill health, he took over as CO in the rank of lieutenant colonel. The unit's work was primarily concerned with retaining the knowledge and skills of escape and evasion techniques that had been built up during the war and applying them to the new circumstances of the Cold War.

In the event of a Soviet bloc invasion of Western Europe, it was intended that specialist reserve troops who were cut off behind enemy lines would form units to carry on fighting in the rear. Local support was to be provided by the same patriots who had sustained the escape organisations. Neave stood down as CO of IS9 (TA) in September 1951, citing the fact that he was a parliamentary candidate in the forthcoming general election. 'Whether or not I am elected,' he wrote in his resignation letter, 'I intend to pursue a political career. In these circumstances I shall find it impossible to give adequate time to my increasing duties in command …'[6] The deputy director of military intelligence agreed, recommending that 'owing to the security nature of IS9, it is not advisable that Colonel Neave should continue to be a serving TA officer after his nomination as a parliamentary candidate.' Neave remained on the reserve list, however, and was expected to play a useful role in any future hostilities. A note in his army file from the Air Ministry dated 3 October 1952 proposed that 'the aforementioned officer be earmarked for the appointment of O/C Escape Section IS9 (UK) in the event of mobilisation'.

As late as May 1974, Neave was giving advice to senior NATO officers from Supreme Headquarters Allied Powers in Europe 'about the possibility of escape and evasion in the event of war with Russia' and putting them in contact with Albert 'Pat O'Leary' Guérisse.[7] Neave's critics would say that his connections with the intelligence world continued long after his formal association had ended.

Neave never fully put the war behind him. He described his exploits in a series of books, beginning in 1953 with the publication of *They Have Their Exits*, an account of his escapes and the journey back to Britain. It carried a foreword by Norman Birkett, one of the British judges at Nuremberg, who described the author as 'a rising young barrister and politician'. At the time, Birkett was a very senior judge, sitting in the Court of Appeal. He was one of the great lawyers of the age, wise and humane, a Methodist preacher and lifelong Liberal who served twice as an MP. He praised the book as 'a story of the most enthralling kind, with here and there touches of humour and even gaiety', and ultimately a 'revelation of the essential nobility of men and women, when faced with the most desperate and dreadful circumstances'.

Birkett's hope that 'this book will be widely read' was amply fulfilled. *They Have Their Exits* was well reviewed and went on selling in very healthy numbers for the next twenty years. This success provided another source of income and paved the way for further works, all of which drew on his wartime experiences. It was followed a year later by *Little Cyclone*, which told the story of Dédée. In 1969, *Saturday at MI9* gave a fuller account of the organisation's work in occupied Europe. In 1972, he went back to the beginning with *The Flames of Calais*. He completed the chronicle with *Nuremberg*, which appeared in 1978. Neave wrote entertainingly and revealingly in an accessible style that, in the case of *Little Cyclone*, could border on Mills & Boon. He also started two thrillers – *Low Profile* and *Green Card* – using his political and intelligence-world experiences to authenticate the plot. Sadly, neither made it into print and the manuscripts have disappeared.

The literary output also served to boost his political profile. Neave had had a good war, but so had many other young Tory aspirants who did not write books. His fellow Old Etonian Peter Carrington, who soared through the party ranks at the same period, never publicly recorded the deeds that won him an MC. Nor did Neave's comrade and friend Hugh Fraser publicise his considerable exploits behind the lines in the Ardennes in the autumn of 1944. But Neave needed all the help he could get. Despite the advantages he had been born with, the rewards were all fought for and hard won. Carrington, by contrast, did not have to go to the trouble of seeking election, on account of an hereditary seat in the House of Lords. Hugh Fraser was selected for the safe Tory seat of Stone in Staffordshire by the time of the 1945 election and won it with ease. Neave had to make his own luck, and reminding the world of his wartime achievements was one way of doing it.

There was more to it than that, though. The war had been the great formative experience of his life, for worse as well as for better. He had emerged from it bearing psychological as well as physical scars (thirty-three years after being wounded at Calais, medical examinations revealed the presence of metal in his chest). In his books, he made only glancing references to terror and anxiety. In the privacy of his intermittent diaries, he was more forthcoming. Many years after the conflict, he wrote that 'it took me twenty years to recover from the war.'[8] The emotional intimacy of his marriage made it inconceivable that he could have hidden his trauma from Diana. Whatever passed between them was not communicated to the children, let alone to any of the vast array of accumulated political and business colleagues and acquaintances (Neave owned to having very few real friends).

Nonetheless, those around him sensed a deep hurt and guessed that the war was to blame. Veronica Beckett, who worked as his secretary in the early 1960s, recalled being told – perhaps by Diana – that he would 'sometimes wake in the night screaming'.[9] The children too have their recollections of behaviour that hinted at hidden scars, such as his irrational fear of airport security scanners. The phobia is confirmed by a diary entry more than thirty years after the 'home run' from Colditz. 'I loathe travel,' he wrote after arriving in Florence for a holiday with Diana in April 1973. 'It reminds me of my escape, with the meticulous preparations to get through controls … I am very neurotic about this and panic easily.' Psychotherapy was in its infancy in Britain, and a Conservative politician who admitted to undergoing it risked damage to his reputation. Writing was one solution. 'It is really my only relief from anxiety neurosis,' read another entry later that year. 'But I can't get anyone else to understand this.'[10]

He was to some degree imprisoned by his wartime history. The paradox was that although war had damaged him, it had also made him what he was, and when he faced the world he leaned heavily on his reputation as a war hero for support. His name and that of Colditz would be linked for ever. He worked hard to buttress the connection. He would talk to anyone who asked him about his exploits, from the Wallingford Rotary Club to the *Daily Mirror*, and over the years delivered hundreds of lectures. He guarded the memory closely, marking each passing anniversary of the escape itself and the crossing of the Swiss frontier. In 1973, public interest in the castle was stoked by the BBC TV series *Colditz*. Annoyingly, from Neave's point of view, the storylines were based on Pat Reid's book and his own escape was barely featured, kindling some resentment and a spark of jealousy.

The relationships he had forged with MI9 colleagues do not seem to have matured into particularly strong peacetime friendships, though he kept in touch with 'Monday' – Michael Creswell – visiting him at his house in Surrey. However, he retained a strong emotional attachment to his old agents and, insofar as it was possible, he kept in touch. After her release from Ravensbrück, Dédée resumed nursing, and spent much of the rest of her life in Africa, working in clinics and leper colonies, so contact was difficult. They had a reunion in July 1974 when she took a break from the leper hospital she was working at in Addis Ababa. 'She looks remarkably well but is obviously not so,' he wrote in his diary.[11] 'Only five years ago did she recover her sense of taste. She is having a difficult time in Addis Ababa … it was a relief to meet someone who faces life so cheerfully.'

The children recall lunches and dinners with modest, discreet middle-aged men and women from Belgium and France, who they later learned were the heroes and heroines of the escape lines. Airey even retained his affection for possibly his most troublesome agent, and Mary Lindell was an intermittent visitor at the Neaves' London flat.

The House of Commons he entered in 1953 was full of ex-soldiers, sailors and airmen. For some, memories of war sat lightly on their shoulders. In Neave's case, the experience would continue to shape his thoughts and deeds until he died. The war provided him with an array of causes, such as his long struggle to win compensation for prisoners and other victims. But, above all, it conditioned his political thinking. What he had seen as a soldier, a prisoner, an escaper, an intelligence officer and a lawyer left him with a profound hatred of totalitarians and a determination to confront them, be they Soviet Communists or Irish Republicans.

The day after the by-election victory, he took his seat in the House to the cheers of his colleagues, 'a well-built fellow of medium height with rugged, clean-shaven features and an air of quiet assurance,' according to one sketch-writer.[12] He was eager to get started. He was thirty-seven years old and many of his wartime contemporaries already had years of parliamentary service under their belts. At 5.44 p.m., on 29 July 1953, only four weeks after his election, he got to his feet to make his first speech, intervening in a debate on defence. It lasted ten minutes, during which he marked out the arena in which he would initially strive to make his political reputation.

As Churchill had stated in his message of support, peace was in the air. The death of Stalin in March, the accession of Khrushchev to the Kremlin and Eisenhower to the White House had raised hopes that Cold War tensions might relax. On the other hand, a nuclear arms race was now under way. Britain had to maintain its defences at maximum preparedness. The new member had some thoughts on one area where improvements could be made. He started by pointing out his qualifications for making a contribution.[13] There was the geographical fact that in his constituency lay 'certain defence establishments, in particular the Military College of

Science at Shrivenham and several other Service establishments, as well as the Atomic Energy Research Establishment at Harwell.'

In addition, there were 'personal reasons' why he was joining the debate. He had 'served for a long time in the Territorial Army, recently leaving it, when I retired about two years ago, and I specialised during the last war in military intelligence.' What concerned him today was training, and how national servicemen, particularly those who had been involved in intelligence, could be persuaded to volunteer for the Territorials when their time was up, in order to build on the skills they had acquired in their two years in uniform. He stressed the need for a high-level cadre of Territorial intelligence officers to boost Britain's contribution to NATO. He also called for increased emphasis on language training and the sending of Territorials abroad as liaison officers, to strengthen links with NATO allies and to see at first hand the terrain in which British troops might one day have to fight. Finally, he proposed equipping reserves with the up-to-date equipment and weaponry that was currently in use by regular troops, and concentrating training on practical skills rather than 'too much in the way of regimental duties or too much foot drill'.

He sat down at 5.45 p.m. It was a sound if modest debut, heavy on verbiage, light on detail and raising obvious practical problems. Where, for example, was the money to come from to pay for all the new kit and guns? However, it produced an ecstatic response from the next speaker, George Wigg, Labour MP for Dudley. 'I count myself most fortunate in conveying to the hon. Member for Abingdon the congratulations of the House on his maiden speech,' he enthused. 'My own first speech was also on defence, and I only wish I could have done half as well and spoken half as lucidly as he has done this afternoon … I am speaking very sincerely when I say to him that he has impressed the House this afternoon with the extent of his knowledge. We shall look forward in the future to many other contributions from him, much more lengthy and more contentious.'

To get such praise from a political opponent was unusual. Wigg, though, was not a typical Labour MP. At fifty-three, he was on the older end of the age spectrum and until his election in 1945 had spent almost all his career in the army. To the annoyance of many in his party, he was a fierce champion of a strong defence budget. He was also known to have close links to the Secret Intelligence Service. However sincere his sentiments, his endorsement can be seen as the tribute of one old soldier with security connections to another.

Wigg's anticipation of many more contributions from the new member would not come to pass. Over the next few years, Neave's utterances in the House were intermittent and often narrowly focused on constituency matters or detailed questions arising from defence and scientific issues. He vigorously defended his constituents' interests, even where they clashed with those of the armed services. His first written question was an unrealistic request to stop the operation of jet aircraft from RAF Benson, near Abingdon, which received a predictably dusty reply from the Ministry of Defence. When the bill to set up the Atomic Energy Authority passed through the Commons, he was quick to seek assurances that the new arrangements would mean no job losses at Harwell, which was a major employer in the constituency.

The laboratory had been set up in 1946, sixteen miles south of Oxford, on the site of an RAF station. It was the country's main centre for atomic energy research and development. Neave made sure to build relationships with the staff and involve himself closely in Harwell's affairs. In his first years in the House he regularly prodded the government to ensure there would be enough houses and schools as the number of employees grew and the laboratory spread itself over the surrounding farmland, to the point where he was teased by the opposition for not missing an opportunity to 'log roll' on behalf of constituents.[14]

His interventions on defence were similarly technical and parochial. Speaking in the debate in November 1953 on a bill to streamline call-up procedures in the event of a grave international crisis, he harked back to his wartime service, asking what it would mean in particular for Territorials serving in anti-aircraft units.[15]

His quiet manner, attention to detail and disinclination to rock the boat was soon noticed by the party managers. In February 1954, seven months after entering the House, he got his first promotion when he was appointed parliamentary private secretary to the Minister for Transport and Civil Aviation, John Boyd-Carpenter. In August the following year, he was made PPS to the Minister for the Colonies, Alan Lennox-Boyd. These posts were unpaid and the lowest rung on the ladder of government. 'You're a dogsbody,' explained one MP from the era. 'You hang around whoever it is, you seek to promote their interests in any proper way you can, and you relay faithfully what the party's thinking.'[16] It was a necessary start, offering hope that there was life beyond the back benches – perhaps in time a ministry.

Neave's assiduous defence of his constituents did him no harm with the electors of Abingdon. At the general election of 26 May 1955, he won an increased majority and returned to a House in which the Conservatives under Anthony Eden now enjoyed a healthy sixty-seat majority. Eden was steeped in foreign expertise and had waited a long time for the top job. Years of steady stewardship seemed to lie ahead. Then, in the summer of 1956, an overseas crisis took a hammer to Conservative complacency.

It erupted on 26 July in Cairo when General Abdel Nasser announced that he was nationalising the Anglo-French-owned Suez Canal and Egyptian troops were taking over the canal zone. Eden was outraged and determined to fight back. However, launching a military operation would be difficult. International opinion was hostile to imperialist adventures, as were many at home. Crucially, the attitude of the United States was uncertain. Washington was unsympathetic to British hopes of maintaining its empire and also concerned that Egypt would fall under Soviet control.

While public attempts to resolve the crisis ground on, the government was plotting secretly with the French and the Israelis. The plan was for Israel, citing a threat to its security, to invade Egypt, giving Anglo-French forces a pretext to intervene and restore peace, in the process regaining control of the canal. The Israeli attack went ahead on 29 October, followed by a phoney ultimatum from London and Paris demanding that both sides pull back and allow their forces to temporarily occupy the canal zone. On 31 October, Operation Musketeer was launched with the bombardment of Egyptian airfields, followed by landings and paratroop drops. Militarily, the operation was a success and within a week most of the canal zone was in the invaders' hands. Politically, it was a disaster. America joined the condemnations in the United Nations. At home, Eden faced a sustained and eloquent assault from the Labour opposition, led by Hugh Gaitskell, whose alarm at the Prime Minister's recklessness was shared by at least some on the government benches.

A week after British troops went in, the US had imposed a ceasefire and British troops were forced to withdraw. The debacle did lasting damage to Britain's standing in the world and its cherished 'special relationship' with America. Eden's reputation was fatally wounded by a lie told to parliament denying prior government knowledge of the Israeli attack. Two months later he was gone, replaced by Harold Macmillan. The crisis ignited passionate debate in parliament, with voices raised stridently in defence and condemnation of the action. A faction of Tory imperialists – the Suez group – first fervently backed the government, then turned against it in disgust when they accepted pressure to withdraw, with fifteen MPs refusing to back their leader in a confidence vote. For Conservatives, Suez aroused atavistic emotions and forced reflection on what sort of Tory you were: a traditionalist, fighting a rearguard action to maintain Britain's world power status, or a progressive, a pragmatist, a realist.

Whatever thoughts Neave had on the episode he did not express in public and he made no contribution to the fiery Commons debates. He followed the bidding of the Chief Whip, Edward Heath, in the crucial divisions of 8 November and 6 December 1956. His reticence set the tone for the rest of the decade. He was a mainstream, modernising Tory, comfortable with the post-war social settlement that was honoured successively by Churchill, Eden, Macmillan and Douglas-Home. At no point did he seem drawn towards the radical right-wing doctrines that would come to be associated with the woman whose ascent he engineered.

Neave's feelings could run deep in private but his public utterances on policy were measured, based on information and analysis rather than instinct and feeling. He was a mediocre speaker at a time when rhetorical ability was highly prized in parliament, preferring the careful presentation of data over phrase-making. He was a technocrat not a romantic, and a patriot but not an imperialist. On the big issues of the day, where he might have been expected to feel the tug of tradition, he sided with progress. From the beginning, he was in favour of Britain getting aboard the great project to unite Europe, telling an audience in the summer of 1950, when the Schuman Plan that laid the foundations of the Common Market was launched, that Britain should join the debate 'instead of standing sheepishly aside'. When Heath launched his campaign to enter the EEC, it had Neave's backing.

There was one issue, though, on which he stood on the right of the party. In 1956, a Labour member, Sidney Silverman, introduced a private member's bill in a renewed attempt to abolish capital punishment. Neave made two contributions to the debate and voted against the bill.[17] It would be another nine years before Britain abandoned the rope. Neave continued to believe strongly that capital punishment had a place in the justice system. His assertion while Conservative spokesman on Northern Ireland that political murderers should face execution would arouse controversy and deepen Republican hatred of him.

In January 1957, he moved another rung up the ladder when he was made joint parliamentary secretary to the Minister of Transport and Civil Aviation, Harold Watkinson. Two years later, he was promoted to be Under-Secretary of State at the Air Ministry. To work effectively required the mastery of masses of technical detail and he set about it with characteristic dedication. It was a good-news branch of government. Work was beginning on Britain's first motorways, and the Gatwick airport project was launched, 'the first airport in the world to combine air, rail and road transport in one unit,' as he proudly told the press.

With his ministerial duties and devotion to constituency affairs, there was little time for anything else. The term 'workaholic' was not heard much in the 1950s, but it accurately described Airey Neave's lifestyle. Diana was scarcely less energetic. The couple had moved out of intrepid Aunt Sylvia's flat at 39 Elizabeth Street in 1945 and into a maisonette around the corner at No. 41, where they lived until 1950. They then obtained a lease on a house at 11 Carlyle Square, not as grand as it is today but still smart. From 1957 to 1965, their town base was a flat in Crescent Mansions, at the top of the Fulham Road. They then spent three years at Marsham Court in Marsham Street, a short walk to Parliament, before crossing the road to another large apartment block, Westminster Gardens.

It took them a while to find a suitable home in the constituency. They started off by renting a cottage in Lockinge, near Wantage, where William was born. Later they spent two years in a wing of Ashdown House, Lambourn, a seventeenth-century mansion over-looking the Berkshire Downs. In 1956, they spent a further two years in another architectural gem, Compton Beauchamp House, near Uffington, which belonged to friends. After four years at Grove House South, in the village of Grove, near Wantage, they bought the place where they felt properly at home. The Old Vicarage, Ashbury, was an elegant white stucco house with pillars at the entrance, five bedrooms and a ring of sarsen stones in the garden. It sat on a hill with wonderful views over the Vale of White Horse. The house gave them both great pleasure and they improved and expanded it, adding extra rooms and installing a swimming pool.

It was a haven but also a place of work. In country as in town, both strove constantly at promoting Airey's career. Despite the cautious figure he presented to the world, Neave's commitment to the political life was deep. In the eyes of his eldest child, Marigold, it bordered on an obsession and it was not just her father who was in its grip. At home, the talk in front of the children was almost exclusively of politics. 'There might be some gossip about local people or something like that,' she remembered, 'but not hugely.'[18] William recalled a friend remarking that 'the Neaves are the only family I know who talk politics at breakfast.'[19] 'Politics concentrated [the thinking] of my parents so much,' remembered Patrick. 'As children, we felt we were supporters.' Once they were old enough, when visitors arrived before their parents had descended, they 'opened the door, introduced the guests – might be a minister, someone important, a constituent. We brought them into the sitting room, offered them a sherry and made small talk.'[20]

There were few interests outside of public life. When staying with his in-laws at Chillington, while the others were off riding, walking or shooting, Airey would stay behind in the comfort of an armchair reading a newspaper or a book. According to Marigold, he 'didn't play games, didn't play tennis. He didn't play anything that I can think of.' She came to think that 'it would have done him a lot of good if he had. He ought to have had an outside interest. It all became a little too introspective, really.' His single-mindedness brought success. But nonetheless, 'It probably wasn't very good for him.'

Airey's absorption in politics extended to his social life. 'He was not the sort of person who enjoys going to clubs or attending reunions,' said Patrick. Nor, at this stage, did family life take up the couple's time unduly. At the age of eight, Patrick and William were sent off down the same educational path trodden by their father: St Ronan's Preparatory School, which had now moved from Worthing to Hawkhurst, then Eton. Marigold went to a local independent school run by nuns, St Mary's, Wantage, when she was 'about twelve or thirteen'. It was only a few miles away from where they lived, but as her mother spent much of her time in London supporting her father, she was sent as a boarder. She was 'rather rebellious' and it was awkward being the daughter of the local MP. She remembers being teased. 'At thirteen you're a bit sensitive, and I'd just arrived from London, and everybody else had been at the junior school and I hadn't, and it was not easy. The dreadful French mistress – I was never any good at French – used to call me "my petite MP", and I was always made to stand up and decline all the French verbs. I didn't like that very much.'

The war had taught Neave to respect women for both their intellects and their moral courage. He had married a woman who had operated effectively in a man's world. Yet neither he nor Diana pushed Marigold towards higher education and a challenging career. Instead, their attitude towards their daughter's prospects was practically Victorian. Marigold 'wasn't encouraged to go anywhere'. She left school at sixteen and went to a crammer to get three A levels, which she managed in a single year. Thereafter, she got a job as a secretary at *Queen* magazine, the style bible of the Swinging Sixties. The very different world she had plunged into provoked Diana's mild curiosity, 'but my father I don't think had a clue. It wasn't a job that involved politics and therefore it wasn't of any interest, really.'

Looking back, she 'would have loved to have gone to university, loved to have done what my children did … But I think that marriage was always what they hoped for. With any luck, find a husband and be off their hands.' And this is what she did, though subsequently through her own efforts she attended the Architectural Association, earned a degree in horticulture, took a postgraduate course in historical landscape, and with her husband Richard established a large and flourishing garden business.

The Neaves' semi-detached approach to parenting extended to the boys. 'You didn't have a family where [the parents] endlessly watched every football match you were playing in,' said Patrick. The same imagery was employed by William: 'They were marvellous parents, but they weren't hands-on [as] parents are nowadays, constantly at the rugby pitch shouting, "Come on, school!"' One of Airey's secretaries remembers him dictating a letter to one of the boys 'amid a whole lot of other letters to constituents and so on.' The couple would turn up at the major school events, however, and on one occasion Airey even took part in the fathers race on sports day. According to Patrick, Diana used to 'dress up quite finely in very tight skirts' and therefore 'wasn't quite prepared for the mothers and sons race'.

Neave was proud of his Eton education but it was not the crucial formative event that coloured the subsequent lives of some of its old boys. He did not conform to any of the popular stereotypes of the Old Etonian. When a senior Tory colleague, Tom King, was interviewed for this book, he had forgotten or never known that Neave was one. Infrequent though they may have been, the boys remember their father's visits to Eton with pleasure. Patrick recalls one occasion which showed Neave's fundamental decency and sensitivity. It was at the school's Fourth of June celebrations, at the time of the 1963 Profumo scandal. In the street Patrick pointed out to his father a school contemporary, David, the son of the disgraced minister. 'He went right up to him and had a friendly chat ... I thought it was rather good that he should do that.'

The demands of politics meant that the children spent a lot of time with their grandparents. Neave's father now played almost no part in his life. His mother was dead and Sheffield had married again. Instead, they spent happy summers at Chillington Hall. 'My grandmother was very supportive, knowing that my parents were so busy with the constituency,' said Patrick. 'My grandfather was very keen that we should learn to ride and we were given ponies ... with Chillington being so large and having stables and all that, we were in a very advantageous position to do all these activities, and the parents used to come up and see us between times.'

Later William formed a close attachment to his uncle Digby, born twelve years after Airey, who had married Ulla Schmidt, a Dane, and moved to the outskirts of Paris, where he worked in the reinsurance business. The couple were sociable and fun, close friends of the Anglo-French businessman Jimmy Goldsmith and his brother Teddy, and active in the Parisian artistic scene. William went to stay in school holidays and later, at his uncle's suggestion, took a course in French civilisation at the Sorbonne. 'Uncle Digby was always rather important to me,' he said, 'a great star, almost like a second father.'

Conversely, Digby and Ulla's daughter Philippa came to hold her uncle in great affection. She knew him as a child when Airey and Diana would come to visit. She remembers someone who was 'very quiet ... quite grave ... you wouldn't jump up and sit on his knee, it wasn't like that, but he paid attention to you. He really looked at you and spoke to you.'[21] John Giffard, son of Diana's brother John, remembered his uncle's 'dry sense of humour ... light laugh and big smile. He wasn't distant from us ... a good family member.'[22] When, after Eton and Southampton University, John decided to join the police, Airey 'was one of the great supporters within the family ... against my parents, who were horrified, and that was really nice.' He told them 'to stop being so silly about it ... it was a good thing that people from all backgrounds should be joining the police.' His faith was justified and Giffard ended up Chief Constable of Staffordshire Police.

In their marriage, Airey and Diana created a space for themselves that they did not feel needed the children's presence to be complete. Patrick remembers an occasion when the couple went on holiday *à deux* on the Continent, leaving him at Chillington. 'I caught a bug and my grandmother was very worried. They didn't know whether to get in touch with my parents. They decided not to. I had to suffer in silence.' However, displaying a stoicism that Airey and Diana would surely have approved of, he concluded that 'they couldn't have done anything anyway, and by the time they got back [the bug] had disappeared.'

Sometimes the Neaves' hands-off approach could raise eyebrows. As a young man, William met an attractive woman at a party who introduced herself as a former temporary secretary to Airey. She told him, 'I was aged eighteen and I was delegated the duty to take you to Charing Cross station to go to prep school for the first time. I put you on the train and I think it was the worst experience I ever had.' She 'vowed then that if I ever had any children I would never, ever' send them away to school.

William says now, 'Do I remember that? No. Did it do me any harm? No.' Like his siblings, he defends his parents' apparent remoteness from the daily lives of their children as a matter of time and place: 'It was a different generation and that's how it worked in those days ... I don't doubt that they loved all their children immensely but they didn't turn round and say so ...' Instead, they gave him 'immense freedom', the liberty to make his own choices and learn from his own mistakes.

As the boys approached manhood and Marigold married and began to have children, the family seems to have grown much closer. The boys spent almost every weekend at the Old Vicarage and Marigold would visit regularly with Richard, and her children,

Kate and Edward. It was perhaps the case that Airey found that he needed to see his children as grown-up equals before intimacy and warmth were possible. Certainly the devotion of Marigold, Patrick and William to their parents' memory is profound and genuine. However unusual the Neaves' approach to child-rearing might seem to contemporary eyes, they were clearly doing something right.

Airey's punishing work rate was combined with a careless attitude to his health. He took no exercise, smoked heavily and drank more than he should have done. His wartime books reveal a close relationship with alcohol and there are indications that, in the post-war years, his intake may have gone beyond the almost ritual consumption of gin, whisky, cognac and wine that was routine in the masculine realms of the military, the law and parliament. This became a cause for family concern and, according to Marigold, 'He did at one point have a minor drink problem.' It was unsurprising that he developed high blood pressure and cardiac problems. In September 1959, just as a general election was looming, he had a heart attack at the then constituency home, Grove House South. He recovered sufficiently to take part in the campaign and on 8 October retained his seat with an increased majority of 10,972. Nationally, Macmillan's decision to go early had been triumphantly vindicated. The Conservatives now had a hundred-seat majority.

However, the coronary had cast a shadow over what should have been a bright future. He was now under doctor's orders to alter his habits. In his usual conscientious fashion he strove to lose weight. He did not find it easy. Patrick remembers a rowing machine which was stored in his room in Crescent Mansions. However, 'I don't think he was terribly enthusiastic about it, because it stayed under my bed all the time.' Drink and cigarettes were definitely out. He stoically abandoned the Du Maurier cigarettes he had smoked steadily for decades and turned his back on the drinks tray and the wine cellar, thus depriving himself of a friendly prop to sustain him through the thousands of tedious official dinners and lunches that lay ahead. It was difficult, and it did not get any easier. 'Unable to enjoy life despite many advantages,' he wrote many years after the heart attack.[23] 'It is hard never to drink or smoke and to work so hard for so little.' He was quieter now, his spirit apparently dimmed. Before, according to Patrick, he had been 'very lively … very amusing'. Afterwards, as the above entry attests, he was often sombre, pessimistic and introspective. Brushes with death force reflection on life's purpose, the audit of what has been achieved and what has been left undone, and a resolve to make the most of the time that is left. He was determined to get back into the swim and press on with what might be only a short career.

It was not to be. Some time towards the end of October 1959 he went to see the government Chief Whip, Edward Heath, at his office in the Commons. In his monumental 1993 biography of Heath, the political historian John Campbell gave an account of what happened next. Heath, he wrote, 'made a lifelong enemy of Airey Neave … who returned to Westminster after suffering a coronary, expecting to be welcomed back with congratulations on his recovery, only to be told bluntly by Heath that he was "finished". Neave never forgave him, but took his revenge in 1975.'[24] The story stuck. When Heath died in July 2005, the *Daily Telegraph* obituary stated that 'Airey Neave … had hated Heath since 1959,' and gave a slightly different version of the same anecdote as the reason.

It is easy to see how the story gained traction, with its satisfying narrative of a throwaway snub resulting in nemesis. It helped to explain what drove Neave's brilliant campaign to unseat Heath and enthrone Thatcher all those years later. Marigold is prepared to give it some credence, speculating that Heath might have made some observation about her father's fitness which he might have taken the wrong way. 'I thought it was all rather silly,' she said. 'My father was sometimes quite quick to take offence. And I think that might have been one of the times.'

There are reasons to question the story, however. Heath himself vehemently denied it. Neave never said anything in public about the meeting. In the diaries he began to keep thirteen years later – a period in which his relations with Heath were crucial – there is no mention of an encounter which, if it had taken place, would surely have still resonated. The evidence there suggests that, however it came about, Neave's return to the back benches turned out to be fortuitous. 'Diana drove me to 149 Harley Street to see Dr Graham Hayward,' he wrote in August 1973. 'He was very impressed at my recovery … he would have expected me to die had I remained in office …'[25]

Whatever the truth, by the end of 1959 he was once again at the foot of the greasy pole and years of frustration lay ahead.

9

Darkest Hour

On New Year's Day 1973, Airey Neave confided to his diary that at the start of the previous year he had 'had serious doubts about remaining in Parliament. After twenty years in the House, it did not seem that I should ever achieve very much.' The defeatist mood persisted. Six weeks later, he was 'extremely depressed' and had decided that the 'next General Election will be my last.'[1] He was 'absolutely fed up with being the scapegoat for everything. It is time I became a professional writer and gave up this arduous, thankless task for ever. I have long wanted to do so but have been persuaded that in some old-fashioned way it was my "duty". I have no political future but a literary one.'[2] When he wrote these words he had just turned fifty-seven and clearly believed that his political life was mostly behind him. In better spirits, he might have judged that his achievement was not so slight. After his ministerial career jumped the tracks, he had pressed on, a hard-working backbencher who butted obstinately against the ramparts of official laziness and indifference on behalf of his constituents and a number of good causes.

Their nature revealed a stubborn decency and a determination to see justice done. At the start of his parliamentary career, he had taken up the cause of about 6,000 Britons who had been placed in Nazi concentration camps, among them Mary Lindell. Nineteen years after the end of the war, thanks in large part to his continual representations, they finally received the compensation that had long before been awarded to French and Belgian victims of the Nazis.

He fought on behalf of widows who had married war veterans after they had left the services and were therefore denied a pension. In 1965, he also introduced a private member's bill to award pensions to very old and often impoverished people who, because they had made no voluntary contributions to pre-war schemes, had been excluded when the Labour government introduced the National Insurance programme in 1948. He took up the cause on behalf of two constituents in 1964 when the Conservatives were still in power. Over the next six years he made forty-three speeches and interventions in the House. His style was low-key and courteous. He did not speak particularly well, a definite handicap in parliament. He made up for it by a grasp of statistics and detail. Beneath the old-fashioned manners, though, there was real passion and iron determination. In February 1969, he told members that 'when I started there were 250,000 of these people ... there are now 125,000. Four hundred of them are dying each week. This is a terrible thing to have to talk about, in the House or anywhere else.'[3] It was more than five years before justice was done, and his efforts won praise from both sides of the House. The implacable processes of bureaucracy and the mean-spirited responses trotted out by ministers sometimes stirred him to lose his customary cool. His persistent questioning of a minister over the case of a seventy-one-year-old woman who had been denied a pension because she had not kept up her National Insurance contributions while detained for nine years in a Soviet labour camp earned him a rebuke from the Speaker.[4]

Neave was determined that the lessons of the war should be learned and not forgotten. He was anxious that diplomatic expediency should not be allowed to sanitise history and that the Soviet Union's war crimes should be remembered along with those of Germany. In the face of furious Soviet denial, and to the annoyance of the Foreign Office, he agitated for years for a memorial to the thousands of Poles murdered by the Russians in Katyn forest near Smolensk and elsewhere in the spring of 1940, part of a systematic programme to annihilate the Polish officer class and 'bourgeoisie'. After many frustrations, a site commemorating them and making clear who was responsible was finally opened at Gunnersbury, West London, in 1976.

Neave's sense of justice was impartial. From early 1970, he began campaigning for the release of Rudolf Hess from Spandau prison in West Berlin, where he had been held since 1947. Hess was one of the defendants to whom Neave had served indictments at Nuremberg. Peering at him through the window in the cell door, he had been shocked 'to see his worn figure ... I immediately felt sorry for him.'[5] When Neave, together with other MPs of all parties and Hess's wife and son, began their campaign, the old Nazi was seventy-nine. Neave did not doubt his devotion to Hitler and the party. However, he had not been found guilty of war crimes or crimes against humanity. Neave felt decency demanded it was time to let him go. Spandau was controlled by the Four Powers and Moscow was implacably opposed to freeing Hess. He outlived Neave, hanging himself in his cell in 1987.

Neave was his own man, with a personal code that meant his views could never be taken for granted. On capital punishment, he stood on the right of the party; on immigration, on the left. Unlike some of his back-bench colleagues, he was unaffected by imperial nostalgia or notions of British or white superiority. Nor was he susceptible to the weird charm that Enoch Powell exercised over some Conservatives. In the period the diaries cover, Powell was already well down the path that would lead ultimately to his deserting the party and joining the Ulster Unionists. Neave watched his progress with pity, tinged with contempt. The Wolverhampton Wanderer, he believed, talked 'rubbish', sounded like 'a complete fool' and would 'end up a tragic figure'.[6] When, in August 1972, Idi Amin expelled Uganda's Asians, right-wing Conservative MPs – and some from the Labour benches – fought the Heath government's decision to open the doors to the 27,000 refugees who held British or Commonwealth citizenship. Neave supported the government move and worked hard to ensure their welfare on arrival.

His war experiences had stimulated a particular interest in the well-being of those whom conflict had swept from their homes. In 1970, he was appointed British delegate to the office of the United Nations High Commissioner for Refugees. The head was Prince Sadruddin Aga Khan, a polyglot Harvard graduate, intellectual and socialite. He was also spiritual head of the world's Nizari Ismailis, the Islamic sect to which many Ugandan Asians belonged. The conservative Englishman and the international jet-setter got on well and Neave was an effective advocate for the UNHCR, intervening many times between 1970 and 1975 to secure British aid for its projects.

None of these activities paid the school fees. With the termination of his ministerial career, he looked around for ways to bring in money. He could not live on the royalties from his books, respectable though they were, and he could never hope to command high fees at the Bar. Like many an ex-Tory minister before him, he cast around for directorships in firms where his parliamentary presence would be an asset. Family connections came to his aid.

John Thompson was a long-established engineering firm based in Wolverhampton. In the mid-1950s they were awarded a contract to provide boilers and pressure vessels for a giant nuclear power station being built on the eastern bank of the Severn, near Berkeley, Gloucestershire, which went into commission in 1962. Sir Edward Thompson lived at Gatacre Park and was a neighbour of the Giffards at Chillington. After Neave recovered from the heart attack, he was appointed the firm's legal and parliamentary adviser and given a seat on the main board. When John Thompson was taken over by another engineering firm, Clarke Chapman, the arrangement continued. The post came with an office in Tavistock House, Bloomsbury, and a secretary, valuable perks at a time when support resources at Westminster were minimal.

It was an excellent fit. Neave's employers were getting someone with close connections to the nuclear industry, and his keen amateur interest in science gave him a degree of technical expertise. He was proud of his scientific bent, remarking in his diary after a lunch at the Royal Society ('nice, clever people') that he 'found I could keep my end up'. His competence was recognised in 1963, when he became a governor of Imperial College. In 1965, he joined the House of Commons select committee on science and technology, which he chaired for five years from 1970. In that time it produced four important papers which shaped government policy. Among them was a report on birth control which recommended that it be available free on the NHS to anyone who wanted it. Another dealt with an issue in which he had a personal and financial interest – the question of which reactors the government should buy for the country's nuclear power stations.

There were other directorships, but the affairs of John Thompson and Clarke Chapman were Neave's main preoccupations.[7] He showed the same persistence in promoting their interests as he brought to everything, yet was scrupulous in declaring the connection and there was nothing insincere about his devotion. He believed in supporting British firms over foreign competitors and shielding them where necessary from international competition. In this respect, as in others, his outlook was in marked contrast to what came to be called Thatcherism. None of his colleagues, then or later, regarded him as an ideologue, including Thatcher herself. 'It was difficult to pin down Airey's politics,' she wrote. 'I did not consider him ideologically a man of the right. He probably did not look at the world in those terms.'[8]

Europe was already a divisive – potentially an explosive – issue. Heath's great ambition was to lead Britain into the European Economic Community, and in January 1973, twelve years after the first application had been made, he succeeded. Neave was in favour of European union as a means of diminishing the potential for future war, as well as opening up new vistas to the British economy. Its capacity for bureaucratic expansion into political space was not then so evident. His devotion to parliamentary democracy, and doughty defence of its rights against the executive, make it unlikely that he would have seen the increasing power of Brussels as benign.

* * *

When, after his death, colleagues and journalists looked back over Neave's career, it was sometimes suggested that he had carried his intelligence connections into civilian life. Later, a novel and a TV series took the idea much further, presenting him as a sinister figure with a hand in all sorts of murky, deep state operations. The known facts are less dramatic. It would have been surprising if he had not kept in touch with former colleagues and done informal favours for the security services. There is also some evidence that he played a small part in one of the great spy stories of the age.

Greville Wynne had been brought up poor in a mining village in South Wales. He trained as an electrical engineer, attending night classes at Nottingham University, where he joined the Officer Training Corps and, according to his own account, attracted the attention of the security services by alerting them to a German agent operating at his workplace, the Ericsson telephone factory.[9] He was recruited by MI5 and spent the war snooping on suspected subversives. Afterwards, he set himself up as a middle man representing British engineering companies on the Continent. In the mid-1950s, he was contacted by his old MI5 controller, who was now working for MI6. He obliquely offered Wynne a chance to get back into the game, working behind the Iron Curtain.

Wynne, although by now successful, wealthy and reasonably happily married with a young son, accepted eagerly. As he observed in his engaging autobiography, 'you become to a greater or lesser extent addicted to the cliché situations of third-rate fiction, all the paraphernalia of dead-letter drops, secret rendezvous and the ever present element of danger. Once you've had a taste of that, you can never be entirely happy living a safe, complacent and prosperous normal life.' Wynne needed commissions to act as the agent for UK companies to sustain his espionage activities behind the Iron Curtain. Among the firms he represented was John Thompson. 'The late Airey Neave, one of the firm's directors at the time, approved my appointment,' he wrote in 1983.

Wynne went on to act as one of MI6's chief contacts with Oleg Penkovsky, a senior officer in Soviet military intelligence, who for a while was the West's most important intelligence asset. From 1961 until his arrest in October 1962, Penkovsky passed on information about Soviet missiles, nuclear plans and the identities of spies, until he was unmasked by KGB double agents working in Washington. Wynne's name soon emerged. He was arrested at a trade fair in Budapest and sentenced to eight years in a Soviet prison. Penkovsky was executed by firing squad. Wynne served one year of his sentence in appalling conditions before Britain arranged for him to be swapped for the Soviet spy Gordon Lonsdale.

Neave could hardly have been unaware of Wynne's MI6 connection when he signed off on his recruitment. Whether his involvement went further than that is unknown. Neave's diaries hint at some sort of intelligence role in the post-war years. On 31 October 1973, he recorded a conversation with Diana in which they 'discussed the growing demoralisation of the country which we believe is due to Communist activity'. He went on, 'I am wondering how to act and wish I were back in the Intelligence Service.'[10]

Whatever the nature of his connection, by the 1970s it seems to have been tangential. His soft voice and retiring manner gave him a conspiratorial air which came in useful when he was managing Margaret Thatcher's leadership bid. It fuelled speculation that he was closer to the security services than was perhaps the case. If he was a spy, he left little trace of his activities. There is nothing in his diaries, and no family recollections, to suggest a secret parallel life. Neave may have thought it amusing, and possibly beneficial, to leave the illusion intact.

His remarks about the Communist menace might suggest an affinity with the movements that sprang up in the period pledged to take charge in the event of industrial strife causing a breakdown in law and order. In the last years of Heath's premiership, the spirit of 1926 was in the air and the prospect of a general strike seemed real. Then, as before, there was a mood among sections of the middle classes to step in to keep the country running. Neave became tangled up in this when, perhaps unwisely, in June and July 1974 he attended two meetings with the right-wing backbencher Carol Mather, who had served in the prototype SAS and also as an intelligence officer. Mather had set up a 'study group' of eight MPs to look at the creation of a citizen volunteer force to impose law and order. Neave described it as a 'civil protection group'.[11] The episode chimed with the eruption onto the national stage of General Sir Walter Walker, a fire-eating soldier of the old school who had just retired after holding several senior posts at NATO. Walker publicly called for a 'dynamic, unifying' leadership above politics to 'save the country from the Communist Trojan Horse in our midst'. He then took over the leadership of a movement called 'Unison', which claimed a 100,000-strong membership, all raring to step in if the unions brought the country to a standstill. Simultaneously, the existence of another band of patriots was revealed, an organisation called Great Britain 75, which was headed by the founding father of the Special Air Service, David Stirling. Both quickly fizzled out, but they played to the excitable mood of the time, and press and saloon bar were soon abuzz with speculation that a right-wing coup was afoot.

A leak in the *Birmingham Post* revealed the Carol Mather initiative. On 30 August, Neave spent hours on the phone trying to pour cold water on the story. The results were predictable. 'The Times had quite a reasonable account of their talk with me and my disclaimer that our "citizens police force" had anything to do with General Walker (Unison) and Colonel Stirling (GB75)', he wrote. 'However, other papers, especially the *Daily Mirror*, suggested fascist tendencies.' Another member of the Mather group, Monday Club stalwart Harold Gurden, had fed the frenzy by 'announcing his scheme for 10,000 plainclothes vigilantes'. Neave, however, had only envisaged 'reform of the Special Constables to combat vandalism'.

This was not a hasty rewriting of events. Diary entries *before* the Mather row blew up make clear his lack of sympathy with the self-appointed saviours. 'Much talk about a "military takeover" by General Walker and disgruntled servicemen who distrust politicians,' he had written on 21 August. 'I think and hope this will come to nothing. The Army should be under the control of Parliament. All this is a symptom of the hysterical state of our society and the break-up of the party system.'

Neave's faith in parliament as guarantor of citizens' rights and curb on executive power was strong. The low esteem in which politicians were held outside Westminster frightened and depressed him. That, along with the tendency of the left of the Labour Party to see themselves as the representatives of the unions rather than the general public, presented a real threat to democracy. Like most politicians, he had an ambivalent relationship with the media, using newspapers and broadcasters when he could to make his points and build his image, but despising what he saw as their frivolousness and irresponsibility, which encouraged the breakdown of respect for the democratic process and the erosion of trust. He deplored the airs that TV journalists were increasingly giving themselves. After watching an edition of the BBC TV *Midweek* current affairs programme on parliament that he had declined to appear in, he complained that 'the programme would have been improved if Ludovic Kennedy had not interrupted the whole time.' The following day he congratulated himself on his judgement: 'The BBC are a ripe lot of bastards and anti-parliamentarian,' he concluded. The media distorted and trivialised, stoking contempt. For that reason, he had been an early supporter of televising parliamentary debates and select committee hearings, regarding the diehards who opposed it as 'stone-age men'.[12]

It is fortunate that Neave chose to resume his diaries in 1973 after a ten-year hiatus just as his life, and British history, was reaching a climacteric. Even for those who lived through them, the 1970s now have a planetary remoteness. Much of what passed now seems surreal and things we then took for granted appear outlandish and even shocking. The central political drama was the struggle by the Heath government to reach a working relationship with the trade unions, who imposed themselves economically, politically and psychologically on the nation in a way they can only dream of doing now.

By 1973, the Heath government had reversed the policy on which it had come to power three years before of setting wage levels through free collective bargaining. After the notorious 'U-turn' of 1972, it was now committed to a prices and incomes policy, backed by legislation, which sought to impose order on wage demands in return for slaying the dragon that menaced almost everyone's life: inflation.

Heath sought to achieve stability by inviting the trade unions to participate in shaping government policy. Agreements would not be imposed: they would be discussed and negotiated in a mature manner which took account of the nation's needs as well as the direct concerns of this or that union. The endless consultations that followed might have seemed democratic in form. Directed by Ted Heath, they often felt more like an army orders group in which the bright, efficient CO he had once been in wartime issued commands and expected them to be obeyed. As Labour leaders knew before and later, it did not really make any difference which party was in charge. The unions were not interested in helping to run the country. Their concern was with the wage packets of their members; the fate of the nation and the well-being of their fellow citizens was the business of others. The conflict between government and unions defined British politics for the next decade and beyond, and the realities and atmospherics of national life could only change after a peaceful revolution in policy and strategy. Airey Neave would play a vital part in creating the conditions to bring it about.

At the beginning of 1973, it was clear that Heath's approach was not viable and that he and his government were facing endless trouble. For all the supposed enmity between them, there is no evidence in the diary that Heath's difficulties gave Neave any pleasure. There was more that united them than set them apart. Like Neave, Heath had visited Germany before the war and witnessed the 'evil emotion' Nazism could generate. He had attended a Nuremberg rally in the summer of 1937, with a seat in the aisle where Hitler almost brushed his shoulder as he marched to the podium to begin his rant.[13] In the war, they both served in the Royal Artillery, in anti-aircraft units. There were points where their paths must have crossed. Heath was in action at Nijmegen in September 1944, defending the bridge against air attack, when Neave was there with IS9. Heath's unit stayed on in Germany after the war and he wangled a trip to the War Crimes Tribunal, where Neave's reputation as a minor star of the proceedings must have reached his ears. After the war, they both continued in the Territorials. In parliament, Neave stayed dutifully within party parameters and gave no cause to attract Chief Whip Heath's ire. Whether he voted for him in the leadership contest of 1965 we do not know. But to his party leader and prime minister, Airey gave more than token support, and, as the diaries attest, he often sympathised with his problems.

As 1973 progressed, there were plenty to contend with. The annual inflation rate rose to a peak of over 25 per cent in 1975. The trade unions were thus pitched into a permanent fight to maintain living standards by pursuing wage awards that at least matched price rises. Naturally, those representing strategic industries wielded the most clout – starting with the National Union of Mineworkers. They would play a crucial part in Heath's decline and fall.

The miners had first challenged the government in the previous year when they went on strike for seven weeks in pursuit of a large pay rise that would restore them to their position in the top stratum of the industrial workers' pay league. Every pit in Britain was closed. Flying pickets pressured other workers to strike in sympathy and tried to block the movement of stockpiled fuel to power stations and factories. The national grid flickered as the fuel supply dried up and Heath declared a state of emergency. After the mass picket of Saltley coke depot in Birmingham and the death of a striker at a power station near Scunthorpe, struck by a speeding lorry, the authorities faltered. The government retreated, conceding almost all the miners' demands. The crisis subsided but it was not resolved, and as the winter of 1973–74 approached, another clash with the miners loomed.

Heath now had the whole union movement against him. In 1971, the government had pressed through the Industrial Relations Act, which sought to rationalise negotiations and make agreements subject to the law. To register as legitimate representatives, unions had to sign up to rules of conduct, particularly on the circumstances in which strikes could be called. The Act was vehemently opposed by the Trades Union Congress, and trying – unsuccessfully – to bring them into line drained much of Heath's remaining energy. Neave supported the government strategy and sympathised with

Heath's travails. He gave praise on the rare occasions when the Prime Minister pulled off a reasonable TV performance and respected his capacity to remain outwardly 'optimistic and buoyant' against all the odds.[14]

He felt for Heath when media-confected distractions such as the Lambton affair blew up. In the spring of 1973, a hitherto obscure Tory peer, Lord Lambton, was outed for frequenting prostitutes. Lambton's haughty manner and dark glasses – worn for medical reasons – made him the picture of upper-class decadence, which to some extent he was. So too did the revelation that he liked to smoke a joint *post coitum*. Lambton's role as Under-Secretary of State for Defence provided a thin public-interest justification for the story, raising the prospect of a breach of security and a rerun of the Profumo affair. Lambton left public life, but before departure confronted the allegations head-on in a television interview with Robin Day, offering that 'people sometimes like variety. I think it's as simple as that.'[15] A subsequent inquiry cleared him of any wrongdoing. Heath handled the rumpus well in the eyes of Neave, who regarded the scandal as a storm in a teacup. 'Is one to be always a security risk if one fucks someone who is not one's wife?' he mused.[16]

What bothered Neave about Heath was not his policies so much as his personality. In this he was merely one of many, inside and outside politics. Heath's grumpiness and glacial social manner have now become legendary. In the current age of faked bonhomie, his indifference to what people thought of him and refusal to follow the advice of early spin doctors seem almost noble. However, even in those times, even among the last generation of Britons equipped with stiff upper lips, his manner was offensive. He managed to alienate everyone, not least Tory ladies. 'Diana said that the Conservative Women were angry because the PM did not come to their tea party,' Neave wrote on 21 May 1973. A few days later, Diana reported that her friend Nancy, wife of Martin McLaren, who was PPS to the Foreign Secretary, Alec Douglas-Home, had declared herself 'very fed up with the PM. He never speaks to anyone.' He noted a 'very strong feeling among our backbenchers, especially the wives, that they count for nothing.'[17] Like everyone, Neave spent time analysing the enigma that was Heath. One day someone seemed to have put their finger on it for him. A local constituency supporter remarked that Heath was 'a kind man, without a heart'.[18] As an epitaph for Ted, it was as good as any.

As time passed, it became clear that Heath's awkwardness was not merely an unfortunate character trait. A growing number of Tories came to think that it was a central element in the endless crises. With his wooden delivery and deficit of charm, he would never rally the nation behind the tough policies on offer. In time he would be a huge electoral liability.

For Neave, the darkening political picture was matched by frequent glooms and lapses into depression. He was often ill with unserious but debilitating ailments that further undermined his morale. He was far more sensitive than his confident exterior suggested. He never seems to have developed the tough hide needed to cushion the push and shove of politics. His former secretary Veronica Beckett, with whom he kept in touch after she joined the Foreign Office, remembered that, even after he was elevated to Margaret Thatcher's front bench as Northern Ireland spokesman, he was 'very, very sensitive to criticism'. She remembered him telling her that after some rough press comment he had called the leader, seeking sympathy. 'She apparently said, "Pull yourself together. If you want to be a politician, that's what happens," or words to that effect.'[19] He harboured little vanities and felt snubs – real or perceived – keenly. On 1 June 1973, he recorded that he had once again failed to appear on the Queen's birthday honours list. He had given up hope of getting a knighthood, which was his due as a long-serving Tory MP, while Heath was in charge.[20] Nonetheless, he confessed he was 'upset'.[21]

This small setback came at the time of one of his periodic resolutions to pack in politics. He had just lost someone dear to him, fellow MP Harry Legge-Bourke, who died the week before. 'If I can be said to have any close friends, he was the oldest,' he wrote. They had started at Eton together in 1929 and he was 'one of the last gentlemen in the wretched House of Commons'. The memorial service in Ely Cathedral was the trigger for further despairing reflections. The hymns and panegyrics were 'sad but rather fine, but I kept mourning my own failure and ineffectiveness.'[22] Religion did not provide much solace. The rituals of the Church of England were part of his routine, and he regularly attended at the church in Ashbury, where he sometimes read the lesson. According to the children, though, he was a cultural rather than a spiritual Anglican, and God gets no mention in his writings, public or private.

Thoughts of retirement continued to seduce. He had embarked on another book – his account of Nuremberg – and again he clutched at the idea that he could abandon 'the booby-trap world of politics' and make a living from his pen.[23] Diana, he recorded, 'does not encourage me ... she is anxious about our old age and the inadequacy of my pension arrangements.'[24] Sensible Diana. Projects for thrillers and a biography of the explorer H. M. Stanley had foundered. The considerable literary success he had enjoyed came from mining his wartime experiences, and the seam was surely nearly exhausted. Interest in Colditz, though, was unabated. Unfortunately, it did not directly benefit him. Every Thursday night throughout the autumn of 1972, Britons were glued to their TV sets by an enthralling new series with a fine cast and powerful storylines. *Colditz* ran for fifteen episodes, and a second series followed in January 1974. Most of the characters were invented, a few clearly identifiable and others an amalgam of several real inmates. None of them was based on Airey Neave, nor did his famous escape feature.

The technical adviser was Pat Reid, who was the model for the escape officer 'Captain Pat Grant', and Reid's escape via the Singen route to Switzerland was the climax of the first series. The huge publicity surrounding the show did bring some media attention Neave's way, in the form of press features about the 'real Colditz', TV and radio appearances and the like. One evening in May 1973, he was the guest of Rupert Murdoch, then a fledgling press baron, at the *Sun* annual TV awards. At dinner he sat at a table with Nyree Dawn Porter of *Forsyte Saga* fame, Mr and Mrs Rolf Harris and the second Mrs Murdoch. He liked Alwen Harris, as he did Anna

Murdoch – an 'Australian Catholic with whom I discussed contraception.' He was pleasantly surprised when *Colditz* won an award and he was called forward to accept it.[25]

This was gratifying, but it did not compensate for the irritation he felt at perceived inaccuracies in the series and at the fact that his own feat had been overlooked. In various interviews, he let some of his dissatisfaction show. He was quoted as saying the harsh conditions had been underplayed, so that the castle seemed more like a holiday camp, and the prisoners looked as if their hair had been styled by Vidal Sassoon (he denied saying the latter – the great hairdresser's name was unknown to him). In private, he was sharp about the way history, as he saw it, had been tampered with. After a party at the Imperial War Museum in January 1974 to mark the start of the second series, he recorded with gratification that he 'met many old friends who recognised that I was the pioneer escaper who led the way'.[26] However, the programme presented 'Pat Reid as someone who made a home run when he spent the rest of the war in Switzerland'. The Colditz escape was still his most cherished achievement. When, a few days later, a letter appeared in *The Times* expressing weariness with the second series, under the heading 'Is There No Escape from Colditz?', he remarked tetchily, 'And so a great episode is now derided.'[27]

There were moments, though, when he recognised his good fortune and was properly thankful for it. 'I never cease to feel how lucky I am in my home and my family,' he wrote in March 1974.[28] He loved the Old Vicarage. Diana had made it 'a dream place'.[29] Whatever emotional distance might have separated him from his children when they were young had faded. Marigold had left home first, married, become a mother and pursued a career path that he had limited interest in, and as a result he knew her 'comparatively little'.[30] He was proud of her intelligence, and the grandchildren gave him amusement and pleasure.

The boys were down at Ashbury most weekends, bringing friends and livening the place up. William's high spirits and adventurous nature, which was combined with sound common sense, cheered up his father. Patrick was less flamboyant, but diligent and determined, and each step as he set off down the path of a career in international banking was approvingly noted. Above all, there was Diana. She never seems to have grown exasperated with his frequent depressions and dissatisfactions with his lot. For, though he might count his blessings from time to time, the banked fire of ambition still glowed. 'I would like to be "somebody",' he confessed in the summer of 1974. 'It is, I fear, too late.'[31] He was wrong. Though there was nothing at all to suggest it, his time was at long last approaching.

'A Perfect Woman, Nobly Planned'

In the summer of 1973, the Neaves prepared to welcome a special visitor to the Old Vicarage. Airey had known Margaret Thatcher for almost twenty years. He had first met her when she arrived as a pupil at Frederick Lawton's chambers in 1954.[1] As aspiring politicians they came across each other at meetings of the Conservative Candidates' Association. Margaret Roberts, as she then was, stood out for several reasons. She was a woman who wanted to be an MP, still a rare species in early 1950s Toryland. She was bright, and she was attractive. Not all of the dark-suited, mainly public-school men who crowded the ranks of hopefuls found her appealing. According to one aspirant, Edward du Cann,* she was 'strikingly attractive, obviously intelligent, a goer', and first on her feet at meetings to ask a question. However, 'most of her fellow-candidates found this habit off-putting: they thought her too keen by far, too pushy.'[2]

Neave's thoughts on first encountering the woman whose fate would become so entangled with his are not recorded. Their paths often crossed thereafter. She helped him with his old-age pensions campaign and for a while they were neighbours in Westminster Gardens. By the time she and Denis made their visit to Ashbury he

---

* Edward du Cann (1924–2017), educated Colet Court, Woodbridge School and St John's College, Oxford; Conservative MP for Taunton, 1956–87; Chairman of the Conservative Party, 1965–67; Chairman of the 1922 Committee, 1972–84; knighted, 1985.

was, unreservedly, a fan. Margaret Thatcher was now Secretary of State for Education and Science, appointed by Heath after his victory in June 1970. She was due to visit some schools in the constituency and Airey and Diana had invited the Thatchers to stay the night. For the Neaves, it was clearly a big event. Thatcher was the only cabinet minister with whom he had a personal connection. Planning began two months before. The couple wanted the stay to be relaxed. When a neighbour tried to lure them and their guests out to dinner on the night of their stay, Airey vetoed the invitation. He felt 'Margaret should be given a rest.'[3] Instead, they would dine at home, with Meredydd Saunders-Davis and Dr Walter Marshall, the witty Welshman who was director of Harwell, and his wife Ann.[4]

The morning of Friday 6 July 1973 was overcast and thundery. Airey and Diana set off at 9.30 from Ashbury for Thameside primary school in Abingdon. They got there a quarter of an hour before Margaret arrived, 'dressed to the nines in a yellow coat and hat'.[5] The school was 'open plan with children doing their own things all over the place and a number of parents helping'. Diana and Margaret 'thought it a mess; no discipline'. The next stop was more to their liking. Radley College was housed in a mansion and set in landscaped grounds. They enjoyed 'a very pleasant visit' and Mrs Thatcher was 'much impressed'. After lunch with the staff she toured the facilities before presenting prizes.

Airey gave the vote of thanks, quoting from Wordsworth. In his diary he gives the name of the poem as 'She was a Transport of delight'. In fact, its title is 'She was a Phantom of delight'. The lines he chose to share with the boys are not mentioned, but any would have been outrageously flattering. The paean to 'a lovely Apparition sent' ends:

A perfect Woman, nobly planned,
To warn, to comfort, and command;
And yet a Spirit still, and bright
With something of angelic light.

The sentiments faithfully reflected Neave's admiration. '[She] is really beautiful and brilliant,' he wrote after watching her charming the Radley boys and their teachers. He was not so taken with Denis, who turned up in the morning, 'an awkward, complaining character, very jealous of his wife'. They got back to Ashbury at 7 p.m. There was champagne before dinner – boeuf en croûte, followed by strawberry meringue. During it there was 'a good deal of talk about select committees', gratifying for Airey, given his chairmanship of the science and technology committee and fervent belief in their value. By the end, 'Margaret was obviously exhausted' and Diana put her to bed. Three quarters of an hour later, as midnight chimed, Denis announced that they would not be staying the night after all, but returning to London, 'since the plumber was coming at 9 a.m. and he wanted a bath!'

Airey came to form a more positive opinion of Denis. His devotion to Margaret would only increase. He seems to have seen in her some of the qualities he admired in his wartime women agents. Indeed, he had drawn on four lines from 'She was a Phantom of delight' in the dedication to *Little Cyclone*, his book on Dédée and Comet. Like Dédée and Trix, she was mentally tough and courageous and undaunted by odds that most would regard as insuperable. They shared an interest in science and saw eye to eye on some political issues. Thatcher at this stage was not firmly associated with the political ideology to which her name would be attached, and, for all that passed between them, Neave would never really be considered as a Thatcherite. What attracted him was her energy and her optimism, which shone out all the more brightly for the contrast it made with the fog of defeatism that frequently swirled over the parliamentary Tories.

He was also drawn to her as a female. Airey liked women. His diary is full of appraisals of their brains and appearance. 'Looks a steady blonde,' he noted of the night sister who brought him his Horlicks as he lay in the London Clinic awaiting a bladder examination. 'The last time I [was] here I was only 21 and after the nurses with great success.'[6] The wives and daughters of colleagues, the girls the boys brought home, women in the publishing world – all caught his admiring or critical eye. He judged Emma Nicholson, a computer analyst who went on to become a Tory MP, 'very intelligent and attractive' after she came to a lunch party at the flat in July 1973.[7] However, 'needs to slim' was the verdict on a girl Patrick brought down to Ashbury for Sunday lunch.[8] Female parliamentary colleagues were given the once-over. 'The new girls elected for the Labour Party all rather attractive, especially Helen[e] Middleweek,'* he reported after the October 1974 election.[9]

Veronica Beckett was the sort of young woman he liked: educated, good-looking and well turned out. She worked for a while as his secretary in the early 1960s, before starting a successful career in the Foreign Office, ending up ambassador to the Republic of Ireland and Commonwealth Deputy Secretary-General. She found he had 'a strong feminine side … he wasn't a man's man, actually. He had a lot of men friends but in some circumstances he found the company of intelligent women more agreeable than that of men.'[10] It seemed that it was not just their minds that interested him and he could be a 'flirter'.

He saw himself as a man of the world, with a full appreciation of the power of sex. In his Nuremberg book, he stated that 'all prisoners thought of sex … it was a reason for escape.'[11] It was an important ingredient in happiness. Following a lunch party at Ashbury attended by several unmarried female twenty- and thirty-somethings, he and Diana decided that 'many of the girls who came yesterday were suffering from depression … sex seems to be the problem with many of them.'[12] The Neaves were no prudes and seemed rather proud of their ability to withstand the studiedly shocking cultural offerings of the time. During a week's holiday in Fiesole at Easter 1973, they went to see Bertolucci's Last Tango in Paris. 'I found this disappointing after the book,' he wrote. 'Marlon Brando does little acting and the explicit sex scenes are almost boring.'[13]

---

* Helene Middleweek (1949–), educated Wolverhampton Girls' High School and Newnham College, Cambridge; Labour MP for Welwyn and Hatfield, 1974–79; created Baroness Hayman, 1996; Lord Speaker of the House of Lords, 2006–11.

If Diana was ever bothered by Airey's devotion to Margaret Thatcher, he does not mention it. However, Marigold suspects there may initially have been a twinge of jealousy. In time, the women would develop an almost sisterly relationship, with Diana, the elder by six years, advising Margaret on her clothes and hair. There was, it seems, little reason for concern. Airey did have certain attributes that would have appealed to Margaret. He was her senior by nine years and she liked older men. His war record was a big commendation. 'His manner was quiet yet entirely self-assured,' she wrote. 'As a writer and a war hero who escaped from Colditz there was an air of romance about him.'[14] What is more, he was upper class, and for all the disruption to the class system she wrought later, Thatcher had no animus towards toffs. Physically, though, Airey was not her type. Her preference was for the tall, the smooth and the handsome; the likes of Ian Gilmour, Cecil Parkinson and Humphrey Atkins, all of whom could reduce her to blushing girliness. Her admiration for Neave did not belong to this category. When the author asked Jonathan Aitken, who has some expertise in the matter, whether 'there was any chemistry' between them, he replied with an emphatic 'No'.[15]

The visit to Ashbury marked the start of a friendship that would soon become an alliance. When politicians returned to work in September 1973, a turbulent year seemed to have settled down and there was reason to hope that an easier passage lay ahead. The industrial scene was quiet, inflation appeared to be under control for the time being and industrial production and export figures were healthy. It was the calm before the tempest, but even before it broke, Neave was recording the first stirrings of a belief that Heath would have to go. 'Diana and I discussed whether we can stand him much longer,' he wrote on 15 September, while on a short break to Brittany. 'He lacks any idea of how to handle MPs or their wives and has annoyed the country by his irritating habit of telling people how good things are ... The country is only going to work for somebody who inspires and leads them, but who is this going to be? Heath has now got everybody on the wrong side.'[16]

In the same passage he made a first attempt to answer his own question. Heath's only rivals, he reckoned, were 'Whitelaw, Barber and possibly Margaret Thatcher.' The first two were fairly obvious candidates for the succession. Anthony Barber was Chancellor of the Exchequer and had presided over the tax-cutting 'Barber Boom', which he (wrongly) claimed would stimulate growth and preserve jobs without fuelling inflation. William Whitelaw was a former Chief Whip and Leader of the House, now Northern Ireland Secretary, widely liked and respected, and a reassuring figure. Both had been loyal to Heath, but if Ted had to go, they might provide stability and continuity.

Margaret Thatcher was a much more radical proposition. In her time as Education Secretary she had become a national figure, but not because of her brilliant handling of the department. She had been branded 'milk snatcher' after cutting free milk for primary school pupils. It was rather unfair. In other respects she had been remarkably open-handed, and education was one of the biggest spenders in a government that came to power promising to slash public expenditure. Her colleagues appreciated her diligence and huge energy. However, she was little known among backbenchers. MPs spent a good deal of time at the House and late-night sittings were frequent. Enforced proximity in the lobbies, tearooms and bars meant they all knew each other reasonably well: their strengths, weaknesses and leadership qualities. Thatcher was much too busy to hang out in the watering holes of Westminster.

Even if she had had the time or inclination, she would probably have been unwelcome. The environment was heavily masculine – there were only twenty-six women in the House – and those who inhabited it were far from fully adjusted to the new climate that the women's liberation movement was creating in the world outside. That Neave was prepared to entertain her as even a possible challenger to Heath is evidence of his prescience and open-mindedness. He had never been constrained by the suppositions and prejudices that his upbringing might have lumbered him with, and his wartime experiences and marriage had provided ample evidence that women were every bit as effective as men in even the most extreme situations.

In the eyes of some Tories, however, Mrs Thatcher had a disadvantage other than her sex. Although she might look like and sound like a Home Counties bourgeoise, and a rather old-fashioned one at that, she was in fact from the lower middle class. Ted Heath declared his origins to be working class, but he was a man. At this time the combination of sex and what Harold Macmillan would have called 'background' constituted a serious obstacle to a bid for the highest office. The social upheavals of the Sixties had made it obligatory for Tories to decry class distinctions. In private, though, snobbery did not die quietly. What class Margaret Thatcher was born into does not seem to have bothered Airey Neave one way or the other. He was not prone to the ancestor-worship that beset some with his upbringing and took only a mild interest in his own antecedents.

The diary entry for 15 September marks the planting of a seed. It would take many months and a succession of dramas before it flowered. In October 1973, the slow downfall of Ted Heath began. It was a combination of the National Union of Mineworkers, the oil sheikhs and his own personality that did for him. The large pay rise awarded to the miners after the 1972 strike had not kept the peace for long. The government dreaded another conflict: one billion pounds had been poured into the industry to prevent closures and preserve jobs and, it was hoped, to win some goodwill. In November 1972, statutory wage controls had been put in place setting limits on pay rises. The policy was to be implemented in stages. The first two had passed off without trouble. Stage three fell in October 1973. The NUM annual conference had passed resolutions demanding a 35 per cent pay increase regardless of government policy. However, during the summer Heath held informal talks with the union's relatively moderate leader, Joe Gormley, in the garden of No. 10. Both believed they had found in the tortuous provisions of the pay policy a formula involving 'unsocial hours' that would allow a settlement which satisfied Gormley's men without embarrassing the government.[17]

The subsequent offer, made by the National Coal Board, which ran the industry on behalf of the government, was the biggest the miners had won without a strike. However, it arrived just after their bargaining power had received an enormous and unforeseen boost. Once again, events in the Middle East had combined to confound a Tory Prime Minister. The Arab–Israel war broke out on 6 October and lasted nineteen days. At the end of it the Israelis had won a great military victory. The Arabs – or those who produced oil – had secured an economic one. Anger, real or confected, at the West's overt or tacit support for Israel required punishment. The Arabs now controlled the oil producers' cartel, OPEC. They cut deliveries to the West and raised the price of crude by 70 per cent.

Britain depended on cheap oil, and production from the North Sea fields had not yet come on stream. The crisis further strengthened the hands of the militants in the NUM whose power had been boosted by the election of a Scottish communist, Mick McGahey, as vice-president. The union's national executive committee rejected the NCB offer and in early November called an overtime ban, which within a few days had cut production by 40 per cent. The government declared a state of emergency, the fifth since the Conservatives had arrived in power.

Heath's reactions were confused. He believed the miners' militancy to be politically motivated, a conviction strengthened by McGahey's class-war rhetoric. He was also determined to preserve the baroque architecture of the incomes policy. But at the same time he was reluctant to go head-to-head with the miners. Some advisers urged him to call an early election, to be fought on the question 'Who governs Britain?' Heath's instinct was always to stress national cohesion. He recoiled from a campaign that seemed bound to aggravate divisions and destroy his mission to recast the Tories as the party of all Britons, employer and worker alike. But the alternative, no matter how it was dressed up, would seem like another defeat. Caution and boldness pulled him in opposite directions. He shrank from the big decision and procrastinated.

On 13 December he went on television, a medium he had avoided for most of the year, to speak to the nation. He insisted that the government was standing firm and emphasised what a good deal was on offer. Yet at the same time he declared there was 'absolutely no question of taking on the miners'. Airey and Diana were not impressed. 'Watched the PM give a wooden appeal to the nation,' he wrote. By now, his feeling that the Prime Minister's days were numbered was hardening into something more than wishful thinking. 'I am quite relieved that he might be forced out,' he had recorded the day before. Even before the broadcast, he had been canvassing his fellow MPs about a possible successor. 'Today I suggested to some members that Whitelaw should be PM but they thought him "too emotional",' he wrote.[18] All this was premature. It would be another thirteen months and many humiliations before Heath was cast out. In the meantime, though, Airey's reputation as an enemy of Ted and an awkward-squad skirmisher grew.

Among the Prime Minister's pronouncements was the introduction of special measures to conserve fuel and reduce electricity consumption. The nation, he warned, was facing 'a harder Christmas than we have known since the war'. The three TV stations were to cease broadcasting at 10.30 p.m. (though restrictions would be lifted for the festive period). This was a further dampener after the announcement two days previously of heating restrictions in schools, offices and shops, and possible petrol rationing. The real bombshell was the revelation that from 1 January, almost all electricity supplies to factories, shops and offices would be limited to three consecutive days a week. The idea was to preserve coal stocks and maintain some level of electricity supply to keep industry going, albeit at reduced capacity. The measure worked surprisingly well, and after six weeks productivity was nearly back to normal, raising the question in some minds as to whether it had been needed in the first place and might not rather be a political stunt designed to demonise the miners.

The Three-Day Week came to symbolise government weakness and indecision and, above all, the absence of a positive solution to Britain's core problem. It created a beleaguered atmosphere that for anyone above the age of forty was all too familiar. On 2 January, Neave drove through central London, noting 'little traffic in the streets as if in wartime'. At his office at Clarke Chapman, he wrote, 'We are allowed neither heat nor light, so it is very difficult for Joy [Robilliard] to type after 3 p.m., when the office under the new regulations is obliged to close.'[19]

There was almost a year and a half before the next election was due by law. But given the challenge to the parliamentary system that the union threat seemed to pose, Neave, like many, thought it 'now clear that an early election has to be seriously considered'. The idea filled him with dread. But circumstances had made one inevitable and it was best to get it over with. The Prime Minister continued to hesitate. He was unwell, suffering from an underactive thyroid which puffed him up and sapped his energy. At first glance the choice seemed a fairly easy one. Polls showed the Conservatives ahead by as much as 4 per cent. The party was united. Yet the more he thought about it, the harder the decision became. Victory would not necessarily change anything. Unless the Tories went into the election with radical new policies with which to confront the crisis, the miners would still be there when the dust settled, and the question of 'Who governs?' unresolved. Negotiations continued through January. The NUM sensed weakness and upped the stakes, calling a ballot to authorise an all-out strike. On 4 February, the results were announced: four out of five members had voted in favour. There were no straws left for Heath to clutch at. Three days later, he announced a general election, to be held on 28 February.

Given the end-of-days backdrop and the dramatic terms in which the contest was framed, the campaign was flat and bland. Heath was reluctant to come out of his corner swinging. The performance of the Labour leader, Harold Wilson, offering the electorate a fuzzy 'social contract' with the unions, was scarcely more dynamic. Airey and Diana blitzed the constituency in their accustomed style. By the end, he had spoken at a hundred meetings, while Diana followed her own programme of visits, doing 'a fine job making her own speeches and answering questions'.[20] This was Airey's seventh election and he felt 'an air of unreality … no communication from anyone else, only the occasional [Conservative] Central Office notes. Presumably one is supposed to take one's cue from the PM on TV. The electorate are naturally confused.' The outstanding impressions were that not 'many people take the "Reds under the Bed" scare seriously'. Voters were unimpressed by televised slanging matches between the main parties. As a result, they were looking elsewhere. After a visit to Botley shopping centre five days before the poll, Neave noted that 'Liberal support is growing. They call themselves "don't knows".'[21]

He expected a 'knife edge' outcome and so it was. The results gave Labour 301 seats and Conservatives 297. The Liberals won fourteen, a poor return for their six million votes. Ulster Unionist parties returned eleven MPs and there were seven Scottish Nationalists. There was 'no overall majority for anyone. The worst possible result.'[22] Neave had got home comfortably with a slightly improved majority of 13,743. However, his share of the vote was down – both the big-party candidates had lost votes to the Liberal.

Heath did not quit No. 10 without a fight. Over the weekend of 1–3 March, the cabinet discussed offering the Liberal leader, Jeremy Thorpe, a junior partnership in a coalition of moderates, in return for an undertaking to look at the Liberals' perennial demand for proportional representation. Only two voices were raised in dissent – the Social Services Secretary, Keith Joseph, and Margaret Thatcher. A large part of the Liberal vote came from disaffected Tories, she claimed. They should not 'sell [the] constitution for a mess of pottage [but] keep our integrity'.[23]

Neave agreed. 'No future in the Liberals, who cannot be trusted,' he wrote in his diary when he heard on Saturday that Thorpe had gone to Downing Street. 'I thought from the start that E. Heath would have been better to resign.'[24] The bargaining soon collapsed. At 6.25 on Monday 4 March, Heath went to Buckingham Palace and offered his resignation to the Queen. She now asked Harold Wilson to form an administration – his third.

Heath's manner of leaving office did nothing to enhance his standing with the doubters. The chances were, though, that Wilson's government would be unable to survive for long and that another election was only months away. The thought of a disruptive leadership contest, when there was no obvious replacement in sight, persuaded many it was better to leave Heath where he was. But positive forces were also in play. Even after an ill-judged and poorly fought election, he still inspired confidence and loyalty, both in his front-bench camarilla and among Tory officials outside parliament. The ticking bomb had been handed to Labour. There was a good chance it would soon go off, leaving Ted and the Tories to resume power in what would surely be improved circumstances.

Heath's problem lay with the backbenchers, and already a cohort was forming to hasten his early departure. Leading the charge was Airey's old wartime comrade Hugh Fraser, who invited him to a conspiratorial dinner at his house in Campden Hill Square, Holland Park. Diana urged caution, counselling him to be 'more reticent' on the subject of the leader and worrying that there would be 'wild talk' at supper.[25] Airey countered that 'I am the one who keeps Hugh in check.' In fact, the table talk chez Fraser was sober and restrained. Neave noted with a touch of regret the absence of his host's wife, the writer Antonia ('much too grand for politicians ... beautiful and arrogant like Lady Glencora Palliser'). Present were Edward du Cann, chairman of the 1922 Committee, Nicholas Ridley and Philip Goodhart. They decided that 'Heath would not go' and expected an election in the summer which 'may be impossible to save'.[26] Some sort of informal alliance seems to have been created, for they decided to 'invite Willie Whitelaw next time to our "club", we none of us having anything to lose by being outspoken.'

They were, for the time being at least, political allies and an eclectic bunch. Du Cann, saturnine and evasive, was a man of the moment, a Rolls-Royce-driving City slicker whose business affairs often carried a whiff of dodginess. Fraser was as straight as a die, but disgruntled after a political career that had prospered under Macmillan and Douglas-Home, but hit the buffers with the advent of Heath, and he belonged, it seemed, to the past. Ridley was an aristocratic Old Etonian free-marketeer, a chain smoker with a caustic tongue who did not mind making enemies, and at the time (though he changed his opinion radically later) pro-European.

Goodhart came from a wealthy American banking family, brimmed with ideas and was a staunch anti-Communist. As Neave's remark suggested, there was little chance of patronage or preferment to lure them into line and they could afford to play the maverick.

Neave was now in a good place from which to exercise some influence in the leadership drama. A few days before – to his delight and surprise – he had been elected to the eighteen-member Executive of the 1922 Committee, which brought together all Tory backbenchers and acted as a forum in which they could make their views known to the party leadership. His voice in party affairs was henceforth amplified, and his new standing is reflected in the tone of his diaries. The references to jacking it all in dwindle, the mood lightens and there is a growing sense that he is enjoying a time in which things are at last going his way.

As spring turned to summer, the nascent conspiracy continued to coalesce. On 13 June, the five dined together with others at the home of Sir David Renton QC, a distinguished lawyer-politician. Continued dissatisfaction with Heath was such that they agreed 'we might have to take action if things blew up. Edward [du Cann] would have to tell Heath that the party would not support him. People do not think we have yet reached this point but I think we soon shall. The difficulty is Heath will fight.'[27]

That meant it would need another crisis before the challenge could be made. In the meantime, Neave watched his leader closely, noting his actions and moods dispassionately, shrewdly and, it must be said, fairly. Someone as scrupulously polite as Neave could never quite forgive Ted his chronic bad manners. Yet he did not write him off and there is no expression of real dislike, let alone hatred, even when he recorded his conviction – undoubtedly correct – that he could expect no honours while Heath was in charge.[28] After seeing him in the House on Budget day, he wrote, 'He looks red, much fatter and depressed. I feel sorry for him.'[29] There were flashes of insight into this most complex among his contemporaries. He was an autocrat but 'seems as afraid of everyone as they are of him'.[30] There was still hope for him if he could only learn to communicate with the back benches and be 'made to understand

Leading lights of 'Comet': top, Jean Greindl (left) and Jean-François Nothomb. Bottom, Peggy van Lier (left) and Florentino Goïcoechea.

Mary Lindell, aka La Comtesse de Milleville.

A good war: AN towards the end of the conflict.

Evaders await rescue in the Fôret de Fréteval.

British troops move through the burning streets of Arnhem.

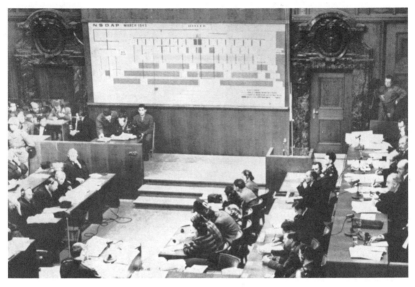

Nuremberg: AN is just identifiable third from right in the row below the judges' bench.

'Really beautiful and brilliant.' Margaret Thatcher applauded by her most devoted fan.

AN and Diana Neave at the Watchfield Free Festival, August 1975. The ideal political wife, Diana was Airey's tireless supporter and loyal counsellor and his career was her life's work.

Edward du Cann, chair of the 1922 committee and one of the 'Milk Street Mafia', 13 October 1974.

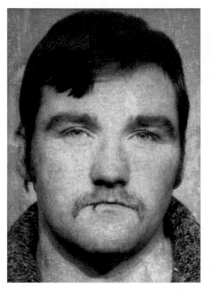

Harry Flynn in 1976.

INLA operative Patsy O'Hara who transported the bomb to Britain. He later died on hunger strike.

The wreckage of AN's car on the exit ramp of the car park.

Mourning a dear friend. Margaret Thatcher at AN's funeral in Oxfordshire.

that he will lose another election if he does not lose his curt attitude. But can he do it?'

The answer, it became clear, was no. In May, the Neaves threw a party at Westminster Gardens for some of the new intake of Tory MPs. When Airey mentioned it to Kenneth Baker, Heath's PPS, he asked him whether his boss had been invited. Caught on the hop, Neave replied they were planning another party after Whitsun to which Ted would of course be asked.[31] Diana saw the event as an opportunity to further her quiet campaign to put more wind in Airey's gently filling sails. There was no harm in seeking a fair breeze, from no matter what direction. 'Plans being made for invitations for 2 July,' he wrote. 'Diana has ambitions to make us popular with the Establishment!'[32]

On the previous day, the pair had set off to Oddbins and bought eighteen bottles of champagne for the thirty-eight acceptees. As well as the new members and their wives (there was only one woman in the intake, Lynda Chalker, and she seems not to have been present), there was a sprinkling of party brass, including the former Solicitor General Geoffrey Howe and his wife Elspeth, and the Deputy Chief Whip, Bernard Weatherill, usually referred to as 'Jack'. Marigold and her husband Richard, Patrick and Joy Robilliard were drafted in to serve the drinks. Heath turned up at the flat at 7 p.m., along with a crush of other guests. Airey wrote that he was 'very frosty for the first 10 minutes. I had a job to get him to talk to anyone. I started with George Gardiner and wife, then Patrick Mayhew and others ... the party went quite well and they drank 16 botts of champagne ... Heath seems rather pathetic but cheered up after the champagne.'[33]

Diana also recorded the event in a very rare journal entry. She was not feeling well but had arranged the flowers, cut from the garden at Ashbury, and bought the food herself. 'Ted ... was a bit sticky to start with,' she wrote. 'However, he took Marigold's glass of champagne which she had just got for herself and cheered up after several more. Airey and I worked hard introducing all the members' wives and in some cases the members who had never spoken to him before. It is certainly not his métier to do this sort of thing, but it was pretty important to him as he needs their support. I cannot make up my mind whether he realises this.'[34]

Airey and Diana were used to Heath's ways. They thought he had done fairly well by his standards. Not so Marigold. Her recollection was that he 'held out his champagne glass … to any passing bottle … When we got to him there was never a word. He never said anything. He was extraordinarily rude [and] he was even ruder to the poor young MPs who he was there to meet up with.'[35]

The party produced a strange example of Ted's usually carefully concealed sense of humour. Among the guests was Winston Churchill, grandson of the great man. Heath asked him what he was doing at the party. Churchill replied with the same question and got the puzzling response 'I am the chief fornicator.' Neave repeated the exchange to Nigel Fisher, his host at a lunch party the following day. 'That's palpably untrue,' he said to laughter.[36] After the party, a bouquet arrived for Diana signed 'Love from the Führer'. Airey remarked to Kenneth Baker that it seemed that Heath did in fact have a sense of humour. It soon emerged that the flowers were actually sent by Richard Webb, Marigold's husband. Two weeks later Heath had still not bothered to thank Diana.[37]

Labour had solved the miners' dispute by the simple means of paying them what they asked. It was clear, though, that sooner or later Wilson would have to go to the country again to seek a working majority. A long hiatus did not mean security for Heath. Neave wrote on 25 July that the leader's position 'is steadily deteriorating'. Endless speculation buzzed about a successor, and to his eyes 'it seems that Margaret Thatcher has a chance.' Neave saw her main rival as Keith Joseph, increasingly her ideological soulmate, whose prospects were damaged by his penchant for ill-timed and needlessly outspoken speeches. There were several other possibles. The names of Ian Gilmour, Willie Whitelaw and even the colourless former Home Secretary Robert Carr were all floated around dinner tables that summer.

In the uncertain atmosphere, Neave was anxious that they should be prepared for all eventualities, urging du Cann to convene the

1922 Executive during the summer recess if necessary. 'If there were any question of the leadership, we should be ready to act,' he wrote. 'Many would be glad to do anything to drop Heath. It is nonetheless important not to damage our election chances. If there is no election in the autumn, we must take things into our own hands.'[38]

But there was a general election. On 17 September, Wilson announced that he was going to the country on 10 October. Once again the Neaves trekked back and forth across the constituency addressing any gathering, no matter how small, in village halls, schools and shopping centres. 'Plenty of apathy, it seems,' he wrote after a day which finished with him addressing a handful of the curious from the war memorial in the village of Brightwell.[39]

It was hardly surprising. Everyone was sick of elections, the leaders included. It was the fourth time Wilson and Heath had faced each other in nine years. Labour's main message was that the 'social contract' between government and unions was working, while the Conservatives offered only more confrontation. Heath derided the arrangement as a 'political protection racket'. The Conservative manifesto instead offered a high-minded but vague-sounding commitment to national unity. They would not govern in a 'narrow partisan spirit' but reach out to the 'leaders of other parties, and with the leaders of the great interests in the nation ... to join with us in overcoming Britain's difficulties.'[40] Neave had thought from the outset that 'our main problem will be the unpopularity (esp. with Conservatives) of our leader.'[41] But as the campaign progressed, Heath found new reserves of energy and seemed unusually cheerful and relaxed.

When the results came in, he had done unexpectedly well. The Tory share of the vote was within 4 per cent of Labour's, but Wilson was home with a majority of three. It was tiny, but in the circumstances Neave felt that 'it surely means that Labour is in power for three or four years.'[42] Ted had fought four elections and lost three of them. No one except himself could justify his unchallenged continuance as party leader.

II

The Arithmetic of Victory

On Saturday 12 October 1974, two days after the defeat, Neave rang around some of his 1922 Executive colleagues to discuss the next move. They agreed that the main reason they had lost was 'E. Heath's unpopularity'. The eighteen-member Executive was due to meet two days later, on Monday 14 October. 'We felt [it] would probably be unanimous that he should go as soon as possible.' He repeated this view to a BBC journalist who rang, saying that 'Heath should announce his resignation,' but cautioning that 'time should elapse before the election of a leader took place.' Neave was only saying what even Heath's closest friends were advising him. On Sunday, he called Sara Morrison, the spirited vice-chair of the party and the nearest thing Ted had to a female friend and confidante, who told him 'she had tried to get Heath to resign on Friday afternoon [i.e. the day the results were announced] and to offer to stand down during the [leadership] election.'[1] He added, 'I doubt if she has such influence with him but who has?'

A further complication was that 'there are certainly people pressing him to stay but the majority are against this and it will seriously split the party if he did.' The Sunday papers frothed with speculation about replacements and Neave was 'rather annoyed at the way that the Press and Television are trying to elect our leader for us'. He noted that among the newspaper comment there was 'some possibility of an official bandwagon for Willie Whitelaw'. Back in June, after the first defeat of the year, he had mused about Heath standing down 'in favour of Whitelaw' but had since come to regard him as an implausible candidate.[2] 'There will be no support for this,' he wrote. 'Most think he could not cope at the Dispatch Box. He is far too bumbling.'

That left Keith Joseph as favourite, but his temperament was also suspect. Neave had been told by Jack Weatherill that he was 'liable to nervous breakdowns'. In the same entry, Neave wrote, 'It looks as though Margaret Thatcher will not stand this time. She thinks the country is not ready for a woman prime minister but I think they soon will be.' Before the election, on BBC radio's *Any Questions?*, she had claimed she did 'not think the country is ready to have a woman leader,' and would not be for ten years. On the day after it, she told the London *Evening News*, 'You can cross my name off the list. I just don't think I am right for it.'

It is highly unlikely that this was her sincere belief. But whether out of conviction that he was the best man for the job, or because she believed her chances were too slim, she now committed to backing Keith Joseph. Progress required surmounting the formidable obstacle of Heath's determination to cling to office, which showed no signs of crumbling, despite the continued entreaties of several friends, among them Toby Aldington, with whom he spent the weekend.*

The press had got wind of the Monday-morning meeting of the 1922 Executive, scheduled at du Cann's house in Lord North Street, and were camped outside when Neave turned up at 11.45. While expressing mild annoyance, he seems to have relished the attention. He was 'photographed several times. A few reporters actually knew my name.'[3] From now on, he would increasingly be identified with the defenestration process under way – and the enthronement that followed.

---

* Toby Low (1914–2000), educated Winchester and New College, Oxford; served in WW2 and in 1944 was the youngest brigadier in the British Army; Conservative MP for Blackpool North, 1945–62; created Baron Aldington, 1962; in 1989 awarded £1.5 million in libel damages arising from allegations concerning his supposed role in repatriating prisoners of war to the Soviet Union.

There was a high degree of unanimity at the meeting. They agreed that parliament was likely to last at least three years under a Labour, or possibly a national, government. 'All thought Heath should go', but with different views on when. Neave was for an early departure, 'preferably after the debate on the Queen's speech', which was due in a fortnight's time. The only dissonant note was struck by du Cann, who 'thought Heath should stay two years'. This surprising attitude, Neave speculated, was perhaps because du Cann had 'thoughts of the job'.

Du Cann now had to relay the views of the Executive to Heath and the Chief Whip, Humphrey Atkins, and tell them that a full meeting of the 1922 Committee would be held in eight days' time. This, some thought, might prompt him to resign beforehand. Du Cann was due to report back the following day with Heath's response. It was agreed that in order to give the press the slip, they would reconvene in secret in the boardroom of Keyser Ullmann (of which du Cann was chairman), in Milk Street in the City of London.

The gathering provided some light relief as a comic example of inept plotting, and those who attended it would be dubbed the 'Milk Street Mafia'. The attendees arrived undetected and du Cann relayed Heath's predictable reaction. As Neave reported it, he had 'made no comment as he [du Cann] told him our opinion that he should resign!! We are being snubbed again.'[4] Heath regarded du Cann not as the elected shop steward of Tory backbenchers, but as an enemy who was abusing his position to undermine the leader. The Executive in general he believed to be dominated by right-wing opponents. While the robust tendency was well represented, there were also a fair few from the liberal wing of the party: the likes of Nigel Fisher, an opponent of capital punishment, supporter of homosexual law reform and opponent of the 1962 Commonwealth Immigrants Act to restrict immigration.* Fisher joined Neave, Angus

---

* Nigel Fisher (1913–96), educated Eton and Trinity College, Cambridge; served in Welsh Guards in WW2 (MC 1945); Conservative MP for Hitchin, 1950–55, and Surbiton, 1955–83; knighted, 1974.

Maude* and Neil Marten† in calling for a meeting of the full 1922 Committee the following week, to maintain the pressure on Heath. However, the majority of the Executive were against it and a date of 31 October was fixed. In the meantime, du Cann composed a letter on the Executive's behalf telling Heath it was 'in the best interest of the party that he should state his intention'.

Even now there was some sympathy for Heath. Peter Hordern, a well-respected City figure and MP for Horsham who was present, recalled there was still significant support for him on the Executive. However, the tactics of the Heath camp worked to undermine it. Hordern says that Humphrey Atkins rang du Cann during or after the meeting and told him, 'You have absolutely no right to have this meeting. You don't represent the party at Parliament. There's going to be an election next week for the executive and we shall make quite sure that you're not re-elected, any of you.'[5]

Ted's men had put their knowledge of the gathering to good use. As Neave and the rest were leaving, they 'heard there were Press and cameras outside and the place of meeting had been again leaked'.[6] Du Cann 'led us to the back door and a key was found'. The scurry to the fire exit reminded several of Airey's great claim to fame and 'there were many jokes about Colditz.' They opened the door to a blaze of flashbulbs. That afternoon's *Evening Standard* revealed the existence of the 'mafia' furtively plotting their leader's downfall. Neave was furious. 'Everything is being put out by the whips to represent the Executive as acting unconstitutionally and to make it look absurd,' he fumed.[7] He later saw Jack Weatherill, who he trusted, and 'explained the situation to him but we have lost the first round'.

---

* Angus Maude (1912–93), educated Rugby and Oriel College, Oxford; journalist before becoming Conservative MP for Ealing South, 1950–58, and Stratford-on-Avon, 1963–83; known as 'the Mekon' because of his dome-like forehead; created Lord Maude of Stratford-upon-Avon, 1983.

† Harry Neil Marten (1916–85), educated Rossall School; in WW2, parachuted into France to work with the French Resistance; FCO, 1947–57; Conservative MP for Banbury, 1959–83; knighted, 1983.

A week after the election, despite doubts about his personal fitness to shoulder the burden of leadership, Keith Joseph had emerged as the front runner. He offered something new: a clear alternative to Heath's centrist approach. All summer, he had been making speeches developing a 'monetarist' theory that argued that control of the money supply, rather than the incomes policies tried by Labour as well as Conservative governments, was the way to beat inflation. Joseph's restless mind ranged in many directions and he was careless of the effect of his utterances. On 19 October, he made a speech in Edgbaston on the subject of population control, a live political issue of the day. 'The balance of our population, our human stock is threatened,' he warned. The wrong sort of people were having the wrong sort of babies, for 'a high and rising proportion of children are being born to mothers least fitted to bring children into the world.' These women 'from classes four and five are now producing a third of all births'. All Joseph was arguing for was better propagation of birth control. The cold sociological jargon of 'classes four and five' made him sound like an early-century apostle of eugenics. It was soon clear that his credibility as a candidate had been severely, and possibly fatally, damaged.

The immediate effect of the media squall that followed was to relieve the pressure on Heath. Joseph had been 'very tactless,' wrote Neave. 'This has raised a storm and will affect his chances of replacing Heath. The latter seems to have recovered his position and I suppose we have to accept the worst.'[8] His fears were confirmed a week later when, following the Queen's opening of Parliament, he saw Heath interviewed by ITN. Heath's message, he recorded, was 'I shall not resign. I am the leader. I have obligations to 11 million people who voted for *me* and the party.'[9] Two days later, on 31 October, the full 1922 Committee convened. Out of twenty-one who spoke, 'only two' were in favour of Heath.[10] However, even those who were critical were 'eminently fair'. The most telling contribution came from Kenneth Lewis, a rare bird in the Tory aviary having been born the son of a Labour-supporting Tyneside shipfitter, who in the course of what Neave regarded as a moderate speech declared that the leadership was 'a leasehold not a freehold'. He concluded, 'Anyone but he would resign after this meeting.'

In early November, the elections for the 1922 Committee Executive were held. There were fifty candidates for the eighteen places, some of them Heath supporters standing to counter what the leader regarded as the existing members' implacable hostility to him.[11] The result dented any hope Heath might have nourished that the threat to him was fading. Despite Humphrey Atkins's warning, all the incumbents were returned – 'triumphantly' in du Cann's judgement.

Even Heath could see that some conciliatory gesture was needed. On 14 November, he met the committee. Neave recorded that he was kept waiting for ten minutes, then received 'coldly but politely'.

The leader told them that he was now prepared to submit himself for re-election. However, in the meantime he would not be standing down. Given that this was an unprecedented situation – the first time a Conservative leader's continued tenure had been openly challenged – he intended to ask Alec Douglas-Home to chair a committee to draft new leadership election rules. This naturally created unease. The fear was that the new arrangements would be fixed to the leader's liking. At a 'kind of anti-Heath rally' at the home of Julian Ridsdale, the Powellite MP for Harwich, on 14 November, where 'many other right-wingers'were present, Airey urged an early election on the existing rules, but failed to convince du Cann.[12]

Neave was now more exposed than at any time since he arrived at Parliament. During his career to date he had steered clear of party intrigues. His dissatisfaction with Heath was shared by many back-benchers, alienated by their leader's rudeness and complete lack of interest in them or their concerns. But now Neave's head was silhou-etted dangerously above the parapet. For all his moaning about 'what hell it is to be an MP',[13] politics was his life. The leadership crisis was becoming a matter of personal survival. 'If Heath wins this battle (which he might) my position will be hopeless,' he wrote on 16 November.

For the next several weeks, Neave pursued a parallel course of seeking to mend fences with Heath, while at the same time positioning himself to be on the winning side when the leadership contest eventually played out. The relationship between Ted and Airey had always been rather more complicated than the old story of the post-heart-attack encounter suggested. Lately it had taken on a disquietingly personal edge that Neave was anxious to blunt. On 21 November, he lunched with the leader's PPS, Kenneth Baker, who told him that 'Heath says "people keep coming to say that Airey dislikes me."' Neave replied that he 'never said I "disliked" him but [had] criticised his style of leadership.' He told Baker he wanted 'to see Heath about this', and the PPS said he would look into it. Later he discussed the matter with du Cann, who suggested that the badmouthing had come from the whips.

There soon came further evidence of Heath's animus towards him. Diana heard via someone who had encountered Heath at the home of Toby Aldington that the leader regarded her husband as 'wicked'.[14] This news prompted Neave to call on Humphrey Atkins the following day, 6 December, to try and arrange an air-clearing meeting. 'He agreed I ought to see E. Heath and "have it out with him",' he recorded. Ten days later, on Monday 16 December, they met. It was, he told Diana that evening, 'an extraordinary interview'. It started – apparently in the Leader of the Opposition's office in the House – at 7 p.m., and Heath offered him a drink, which he refused. Heath, he noted primly, 'took 2 whiskies during the 35 mins I was with him.'

Neave began with a forthright declaration that 'I thought that I should tell him my views and that over Christmas he should consider standing down,' as 'it would be impossible for him to reconcile the differences in the party.' This was a vague formula which avoided the assertion that the central issue was Heath's personality and the perception that he was an electoral liability. Neave suggested that he should do this (i.e. stand down) 'before campaigns for individual candidates began'. Heath replied that Neave was 'ingenuous' to think that campaigns had not started 'the day after the election'.

There followed some conversational *va-et-vient*. Airey suggested that Heath might want to take up some 'position in Foreign Affairs', given that 'he was so important in Europe'. As Britain's membership of the EEC had finally been agreed, it was obviously vital to have a senior figure overseeing the entry process. Ted smartly knocked back the idea that he might serve under a new leader, replying that 'if people didn't want him, he was still young enough to get another job.' (He was then fifty-eight.)

They locked horns when Neave asserted that the party machine should remain aloof from the leadership process and 'Central Office should not promote any individual candidate.' Heath replied that 'Central Office supports the Leader,' while admitting there could be some there who 'might support a particular candidate' – which Neave took to be a reference to Willie Whitelaw.

So it went on, but although minds never met, the atmosphere seems to have been civil enough. Ted 'became more friendly when I said I had no axe to grind and could not hold office because of health, and he referred to my visit to him as Chief Whip in 1959.' That Heath was happy to bring this up is surely further proof that the encounter was not the seismic event of legend. He made a last attempt to get Neave to understand his point of view, asking him, 'Would I not "as a friend" agree that the 1922 ctee were aiming to overrule him and the Shadow Cabinet? I said they were more moderate than he thought. As I left he said, "We must fight on."'

The meeting – the most prolonged encounter they had had in years – ended at 7.35 p.m. On his way out, Airey passed on his thoughts about Ted to Humphrey Atkins: 'I told the Chief Whip I was sorry for him.' It went further than that. 'I feel he is in no fit state to lead a political party,' he wrote, 'but I could hardly expect him to agree with what I said.'

Heath was, of course, right in saying that the campaign to oust him had started as soon as he lost the election. By now there were clear runners in the field, but as yet Neave had yet to make up his mind which one to back. It was a crucial decision, on which his future depended, and heart and head were in constant conflict.

He had first come to think of Margaret Thatcher as a possible replacement for Heath a full fifteen months before, in September 1973. Recording a conversation with Diana in which the usual complaints about his 'lack of any idea of how to handle MPs or their wives' were aired, they discussed 'whether we can stand him much longer'. Then the only possible rivals were 'Whitelaw, Barber and possibly Margaret Thatcher'.[15] Since the visit to the constituency in July that year his admiration for her had only increased. There had been a further local encounter at the end of September when she toured Harwell, where 'Margaret made a hit with the scientists and it all went very well.'[16] The Thatchers stayed the night and the following day visited Uffington churchyard to inspect the graves of 'several members of the Thatcher family ... They appear to have been local farmers dating back to the 18th century.'[17] There was a jolly lunch at the Old Rectory with Philip and Val Goodhart and others ('smoked salmon, curried chicken and ices, champagne to begin with, red and white wines'). The visit was 'a tremendous success' and Margaret raised the prospect of the Thatchers buying a cottage in the Vale of White Horse, handy for Swindon, where Burmah Oil, of which Denis was a director, had its headquarters.

During the fevered months between the two Conservative defeats of 1974, Neave made several remarks in his diary about her cleverness and at a lunch in April assured her 'she had great political future'.[18] At that time she had no intention of letting her ambition shine too brightly and, as the summer passed, let it be known that if it came to a contest, she would be backing Keith Joseph, now seen as an ideological ally.

In the meantime, Neave had been pulled into the orbit of Edward du Cann. He had been impressed by his deft performance as chairman of the 1922 Committee, and soon after the second defeat it seemed likely that he had enough potential support to be a serious contender to replace Heath – an impression du Cann encouraged without explicitly confirming. He exercised a curious attraction on Airey, who was normally unimpressed by City types. He was emollient and sympathetic, a smooth-haired and impeccably tailored tribune of the back-bench plebs. He was also emotionally intelligent and a skilful flatterer. One July evening, despite suffering from a recurrent throat infection, Airey struggled into the House for a vote. There he ran into du Cann, who urged him to get well soon, 'as I had an important part to play. "There were no big men left."'[19]

Neave felt du Cann took him seriously, and he – always troubled by the feeling that he was overlooked and undervalued – responded warmly to the attention. When the October plotting commenced they were as thick as thieves. Airey had detected the first faint creaking of a Thatcher bandwagon preparing to roll. Even before the election, he had reported whip Jack Weatherill's conviction that 'she can be leader of the party.'[20] But he was not yet aboard, and would not be until du Cann's possible candidacy was played out.

As the autumn progressed, he was pulled in different directions by the forces of loyalty, ambition and self-preservation. It was an agonising time. Du Cann was a difficult man to pin down – Heath had attached the word 'slippery' to him.[21] Keyser Ullmann was rumoured to be in deep trouble and Labour were said to have compiled a dossier on its dealings that would blow a possible du Cann leadership bid out of the water. On 13 November, Neave was present at a meeting at the House chaired by Nigel Fisher to discuss du Cann's candidature. 'It appears he is not yet willing to stand, partly owing to his wife's dislike of politics,' he wrote. It was apparent that there might be other reasons for his hesitation. They 'discussed how rumours about his reputation in the City can be countered, as inquiries show nothing against him, though Keyser Ullmann has a doubtful reputation.' They decided that it was 'premature to start a campaign'.

On 20 November came the first reports that Margaret Thatcher had decided to declare her candidature, and the following day Neave was told by Geoffrey Finsberg, a Tory MP whose Hampstead constituency was next door to Thatcher in Finchley, that 'Margaret would definitely stand.' How Finsberg knew is unclear, but it emerges from Charles Moore's biography that by her own account it was indeed on that day that she made up her mind.[22] The decision followed an early-evening meeting with Keith Joseph at his office in the Commons, where he told her that the furore that followed his Edgbaston speech, and the effect that it had had on his wife Helen, had dissuaded him from taking on the challenge.

Despite their good relations, Airey was not involved at all in Margaret's decision. On 26 November, he went to see her in her room in the House and she confirmed the news. 'She seemed rather apprehensive about the effect on her Shadow Cabinet colleagues,' he recorded. In her autobiography Thatcher referred to a meeting which took place at about this time. 'Airey had come to see me shortly after my decision to stand was known,' she wrote.[23] At that time, though they 'got on well' and she was 'conscious of mutual respect … we were not yet the close friends we were to become.' Neave told her that he 'hoped to persuade Edward du Cann to stand', but 'until Edward decided one way or the other it was not, of course, possible for Airey to support me actively.' However, she 'knew that I could rely on his advice and he promised to stay in touch, which we did,' coming to her room in the House 'to exchange notes on several occasions between then and the end of the year'.

Neave left the meeting reckoning that 'she has a good chance.' This was still not enough to persuade him to abandon his support for du Cann, around whom stories of Keyser Ullmann's financial difficulties continued to swirl. They had prompted Neave to consider asking a constituent, Paul Paubon, who he described as a member of the Secret Intelligence Service, to make some checks – though if he did so and what resulted is not recorded.[24]

As the days passed, the odds changed continuously. On Friday 29 November, he lunched at the House and, ear to the ground as always, 'talked to some members about Margaret Thatcher, about whom there is not much enthusiasm.' A week later, another encounter with her persuaded him that 'I shall back her if Edward Du Cann* does not stand.'[25]

On Thursday 12 December, he saw Thatcher again. She too seemed to believe that du Cann was the best candidate. They 'had a private conversation … She made it clear that if Edward Du Cann were to stand she would drop out.' Much depended on the form of

---

* Neave, whose spelling and accuracy with names is usually punctilious, chose to spell it thus, although the correct form is 'du Cann'.

the election system Alec Douglas-Home was due to reveal the following week. The new proposals were announced on Tuesday 17 December. Home's committee came up with two changes to the rules. One was a provision that made it possible for the leader to be challenged by MPs every year. The other was to change the existing system by which, to win the first ballot, a candidate had to have an absolute majority, plus a 15 per cent margin over their nearest rival. This was now to be modified so that the 15 per cent would be calculated on the total number of MPs eligible to take part, whether or not they did so. The proposals were to be voted on in the New Year. 'Everybody quite cheerful but confused,' Neave recorded. However, the general view was that Home had not favoured his boss and 'pro-Heath people complain that he is given too hard a task to win on the first ballot.'

In the run-up to Christmas 1974, the Westminster weathervane was swinging to all points of the compass and it was impossible to detect a strong prevailing wind that favoured any particular candidate. Mrs Thatcher had recovered easily from an early low blow by the Heath camp which publicised an old interview she had given to a small magazine called *Pre-Retirement Choice* in which she revealed that she stockpiled tins of 'expensive proteins: ham, tongue, mackerel ...' as a strategy to beat inflation. This was immediately presented across the media as evidence of 'hoarding'. Stockpiling was something only the well-off could afford and the word still carried pejorative overtones from the last war.

When the story broke, Airey had thought it 'very silly of her to talk to the Press', not realising until later that the interview had in fact taken place before the election.[26] Though he felt 'disillusioned', he told himself 'not to take it too seriously'. He was right to do so. Mrs Thatcher turned her thrift into a virtue. She told the BBC that, though others might call it stockpiling, 'I call it being a prudent housewife,' and invited the media in to inspect the shelves of the larder in the Thatchers' home in Flood Street, Chelsea.[27] Neave, who was always careful to note the effect that she had on women voters, believed that the brisk counter-attack had worked and 'many housewives think she is taking a commonsense precaution.'[28]

Margaret undoubtedly had spirit and determination, yet Airey must still have not rated her a winner, for late on 18 December he went to a meeting organised by Nigel Fisher at which 'we all signed a letter urging [du Cann] to stand in the first ballot.' He advised the gathering that 'if [he] did not stand ... we should all support Margaret, but there is no unanimity. She has less chance at present. Heath's stock is rising again.'[29]

On Christmas Day, the great 'will-he-won't-he' was unresolved. 'Not too happy about E. Du Cann,' he wrote. 'Since his bank Keyser Ullmann is clearly in difficulties. I plan to ring him in a week's time to discover whether he has decided to stand. If not, we must clearly back Margaret.' The day was windy, cold and wet. Airey rose early and brought tea to Diana, then walked next door to St Mary's church to attend matins and read the first lesson. They had a 'happy Christmas lunch' and he 'discussed the future with the boys and we feel we shall somehow fight our way through.' Airey's home life could hardly have been happier. On 29 December, he looked out on the garden of the Old Vicarage, at 'the Christmas roses, the best ever'. It was a date he never forgot: 'Our wedding day, 32 years ago and still very happy.'

Beyond the walls of the Old Vicarage, the scene was dark. Reviewing the year ahead, he wrote, 'Everyone expecting the worst in 1975. They do not seem to realise how much they have brought these misfortunes on themselves.'[30] He listed the figures that spelt out Britain's woes: 20 per cent inflation, a £4 billion balance-of-payments deficit and many major enterprises heading, it seemed, for bankruptcy, including British Leyland.[31] The car-maker was beset by strikes and had a reputation for lousy workmanship. He had his own personal experience of its shortcomings. Two days before Christmas, he had taken delivery of a new Austin 1800, provided after some haggling as part of his remuneration by Clarke Chapman.[32] On driving out of Lex Motors in Swindon, he 'had a premonition that it would not last the day'. Sure enough, 'as I was driving Diana back from Farringdon there was a bang ... it proved to be the suspension. I took it back after lunch all down on one side.'[33]

The seemingly permanent national crisis affected all but the very rich, and even among the upper-middle classes there was a strong feeling of precariousness. In Neave's diaries there are many references to money, or the lack of it, and at the start of the New Year he calculated they would have to borrow £6,000 to get through it.[34] As he prepared to return to Westminster after the break, nothing had been resolved. On Sunday 5 January, du Cann rang him and they spoke for forty minutes. Du Cann told him that he had seen Margaret Thatcher and advised her that for her campaign she needed a 'strong group' around her. He found her 'naïve but admired her character'. His willingness to dispense advice to a potential rival seemed evidence of a lack of seriousness and, indeed, he confessed that he 'still had not made up his mind whether to stand'. He proposed a 'head count as soon as possible so we know what the probable figures are', and Neave agreed to talk to Nigel Fisher.

He was in an awkward situation. He had encouraged Margaret and, as he revealed later, had 'promised her support' – but had also signed a letter effectively declaring his loyalty to du Cann. The latter's endless dithering, however, meant he was restrained from honourably switching allegiance. He told du Cann as much, saying 'it was difficult to commit myself entirely to Margaret and he said I must do what was right for the country!' This, Airey concluded, 'did not help. Until we know how many will back Margaret Thatcher I do not think any decisions will be made.'

He was due to have lunch with her in four days' time. On Thursday 9 January, he and Diana drove to 19 Flood Street, 'a very nice house, a bit too tidy with everything wrapped in cellophane'. There was some preliminary discussion about tax exemption on historic houses, a cause he had recently taken up, before the real subject was broached.

Margaret revealed that she had gained an important supporter – the social services spokesman Geoffrey Howe, along with 'one or two' other members of the Shadow Cabinet.* They shared her view

---

* Her belief that she had Howe's backing in the race would turn out to be mistaken.

that 'a change was essential'. Once again it was personality rather than policy that was the problem. Heath had never run 'a real cabinet' and 'never confided in anyone'. Then it was down to brass tacks.

Thatcher agreed with Neave's proposition that, before a campaign could be launched, 'a headcounting must come first and it was possible that she and E. Du Cann might get the same type of support. There was so far no campaign structure. I said this was not possible until a provisional assessment of the figures could be made. She had heard from the Press that E. Heath would get 120 (he would have to get 159 to win on the first ballot). I said 70 or 80 was more like it. The numbers for E. Du Cann and her could be close, in which case they would have to settle whether both should stand. I find it difficult because having promised her support, I have also signed the letter to E. Du Cann but do not yet know if he will stand.' They also discussed whether or not 'W. Whitelaw who is ambitious would stand. I did not fancy his chances but it was possible that Central Office would influence MPs on his behalf through their constituency associations.'

On Monday 13 January, Nigel Fisher made a further effort to squeeze a decision out of du Cann. Neave had learned from Fisher that their man was citing his wife as a reason for his prevarications. She 'did not want to give up their beautiful home in Somerset, which they could not afford without the bank'.[35] Fisher called a gathering for Wednesday evening at the House, by which time it was hoped things would be clearer. In the meantime, Neave's thoughts and energies were focused on Margaret. He updated her on developments and told her he would ring her on Thursday with a readout on the meeting. 'It looks as though we should mobilise support for Margaret after we have organised a counting of heads,' he wrote. Despite the assumed backing of Howe, he was 'still doubtful of the outcome'.

The following day, Tuesday January 14, du Cann at last made up his mind. '[He] told me he would definitely not stand,' wrote Airey. 'He could not "let down" his wife. It seems she was against his becoming Chairman [of the 1922 Committee] years ago.'

This was a liberation. Neave expressed no word of regret at du Cann's decision. For the next few weeks he would be absorbed in an adventure that rivalled the great dramas of his life, a game of high stakes and potentially rich political rewards. Over lunch with Margaret, he had revealed a talent for electoral number crunching. Added to that were skills he had developed in his wartime secret service days. Among them were an ability to divine people's intentions and a capacity to nudge them in directions they might not otherwise have taken. His campaign would also involve a degree of deception, another art of his old trade.

On Wednesday, 15 January, a brief encounter with Nigel Fisher between divisions in the House produced an agreement 'that I should chair a new group to support Margaret Thatcher'. That evening, in Interview Room J, he took the first steps in building her parliamentary campaign machine. 'After 1½ hours, with contributions by Bernard Braine,* Billy Rees-Davis† and many others, it was agreed that a Campaign organisation should be set up in favour of Margaret,' he wrote. 'Many expressed disappointment that Du Cann will not stand and that the choice was so narrow.' He recorded several 'anti-woman' voices being raised, including that of Betty Harvie Anderson. The dissident was a 62-year-old Scotswoman, member for East Renfrewshire, who had commanded an anti-aircraft regiment on the Home Front during the war. As Neave was to discover in his own constituency, Conservative women did not necessarily look kindly on the idea of one of their own sex leading them.

---

* Bernard Braine (1914–2000), educated Hendon County Grammar School; served North Staffordshire Regiment WW2; Conservative MP for Billericay, 1950–55, South East Essex, 1955–83; created Baron Braine of Wheatley, 2000. For many years unofficial UK ambassador to the Polish Government-in-Exile in London.

† William Rees-Davies (1916–1992), educated Eton and Trinity College, Cambridge; commissioned Welsh Guards, 1939; invalided out after losing an arm in 1943; flamboyant barrister and QC, nicknamed the 'one-armed bandit'; Conservative MP for Isle of Thanet, 1953–74, Thanet West, 1974–83.

Margaret Thatcher already had the nucleus of a campaign team in the shape of two back-bench supporters: Fergus Montgomery, a right-wing former teacher from South Shields who had served as her PPS, and Bill Shelton, the hard-working and likeable member for Streatham. Neave approached them both that evening, though the precise details of what passed are not noted in the diary. According to Thatcher's account, he told Shelton that if they 'could come to some agreement', he would bring over du Cann's supporters to her camp.[36] 'In fact,' she wrote, 'the "agreement" simply consisted of Airey taking over the running of my campaign with Bill assisting him.'

Later Neave came to her room and they 'performed a diplomatic minuet. Slightly disingenuously, he asked me who was running my campaign. Hardly less so, I replied that I didn't really have a campaign. Airey said: "I think I had better do it for you."' She 'agreed with enthusiasm … Suddenly much of the burden of worry I had been carrying around fell away.'

A parallel effort to manage her image outside Westminster was directed by Gordon Reece, a PR consultant, whose success or otherwise would give some indication of how Mrs Thatcher would play with voters. Neave arranged with Shelton 'to hold a meeting to discuss "identification"' of her supporters the following Monday, 20 January, at 9 p.m.

The day after his role at the head of the Thatcher campaign was formalised, the 1922 Committee endorsed the new rules to elect the leader. The game was now afoot. Henceforth Neave would be roaming the corridors, restaurants, cafeterias and bars of Westminster, saying little, hearing much and, with Bill Shelton, endlessly computing the arithmetic of victory.

A slightly complicating factor arose when, on 16 January, Hugh Fraser told Airey that he too intended to stand. The idea had been incubating for weeks. As long ago as 3 December, over lunch with Neave in the Members' Dining Room – where Airey rarely ventured – he had expressed distaste for both Thatcher and du Cann. He had considered supporting Whitelaw, but after some prevarication had now decided to make a stand himself. It was a quixotic gesture, to raise the standard of traditional Toryism, which Fraser himself knew had zero chance of success. For all the affection Neave felt for his old comrade, he would not be rallying to Fraser's flag. After their lunch he had remarked that 'Hugh is invariably eccentric (and wrong).' Fraser's intervention 'would certainly take votes off Margaret and Heath but what would it avail?'[37] After this there were no further nominations and it was clear that it was in effect a two-horse race – between 'a filly and a gelding', as the joke had it.

Flushed with the excitement of his new role, Airey went down to Ashbury on Friday 17 January and that evening addressed a private meeting of Conservative supporters at Wallingford town hall. The experience 'was a near disaster'. After explaining why he wanted Heath out and his role in the Milk Street affair, he 'foolishly' declared that 'since there were only two candidates I would support Margaret. I was immediately attacked for deserting Heath, why was there only a woman and so forth. Some of the questioners were quite rude afterwards, especially Mrs Douglas-Pennant of Aston Tirrold. I expect some resignations from the branches. I miscalculated badly.' The audience seemed particularly aggrieved that the choice of candidates was so narrow and he chided himself that he had 'not implied that other candidates would stand and otherwise wrapped it up'.

Afterwards he was 'extremely upset' and the following day was no better. It was 'miserable for me and the aftermath of the Wallingford meeting stayed with me all the time. If only I had had time to think how to present the leadership crisis. They were angry because I gave my views instead of allowing them to state theirs.'[38]

The episode illustrates the sensitivity to criticism noted by Veronica Beckett and by his own family. It is also evidence of a respect for other people's feelings and opinions, suggesting a far softer personality than the calculating Machiavellian of caricature. Nevertheless, guile would be needed if he was to pull off the feat of propelling Margaret Thatcher into office. She aroused mixed feelings among the 276 other members who sat on the Tory benches, all but six of whom were men. To some she was too suburban, to others too shrill. Those who shared Heath's centrist, corporatist outlook were suspicious of her identification with the emerging Tory counter-culture of monetarism. Yet those who might be attracted to her emphasis on shrinking the state and rewarding individual effort were, on the face of it, the most likely to be nervous of the idea of a woman leader.

Neave had grasped the crucial factor in the contest, which was that, one way or another, Ted Heath was finished. Even his strongest supporters, and they were still surprisingly numerous both inside and outside parliament, realised that, no matter how much they might admire his abilities and share his opinions, he was ballot-box poison and sooner or later he would have to go. Whatever her faults, Margaret Thatcher was the agent of change. What was more, a vote for her did not mean her inevitable translation to the leadership. Neave and his team would emphasise her qualities to potential converts. But they would also employ a subtle argument to the less enamoured: by voting for her in the first round, you would not necessarily be getting her as leader. But you *would* be getting rid of Ted and forcing a second round, which would open the field to other candidates.

On Sunday 19 January he got down to work. That morning he spoke on the phone to Mrs Thatcher, who was 'pleased we are getting started', and told her who was in the group. She told him that Keith Joseph was backing her. He felt they were off to a good start because 'that meant that supporters of Joseph, Thatcher and Du Cann were now united'. He 'told her to forget it and stick to the Finance Bill'. By that he meant she should leave the campaign to him and concentrate on opposing the government legislation going through the House. It was sound advice. In the coming days she pulled off some sparkling performances in her clashes with the Chancellor, Denis Healey, standing up to his special brand of brutal sarcasm and hitting back with some wounding sallies of her own.

On Monday night the Campaign Group, as Neave was now calling it, met at the House. There were twenty present. Names were farmed out among them 'on the basis of personal knowledge', so that intentions could be canvassed.[39] Neave wrote that the group was 'formed of people of all shades of thought in the party'. There was a sense of excitement in the air. 'So the balloon has gone up,' he wrote with satisfaction.

To pursue the imagery of the turf that was constantly employed during the contest, on form Margaret Thatcher was the outsider. Her political experience was limited and she was a woman, one whose appearance and manner were not universally appealing. Her stable was a scratch squad and she had put in little time on the gallops. But as Neave was soon telling Arthur Palmer, his Labour colleague on the science and technology select committee, and the Scottish Old Etonian Labour MP Tam Dalyell, 'As particular friends of mine, I'd put your money on the filly.'[40]

During the course of the day following the Campaign Group meeting, Tuesday 21 January, he wrote that 'It became evident that Margaret was in the lead and I told her so.' When they gathered again on the Wednesday evening and compared notes, they decided to 'release the news that she was ahead on ballot 1 according to our present count'. Neave passed the news on to the BBC Political Editor, Peter Hardiman Scott, and the *Daily Mail*. When the news was broadcast next morning on the *Today* programme, it 'caused a sensation and sent the Establishment into a flat spin'.[41] That evening Heath 'came to the 1922 Committee and woodenly announced that he accepted the rules for election'. It was his prerogative to choose the date and he announced it would be in twelve days, on Tuesday 4 February. Neave felt this was another dirty trick. 'The Establishment' had 'deliberately advanced the date to put us at a disadvantage.'

While his lieutenants fanned out through Westminster seeking pledges of support, Neave arranged for Margaret's voice to sound in the Tory press, fixing with the *Telegraph* editor and former Conservative MP Bill Deedes for her to write an op-ed (in fact penned by Angus Maude) the following week. He also fielded a request from BBC *Midweek* for Margaret to be filmed for a programme on Thursday 30 January, in which Heath and Hugh Fraser would also appear.

Neave had little time for the new media aristocracy ('I hate these arrogant, selfish TV teams'),[42] but it was all part of the game and he agreed. This put him in conflict with Gordon Reece, to whom he seems to have taken an immediate dislike, referring to him in the diary as 'one Rees'. Reece complained that by appearing on *Midweek* she would upset Granada's *World in Action* programme, who had already spent five hours filming her.

Neave replied robustly that 'They could not possibly have monopoly of the whole week. *World in Action* does not come on till next Monday. I eventually won the day.'[43] Mrs Thatcher duly appeared on both, interviewed while having her hair done on *Midweek* and talking widely and confidently on her background, her beliefs and her conviction that she could cope with the strains of leadership 'every bit as well as my colleagues' in the *World in Action* programme broadcast on the eve of the poll.[44]

Neave spent the weekend of Friday 24 January in the constituency. He attended another meeting of Tory supporters in Abingdon. To his relief, the mood was much more friendly than it had been the week before in Wallingford and 'nobody opposed my right to come out for Margaret and act as her manager.' He noted that people were 'not yet used to the idea of a woman leader'. He returned to London on Sunday afternoon and went with Keith Joseph and Bill Shelton to Flood Street to see Thatcher. They sat in the drawing room and Neave revealed the latest figures. Their polling gave her 112 pledges and Heath fewer than 80. To win on the first ballot, she needed 159. The figures, he judged, 'must be too optimistic'. He knew very well that statements of intention were not to be trusted and that there was a tendency for members to give questioners the answer they wanted to hear. 'One has to remember,' he told himself, 'that practically all canvasses are overoptimistic and that in the [1965] Maudling/Heath contest Maudling was told he was in by 30!'[45] The numbers possessed the power to shift events one way or the other as MPs weighed the odds. Such data was precious and had to be guarded. Henceforth, he decided, 'it is essential to give out no figures.'[46] The line would be that 'Margaret was in a "strong position" and leave it at that'.[47]

With a week to go, the demands on Neave's time and energy meant he was no longer able to maintain his diary. The last entry is for Tuesday 28 January. It records a new addition to the team, Joan Hall, who had been elected MP for Keighley in 1970 but lost her seat in February 1974 and to whom Neave had taken a shine. She was thirty-nine, 'most competent and popular', and would man the phones as well as driving Mrs Thatcher around in her MGB GT sports car. That day, the see-saw of opinion seemed to have tipped Heath's way. After all, he had 'all the patronage and Establishment organisation behind him whereas we are amateurs'.[48] But nonetheless he noted that though 'there are allegedly signs that Heath support is growing and that he may win outright, our canvass does not support this.'

If Neave and his team were amateurs, they were energetic and skilful ones. He was generally regarded as quiet and unobtrusive, and in the opinion of Richard Ryder, who worked with him in Margaret Thatcher's private office, 'a shy man with men as well as women'.[49] To succeed, Neave now had to transform himself into something he had never been – a schmoozer.

He proved unexpectedly good at it. Norman Tebbit recalled his experience of the Neave technique. 'Airey suggested to me that Margaret Thatcher was the preferred candidate and I scratched my head a bit ... I was of the view that we needn't make our lives more difficult than [they] had to be and that selling a woman candidate to the Conservative Party would be a big step. Airey said, "Well come and talk to her ... these reservations could be overcome." I think most people thought that it would be inevitable that there would be a woman party leader before long, but most ... took the view that it would be the Labour Party [that produced one] ... I decided that was not the case and then I worked with Airey ... to get Margaret elected.'[50]

Tebbit was not alone in having little personal knowledge of the candidate. There was no social ground in the Commons on which they were likely to meet. Neave arranged for small gatherings of backbenchers in the rooms of a West Country MP, Robert ('Robin') Cooke, for a cup of tea or a glass of wine, where they could form an impression of her. With the help of David James, MP for North Dorset, he also organised a series of lunches at the 'ladies side' of

Boodle's club, a private dining room where MPs brought their wives to meet Mrs Thatcher. Diana Neave was in support. According to one who was close to the arrangements, things 'went very nicely' and 'a number of waverers were persuaded'.[51] These events were markedly more successful than Ted Heath's belated attempts at bonhomie. It was too late to start being nice now, and the lunches, dinners and visits to the Smoking Room that his team pressed him into did more harm than good.[52]

Neave was meticulous in his list-making, never taking a pledge at face value. 'People were not straight,' remembered Jonathan Aitken, then a young backbencher.[53] 'They were fearful that Heath would take revenge.' Thus 'people were sent off to double check. "We know X says he is going to vote Heath, but is he really?" They would go off to X's best friend and grill them to find out his real intentions.'

All this was simply common sense and perfectly above board. There are many stories, though, of cases where Neave was more inventive, provoking subsequent accusations that he had employed 'dark arts' acquired in his intelligence service days to swing the result.

Aitken remembers being cornered by Sir John Rodgers one night in Pratt's club when the sixty-eight-year-old member for Sevenoaks, who had broad intellectual interests and was by no means a reactionary, was in his cups. Rodgers disliked Heath but nonetheless felt he should continue as leader. He told Aitken that he had been approached by Neave and told, 'John, you know Margaret's not going to win but we've got to give Ted a jolt.' Rodgers agreed and 'Airey persuaded [him] to vote for Thatcher on the grounds that Heath needed a kick up the bum and then he'll behave much better.' When the results came through, 'John was furious. "That fucker Neave – he said there was no chance of her winning!"'

Neave used the same technique when engaging in a clever piece of media manipulation. According to Richard Ryder, the night before the poll he spoke to Bob Carvel, political editor of the *Evening Standard*, an important publication in the pre-internet age, when its early editions could set the news agenda. He told the reporter that Heath's figures were higher than his own canvass suggested. The story was carried in the first edition, which appeared before lunch, and Neave arranged for extra copies to be distributed around the Commons facilities. The idea was that members who wanted Heath out but intended to back candidates other than Thatcher who would emerge in the second round would get the message and make sure Ted did not survive.[54]

On Tuesday 4 February, in Committee Room 14 in the House, polling began. It closed at 3.30 p.m. and the first results based on ballots cast on the spot produced a tie. Postal votes determined the outcome. When they were counted, Thatcher had 130, Heath 119 and Fraser 16, with six abstentions and five spoiled ballots.

Mrs Thatcher had not won outright and there would have to be a second ballot. Nonetheless, that night the Neaves gave a party at Westminster Gardens. There was champagne and the TV cameras were allowed in. The celebrations were premature but understandable. Margaret Thatcher had defeated the incumbent, who now resigned. Whatever happened next, she was the moral victor. She had demonstrated those qualities that Neave had long identified in her: courage, boldness and determination. That did not mean that she would necessarily win the next round. But by hanging back, the candidates who now came forward made unconvincing leaders. A week later the second ballot was held. Thatcher got 146 votes, Willie Whitelaw 79, Jim Prior and Geoffrey Howe 19 each and John Peyton* 11. She had won by the margin required, and with higher support than Neave and Shelton's figures had estimated. It was fitting that it was Airey who brought her the news as she waited in his small room in the Commons.

---

* John Peyton (1919–2006), educated Eton and Trinity College, Oxford; commissioned in 15/19 Hussars, 1939; captured in Belgium, 1940, and POW until 1945; barrister; Conservative MP for Yeovil, 1951–83; created Lord Peyton of Yeovil, 1983.

12

Warrior in a Dark Blue Suit

As Margaret Thatcher began selecting her Shadow Cabinet, she told Humphrey Atkins she felt 'a special obligation' to Neave, as well as to her other staunchest political friend, Keith Joseph.[1] The implication was that he would occupy an important place in her shadow front bench and that his desires would, if possible, be accommodated. A week after her triumph, the appointments were announced. Neave was to be spokesman for Northern Ireland.

According to his family, the choice was his. 'Mrs Thatcher said, "You can have anything," and he said, "I'd very much like to have Northern Ireland,"' was Marigold's recollection.[2] Mrs Thatcher suggested later that the initiative had come from her. She wrote that his killing had been 'a terrible blow, because I'd never thought of anyone else for Northern Ireland … He understood the "Irish factor". He'd studied it.'[3]

In fact, before he asked for the job, Neave had shown very little interest in Northern Ireland. Judged on his experience, he was surely better suited for Defence, which went instead to George Younger, who had no obvious outstanding qualifications for the post and lasted less than a year in it. Instead, Neave chose a task that seemed to promise only frustration and failure, along with a high level of personal risk. In 1975, Northern Ireland was stuck in a routine of almost daily bombings, attacks on the security forces and sectarian tit-for-tat murders that a massive British Army presence seemed to be incapable of ending. The political landscape was barren. The

Sunningdale Agreement overseen in 1973 by the then Northern Ireland Secretary, Willie Whitelaw, by which Nationalists and Unionists would share power in a devolved assembly, had collapsed less than a year before and the province was under direct rule from Westminster. Why had Neave been so eager to grasp the poisoned chalice?

The family was as surprised as everyone else. 'I've been asking myself that question endlessly,' said William Neave. 'Why did my father take on what at the time must have been the most unattractive job [in politics].'[4] Neave, though, 'never spoke about it'. In the end, William could 'only assume that this was all something that came back to the war. Colditz and [IS9].' Marigold too felt that he saw it as somehow a continuation of his wartime service. 'It was partly the element of danger,' she said. 'He didn't want to be in a cushy [job]. He wanted to make a difference.' The war had 'coloured it for him. He'd done so many [seemingly] impossible things and succeeded in them and maybe thought he could do this.'

As well as his Northern Ireland responsibilities, Mrs Thatcher also appointed him head of her private office. It turned out that his involvement was only limited. The real work was done by a young former *Daily Telegraph* journalist, Richard Ryder, and his assistant, Caroline Stephens (the couple later married). Diana, however, kept a benign eye on the employees. According to Caroline, she was 'very much around and incredibly kind and friendly to the staff', often inviting 'us girls' over to the flat for a drink.[5] As Airey's importance grew, so did her role as his supporter and promoter, and her presence softened his image. Grey Gowrie, poet, intellectual and a romantic figure on the Tory front bench during Heath's premiership who went on to ministerial office under Mrs Thatcher, thought Neave a 'rather uptight, buttoned figure'. Diana, however, was a 'very, very charming woman ... she wasn't at all self-centred. She was really interested in other people and what they were doing.'[6] Neave needed a goodwill ambassador. He did not fit in comfortably with the party machinery, and according to Alistair Cooke, his political adviser from 1977, was 'distrustful of many elements of [it] because it had served Heath'.[7] Nor, in Ryder's view, did he 'have a close relationship with any other members of the Shadow Cabinet'.[8] The monetarist theories which preoccupied the team around Thatcher were 'out of his eyeline … He wouldn't have read [Milton] Friedman or [Friedrich von] Hayek or anything like that.' Instead, he was 'very self-contained', preferring to concentrate on the new job. 'Ireland took up a hell of a lot of his time. He was totally committed … absolutely dedicated to it.'

He was starting off with a mind unclouded by expertise. Between January 1973 and February 1975 there are fewer than thirty mentions of Northern Ireland in his meticulously kept diary, and these are mostly passing references to outrages or big political developments. What they reveal is a broad sense that political initiatives are unlikely to work until the gunmen have been defeated. Commenting in August 1973 on newspaper reports of a 'breach between the government and Eire', he declared that 'no one seems to be able to concentrate on what matters – to get on top of the IRA in Northern Ireland'.[9]

They also show him to be a supporter of the death penalty for political murder. On 11 March 1973, he was 'horrified' to learn of the killing of Sir Richard Sharples, the Governor of Bermuda, by assassins belonging to a black power group. Sharples was a former Conservative MP and an Eton contemporary. The *Daily Express* called Neave to ask his views on capital punishment. He told them 'things had changed since abolition and there should be the death penalty for political murder.' The launch of a campaign in mainland Britain by the IRA strengthened this view. After the Birmingham pub bombings of 21 November 1974, which killed 21 and injured 182, he noted, 'Demand for the death penalty is growing everywhere and even Labour MPs think the IRA terrorists should be executed.' He felt that 'references to "hanging" confuse the discussion. The penalty if it is a war, which it is, should be shooting.'[10]

The last sentence summed up Neave's attitude. Britain was at war with Republican terrorists who wanted to impose their will on the majority by violence, both in Ulster and Britain generally. Thus it was *à la guerre comme à la guerre*, and the rules of peacetime no longer applied.

Pitiless opposition to the IRA did not imply any particular liking for the Unionists. In March 1974, he remarked that the United Ulster Unionists who opposed the Sunningdale Agreement in parliament 'looked like gangsters'.[11] When, in May, a combination of parliamentary pressure, paramilitary violence and a strike by Protestant workers that brought the province to a standstill killed off Sunningdale, he wrote that 'many people would be glad to see these people out of the House of Commons.'[12] Neave's attitude soon changed, and he came to be seen as one of their most reliable champions at Westminster.

In forming his policies, Neave's outlook appears to have been influenced by a booklet produced by the Bow Group called *Do You Sincerely Want to Win?* It was written after a visit to Ulster in the summer of 1972 by four young Tories who interviewed leading players, including the IRA commander in Londonderry, Martin McGuinness.[13] One of the authors, Peter Lilley, claimed that he had been told by Neave's friend Ian Gow (who from 1978 shared his NI spokesman duties) that 'it was his bible.'* There are certainly many similarities between the report's thesis and Neave's subsequent approach.

It declared that it was a mistake to assume that 'a minimum military response to terrorism would facilitate negotiation and the achievement of a settlement acceptable to both communities', Nationalist [Catholic] and Unionist [Protestant]. Similarly, it was wrong to think that intensifying counter-insurgency measures would automatically freeze any progress on the political front. Thus 'the logic of the situation … demands that from now on no effort be spared in rooting out the IRA … Can terrorism be defeated? The answer must be an emphatic "yes."'[14]

These words were written in 1972, but given Neave's existing views, what had since passed can only have increased their relevance. After seeking to snuff out the IRA by rounding up and

---

* Ian Gow (1937–90), educated Winchester; served in 15th and 19th Lancers, Malaya and Northern Ireland; Conservative MP for Eastbourne, 1974–90; killed by the IRA, 30 July 1990.

interning suspected members (a policy that increased Catholic sympathy for the gunmen), the Heath government had tried conciliation. In July 1972, the Northern Ireland Secretary, Willie Whitelaw, flew an IRA deputation to London for talks. IRA and Loyalist prisoners were granted 'special category status' which, despite government denials that this was the case, was taken by the paramilitaries to mean official recognition that they were 'political prisoners' or prisoners of war.* There was little to show for the concessions. Ceasefires had come and gone but the respites were always temporary. The number of deaths among civilians, security forces and paramilitaries had reached a peak in 1972 with 496.[15] But 263 were killed in 1973, 303 in 1974 and another 267 would die in 1975.

On the political front, there seemed little or nothing to lose by taking a tough line on security. The brief moment of hope offered by Sunningdale, when moderate Unionists and Nationalists came together, had been illusory. Neave soon came to believe that for now there was no point in pursuing new initiatives and the priority was to smash the IRA.

Since the beginning, both main parties had agreed on a bipartisan approach to dealing with the Troubles. Security policy and political initiatives in Ulster were removed from the political battlefield and the convention had been established that Government and Opposition should strive to show a united front. From the outset, Neave's attitude put strains on the understanding. He was soon a persistent critic of what he regarded as the placatory approach of the Northern Ireland Secretary, Merlyn Rees. Since January 1975 there had been a fitful ceasefire by the IRA, whose leadership believed that the British government was considering disengagement.[16] In return, Rees agreed to start 'the phased release of those detained under internment'.[17]

---

* Following the 1975 Gardiner Committee recommendations, the government announced in March 1976 the phasing out of SCS. Henceforth anyone convicted of a terrorist offence would be treated as an ordinary criminal.

Neave had initially supported the process but was soon questioning Rees about the wisdom of releasing 'potentially dangerous people' and 'hard-core terrorists' when the ceasefire was so precarious. He maintained that 'we should be deluding ourselves and the people of this country if we were to pretend that there is yet convincing evidence of a plan for a permanent end to the Provisional campaign.'[18] On 10 July 1975, after three bombs exploded in Londonderry, he asked Rees to agree that 'Provisional IRA violence is being resumed' and told him he should 'think again about continuing his policy of release of terrorists from detention'. Neave's sniping created friction between the two and brought the first charges that he was seeking to undermine bipartisanship. Rees felt Neave had become 'increasingly sceptical and was sometimes outright hostile to our policies'.[19] The antipathy was mutual. After Rees's departure, in 1976, Neave would claim that his 'approach to terrorism was that of a distraught curate'.[20]

On 24 November 1975, Stan Orme, the Northern Ireland minister of state, spoke to the House about the killing of three fusiliers who were manning an observation post near Crossmaglen in South Armagh, close to the Irish border. Neave replied aggressively with an attack on Rees.

> Is the right hon. Gentleman … aware that much of what he said about the state of affairs in South Armagh will not be received very well on this side of the House … his right hon. Friend the Secretary of State for Northern Ireland said yesterday that it is bandit country where there has never been a cease-fire? If that is so, why is not the Army being given clear orders to counter-attack and clean it up?
>
> Is the right hon. Gentleman aware of our astonishment at the Secretary of State's comment that his release of committed and dangerous terrorists has nothing to do with South Armagh when a great many of those detained came from that area?
>
> Finally, when will the Government give evidence of leadership and decision in fighting terrorism, which is the least they owe to the security forces and the people of the United Kingdom?[21]

This was strong stuff and it produced a rebuke from Orme, who told him he was 'playing politics with the situation ... playing politics with the British Army'. Neave had always been sensitive to personal criticism and careful of parliamentary etiquette. Late in life his concern for correct form seems to have faded, to be replaced by a new boldness and disregard for niceties.

In a way, the new job had taken him back to where he began: doing battle with what he saw as the forces of evil. He seemed to Alistair Cooke, his political adviser, 'an elderly man ... It was hard to resist the impression that ... the prominence he had secured had come too late.'[22] But Neave still had fire in his belly. He had been given the chance to be a soldier again, a warrior in a dark blue suit. For him, the lines in the conflict were clearly drawn. His sympathies were with the Unionists and their Protestant culture. He respected their identification with Britain and their history of sacrifice in its interests. His views were reinforced by John Biggs-Davison, who was his deputy from 1976.* Biggs-Davison, a Catholic, believed that the historical alliance between Conservatives and Unionists had been betrayed by the Heath government's abolition of the Protestant-dominated Stormont parliament, which had governed Northern Ireland from 1921 until 1973. There would be no dissenting voice from Ian Gow, who joined the team in 1978. A former soldier, he had developed strong Unionist sympathies while serving in Ulster during the IRA's border campaign of the late 1950s and early 1960s.

Neave showed little obvious interest in or empathy with the Nationalist aspect of the conflict. Despite his belief that Britain was engaged in a war with violent Republicanism, he was never prepared to ascribe any honourable motives to the enemy or grant them the status of soldiers. He had no understanding of how men from the council estates of Belfast and Londonderry might regard the British and the Loyalists as oppressors and see themselves as patriots in the

---

* John Biggs-Davison (1918–88), educated Clifton and Magdalen College, Oxford (where he was a member of the Communist Party of Great Britain); Conservative MP for Chigwell, 1955–74, for Epping Forest, 1974–88; knighted in 1981.

mould of the French resisters who had fought the Germans. For Neave, the roles were reversed. It was the gunmen who were the fascists and the security forces who were the freedom fighters. He wrote about them in the same way he had described Germans in the Second World War. On a trip with the army to Armagh in December 1977, he was 'shocked by the photographs of wanted young people in operations rooms and police stations. The girls look the hardest. There is a fixed look of hatred and malevolence in their eyes.'[23]

It followed that there should be no negotiations for ceasefires or amnesties, and it was 'fundamentally wrong' to hold talks with Provisional Sinn Fein, the political face of the IRA.[24] Peter Lilley recalled hearing a story of how Neave was asked whether he would be prepared to talk to the IRA. 'He said, "Yes. I'd say, 'Come out with your hands up."'[25] This attitude might have endeared him to the Unionists but it raised the hackles of Northern Ireland's Nationalists who, however much they disliked the IRA, still felt a tribal sympathy towards them. It invited the enmity of the politicians of the Republic, who saw his remarks as evidence of innate anti-Irishness. Taken together with his advocacy of capital punishment for terrorist crimes, it made him a prime target for Republican gunmen.

Neave's reputation as a hardliner on security has distracted attention from his attitudes to political policy in Northern Ireland. The impression has formed that he took little interest in moves to end direct rule and reintroduce some measure of democracy and that he shared Biggs-Davison's view that Ulster should be as fully integrated into the United Kingdom as Yorkshire or Cornwall. Dr Stephen Kelly, an expert on Conservative policy in Northern Ireland during the period, asserts that 'Neave remained committed to finding a workable solution amongst the political parties in Northern Ireland in the hope of ending direct rule.'[26] However, again his interventions created controversy both at home and across the Irish Sea.

Initially, he endorsed the government's continued commitment to establishing devolution in Northern Ireland, telling the House of Commons in October 1976 that 'Our policy is for a devolved Government within the province.'[27] However, Neave maintained that the violent opposition shown to Sunningdale by the Unionist majority had demonstrated that 'power sharing on the 1974 model is not practical politics.'[28] He began floating his own proposal for the restoration of some substantial local powers to Ulster through an elected regional council or councils in which all parties could get involved. When he laid it out formally in a speech to a Conservative women's group in Surbiton on 1 February 1978, it generated indignation and alarm in the Northern Ireland Office.

Neave had not given its chief, Roy Mason, any advance warning that it was coming. The speech had provided no details of how sectarian differences were to be managed. An official noted that the plan 'has no built-in safeguards for the minority community … it would be resolutely opposed by the [mainly Catholic] SDLP* and by the Irish Government. It would be seen as a reversal of all those steps taken since 1969 to prevent discrimination and unfair local government.'[29] A few weeks later, as Neave further publicised the plan, an NIO briefing document judged that he had 'moved perceptibly nearer OUP [Official Unionist Party] policy and stretched bipartisanship further … [he] says virtually nothing about the crux problem of acceptability, participation and partnership.'[30]

Neave always denied the charge that he was breaking ranks, maintaining that his plan differed little from the government's own proposals. He continued to promote the regional council initiative with vigour. In June 1978, Margaret Thatcher told the Ulster Unionist Council that she backed the policy and it was included in the Conservative manifesto for the 1979 election. In the eyes of the NIO civil servants, there was no doubt about where Neave's sympathies lay. One noted 'an unusually strong Unionist tinge to Mr Neave which he would be wise to correct'.[31]

Nonetheless, security remained his prime concern. The 'first priority' was 'the defeat of the fairly small, but utterly ruthless, groups of terrorists who are mainly responsible for the present troubles'.[32] He believed that when he took over his new role, official

---

* The Social Democratic and Labour Party, founded in 1970 by six Stormont MPs and a senator to fight for Catholic civil rights and regarded as the voice of constitutional Nationalism in Ulster.

military strategy was wrong. 'One of the great mysteries is why no one at the Ministry of Defence discovered for so long that this was a guerrilla war,' he wrote at the end of 1977. As late as 1976, he had been 'tartly informed at the highest level that it was an "ordinary infantry operation".'[33] He was soon urging the greater use of unorthodox special forces and the intensification of counter-insurgency intelligence-gathering. According to Alistair Cooke, 'Neave wanted to employ undercover methods in defence of democracy, just as he had during the war.' He 'brought a vital new ingredient to the quest for victory, an insistence on the full deployment of the intelligence services with which he always had close connections. He spent much time with generals, senior policemen and spooks.'[34]

Early in 1976, government policy had hardened, moving in a direction that was much more to Neave's liking. In January the Prime Minister, Harold Wilson, announced that the SAS were to be officially deployed in Northern Ireland (they had in fact been present in small numbers on surveillance operations since 1973). The Minister of Defence responsible for directing them was Roy Mason, a former miner who in September replaced Rees as Northern Ireland Secretary (Rees was moved to the Home Office). Mason's arrival brought a marked change in the Ulster atmospherics. The province, he declared, 'had had enough of [political] initiatives', and 'Republican terrorism [would be] treated as a security problem and nothing else.'[35]

Neave admired the new man, judging that 'on security at least Mr Mason is a Tory.'[36] SAS units took the fight to the IRA in the 'bandit country' of South Armagh, forcing them onto the defensive and, according to one member of the regiment, inducing paranoia in the gunmen, so they came to believe 'there was an SAS man behind every bush.'[37] The policy seemed to work. Casualty figures began to fall. In 1976, the death toll was 308. In 1977, it was 116 and in 1978, 88. On a visit to South Armagh in December 1977, Neave 'felt for the first time that the terrorists were in trouble'. He took backhanded credit for the development, saying that the special counter-terrorist training and covert role for soldiers had 'brought quick results since Roy Mason took over the office of Secretary of State … and the Security policy of the Conservative Party'.[38]

The formulation of that policy was largely left to Neave. Margaret Thatcher had little interest in Northern Ireland and let him get on with it. When in 1978 he accompanied her on a fact-finding visit, she did not impress the military with her grasp of the situation. She started by calling at Army HQ for a briefing with the GOC, General Tim Creasey, a burly, shrewd Second World War veteran whose nickname was 'the Bull'. Michael Rose, then serving as the general's military assistant and soon to take command of 22 SAS, remembered Thatcher and Neave turning up fifteen minutes early, while his boss was 'in the loo'. He 'banged on the door, telling him they were coming up the stairs. She arrived to see the general running down the passage doing up his trousers.'

She greeted him with the words 'General, I thought the army were never late.' Creasey was 'livid'. He replied, 'The army is never late, but you have had the discourtesy to arrive fifteen minutes early.' Things did not improve. At the 'icy and unproductive meeting' Mrs Thatcher asked 'some pretty odd questions', wondering what use the security forces were making of satellites to track terrorists. It was pointed out that there was quite a lot of cloud cover in Northern Ireland and that there was some difficulty identifying from the exosphere who was a terrorist and who an innocent farmer. Although Creasey was still fuming when they left, the general and Mrs Thatcher later became 'inseparable friends'.[39]

Neave's outspoken hostility to the IRA and his advocacy of fighting fire with fire put him, with Mason, at the top of their death list. The first hard evidence of a plot to kill him came only ten months after he took on the Northern Ireland role. In December 1975, the police cornered four members of an IRA 'Active Service Unit' in a flat in Balcombe Street, Marylebone. They had taken hostage the couple who lived there and a siege ensued which ended after four days, when the gunmen gave themselves up. Among documents found on them was a sketch map of the Old Vicarage, Ashbury.

There had been security fears a few years before, following a spate of burglaries in the area, and Diana did not like staying there alone.

Patrick Neave remembered the security arrangements after his father took the Northern Ireland job as consisting of 'a policeman coming round in the evening, turning up at the front entrance, turning round and going off again'.[40] With Airey's new duties, his absences would be frequent. Leaving Ashbury would be an enormous emotional wrench. Diana had turned it into a haven, where despite periodic worries about the maintenance costs, they had planned to see out their days. In the end, they decided they had no choice. Even so, they did not depart until November 1976.[41] From then on, their constituency base was Old Rectory Cottage, attached to a larger house at Hinton Waldrist, ten miles south-west of Oxford, which they rented from friends.

A few months after the Balcombe Street siege, Republican prisoners pulled off a feat that in other circumstances might have attracted his admiration. On the night of 3–4 May 1976, nine members of the Irish National Liberation Army (INLA) broke out of the Maze prison, south of Belfast. This was formerly the Long Kesh detention centre, which had been set up on a disused RAF airfield to hold paramilitary members; first as detainees, then, as internment was phased out, from 1976 as convicted prisoners. With its wire fences and huts, it looked like a German Stalag and, as in wartime POW camps, the prisoners to a large extent organised themselves. The operation had a strong wartime flavour and the methods used by the INLA men would have been familiar to any Colditz old boy. It began in Compound 5 in November 1975, directed by an 'escape committee'.[42] The plan was to dig a tunnel under the floor that would stretch beyond the surrounding fifteen-feet-high fence. On the other side lay a zone of open ground twenty yards wide that was overlooked by watchtowers and floodlit by night. The last obstacle was a breeze-block wall twenty feet high.

By mid-April 1976, everything was in place and digging began. For three weeks the escapers worked day and night in teams of two, using tools from the camp workshop or smuggled in by visitors, excavating the sandy soil and dumping the spoil between the corrugated steel walls of the hut. The entrance was covered by a trap door made of floor tiles fixed to a thick block of wood. The tunnel was only eighteen inches wide and ventilation was supplied by a pipeline fashioned from bean cans, attached to a blow-heater acquired from the prison authorities. On 3 May, a prisoner noticed a crack in the ground above the path of the tunnel. To hide the evidence, a mattress was thrown on top of the fissure, with the explanation that it had been put there to dry in the sun. But discovery or collapse could come at any time and it was decided that the breakout would take place that night. Ten prisoners were chosen, organised in pairs. First down the tunnel were Harry Flynn and John 'Eddy' McNichol. Flynn was from Belfast and had been charged the previous year with robbing a bank in the city and possession of firearms. While awaiting an appearance in the Crumlin Road courthouse, he and some accomplices had escaped through a skylight.[43] He made his way to Dublin but, frustrated, penniless and disillusioned, he had returned to the North, where he was arrested at his mother's house in Belfast. He arrived in the compound some time in February or March 1976, along with a batch of INLA prisoners who included McNichol, a country boy from South Derry.

The premature departure meant that, on breaking ground, the escapers found they were still short of the fence. That contingency had been foreseen and they were able to cut through it with a pair of wire-cutters fashioned from smuggled-in blades and sections from tubular steel chairs. They darted across the floodlit zone without the alarm being raised. Their grappling hook failed to get a purchase on the breeze-block wall, but Flynn made use of a plank lying handily nearby to scramble up and attach it. One man turned back after hurting his leg, but with three hours to go before morning roll-call, nine prisoners were free. Two were quickly recaptured, but the rest got away, with Flynn and McNichol making it safely to Dublin. This was powerful propaganda for the INLA, and their political wing, the Irish Republican Socialist Party (IRSP), presented the feat as their own 'Great Escape'.

The INLA had emerged from the successive schisms that fragmented the Republican movement once the Troubles broke out again in 1969. The riots that followed the peaceful agitation for civil rights for the Catholic minority in the North demanded a response from the IRA. The Dublin-based leadership was focused on a radical socialist agenda and had turned its back on 'physical force' Republicanism, regarding violence as an obstacle to building the alliance of Catholic and Protestant workers needed to achieve their goals. What remained of the IRA in Belfast saw their principal role as defending Catholics from Protestant mobs and a prejudiced police force and had no time for the Southerners' theorising. In 1969 they split into the 'Officials' (OIRA) and 'Provisionals' (PIRA).

Five years later the Officials split again. In mid-1972, the leadership had called a ceasefire in response to popular pressure following the shooting of a Catholic British Army soldier while he was home on leave in Londonderry. The policy was resented by a hard core led by Seamus Costello, an articulate, good-looking and charismatic veteran of the IRA campaign along the border in the late 1950s. In December 1974, they broke away to form the IRSP. Initially, they denied having any paramilitary wing, and it was not until January 1976 that responsibility for violent actions was claimed in the name of the INLA. In the meantime, though, its members had been active, largely engaged in robberies, sectarian killings and a murderous feud with their former comrades in the OIRA.

The INLA combined high-flown left-wing rhetoric with crude gangsterism. Their operatives were mostly poor and ill-educated, drawn from the Catholic ghettoes of Belfast and Londonderry and the small rural communities of the border counties. However, the group also attracted men and women who saw themselves as socialist intellectuals. The contradictions were encapsulated in the figure of Ronnie Bunting, who taught history after graduating from Queen's University, Belfast. He was the son of Major Ronald Bunting, a former British army officer and an erratic figure who had at different times been political agent for the SDLP politician Gerry Fitt and a lieutenant of the rabble-rousing loyalist leader Ian Paisley. Ronnie Bunting saw himself as an Irish patriot in the tradition of Theobald Wolfe Tone and Henry Joy McCracken, two eighteenth-century Protestants who, like himself, had risen above sectarianism to embrace the cause of a united Ireland free from British dominance and had died in the effort.

He could be charming but was also manipulative and careless of the damage to those around him that resulted from his actions. According to a childhood friend and distant relation, Walter Ellis, 'the aura of barely contained violence around him was overwhelming.'[44] He identified as an international revolutionary, and looked the part with his bushy sideburns and Zapata moustache. A 'whole hog man, he had no time for … compromises.'[45] What he sought was 'the creation of a 32-county terrorist Republic ruled by commissars like himself'. He first joined the Officials but was expelled after opposing the ceasefire and became part of a group of enthusiasts for action that coalesced around Seamus Costello, which eventually morphed into the IRSP and INLA. Marriage to a long-suffering girl from a Protestant background, Suzanne Murphy, and the arrival of a daughter did nothing to calm a wild streak that often seemed to border on insanity.[46] The feuds that followed the splits meant he had as much to fear from his former comrades as he did from the security forces. In March 1975, he escaped being killed by an OIRA hit squad who shot at him as he was driving near his home in Turf Lodge, Belfast. It was the third attempt on his life and he fled with the family to Wales, before moving to Dublin in July 1975.

When, after their spectacular escape, Harry Flynn and Eddy McNichol arrived in the city, they moved in next to the Buntings, squatting in an apartment in a small block of flats in Pembroke Lane, just south of Dublin city centre. 'Basher' (as Flynn was known) and Bunting were Belfast comrades with a shared thirst for action and loyalty to Costello. They had been involved in a number of 'jobs' together. The group's activities had been hampered by a lack of weapons and they had been denied access to the Officials' armouries. Costello then mounted a series of robberies to finance arms purchases, starting in early 1974 with the ambush of a post office van near Dublin airport. In May, a more ambitious project to rob a mail train near Mallow in Cork was aborted when the inhabitants of a house that the gang tried to take over alerted the police.

Bunting's companions fled, leaving him in a field by the railway line. It was Harry Flynn who went back to rescue him.[47]

Life in Pembroke Lane was squalid. The flats served as a doss-house for itinerant INLA men. There was no money and the land-lord was too frightened to press for the rent. There were frequent drunken fights and Costello's visits to check on his men were some-times greeted with showers of empty cans and bottles.[48] This was their way of expressing their displeasure at their leader's failure to come up with weapons or a concerted plan of action against the 'Brits'. Frustration with Costello was widespread. By the end of the summer he had lost the support of the Belfast men. He was ousted from his position as the INLA 'chief of staff' and replaced by Eddy McNichol. A year later Costello was dead, shot by a gunman from the Official IRA.

By then Bunting was back in Belfast. He had returned in late 1976, to take over as the INLA 'OC' in the city, which he would remain until his death. Flynn too returned after the Irish police began seeking him in connection with a bank robbery.[49] He was one of the North's 'ten most wanted' men but had managed to stay at liberty for two years, constantly moving from house to house, until returning to Dublin.

For all its revolutionary rhetoric, the INLA had so far failed to make much impact on its enemies. Shortages of material and personnel – in late 1976 the IRSP had only forty members[50] – meant that its violent activities were limited to the odd attack on the secu-rity forces, carried out primarily to maintain morale and advertise the group's continued existence. Costello and Bunting agreed that whatever resources they mustered would be better used against high-profile political targets. Their capacity to mount such opera-tions was boosted by a robbery carried out in June 1977. After meticulous preparations, a twelve-man team ambushed a Brinks-Mat security van at Barna Gap, County Limerick, which was stuffed with money after doing the rounds of local banks. The gang included Ronnie Bunting and a young INLA member from Londonderry, Patsy O'Hara, who had fled to the South and will feature later in the story. The operation netted £460,000. They now had the money they needed to buy weaponry and mount a spectacular operation.

The INLA already had friends in the right places. Three years before, the IRSP had been adopted by the 'West German Ireland Solidarity Committee', one of whose members belonged to a violent group called the Revolutionary Cells. They in turn were connected to the Fatah wing of the Palestine Liberation Organisation and they put INLA in touch with its intelligence section. The connection had already borne fruit. In 1977, using the £25,000 ransom money extorted by the kidnapping of the son of a Belfast bank official, they bought a small consignment of rifles and grenades, supplied by the PLO and smuggled in by a German sympathiser in his father's Mercedes saloon.[51] Armed with the Brinks-Mat funds, two INLA men, Seamus Ruddy, a 25-year-old language teacher from Newry, and Phelim Lally, a Dubliner, made two trips to Beirut in the summer of 1978. They returned by van with a batch of Kalashnikov rifles, and most importantly in view of what was to come, a cargo of plastic explosive, which they packed into the vehicle's door panels. It was of Soviet manufacture, a mixture of penthrite and TNT, grey-pink in colour and undetectable by security scanners.

The material was too valuable to be used in conventional operations. The September 1978 issue of the IRSP newspaper, the *Starry Plough*, gave some indication of the INLA's plans for it. It reported a speech by Miriam Daly, a left-wing academic and the party's chairperson, in which she pointed out the discrepancy between the fortunes of 'Airey Neave [who] built his career on his escape from Colditz Prisoner of War Camp' and one of the participants in the May 1976 escape from the Maze, Jake McManus, who after recapture had been sentenced to two more years' imprisonment.

By now Neave was established in the minds, not only of violent Republicans, but of the Nationalists of Northern Ireland and the politicians of the Republic as a friend of Unionism and an implacable opponent of compromise. He approached his task with zeal, disrupting the bipartisan consensus in Westminster and causing irritation and alarm in Whitehall and Downing Street.

Almost painfully polite in private, he could be rough in public with politicians, officials and journalists whose views or attitudes he opposed. He came to loathe the BBC. He regarded their studied even-handedness as little short of treasonable. When, in January 1979, TV crews filmed the IRA showing off recently acquired M60 machine guns and setting up checkpoints in a propaganda stunt staged in Londonderry, he claimed they had 'nurtured the recovery of the terrorist element in Northern Ireland'.[52]

Before his arrival on the Ulster scene, Conservative and Labour governments alike had trod carefully around the sensibilities of the Northern Nationalists and the Southern government. They received no special consideration from Neave. He saw no significant place for the Republic in the affairs of the North and regarded even theoretical talk of unification of the island of Ireland as provocative and inflammatory. The responses from Dublin were equally robust. Richie Ryan, foreign affairs spokesman of the opposition Fine Gael party, described remarks in one of his speeches as 'ill-informed, anti-Irish and rabble-rousing'. Neave, he said, belonged to a small group of English politicians 'who knew little about Ireland and understood even less'.[53]

Was there any truth in this? The bipartisan approach to Ulster's problems seems unusually delicate in retrospect, and Neave was surely justified in challenging government policy where he saw fit without worrying about established protocol. His own main political proposal for a regional council never looked viable, however. Politics in Northern Ireland were governed by the mutual fears and suspicions of the two communities. No Nationalist party was likely to enter into new governmental arrangements unless they felt their interests had been constitutionally copper-fastened. Neave's plan, with its vague talk of an 'appropriate committee system', came nowhere near providing such reassurance, and when the Thatcher government arrived in power the proposal was soon dropped.

With his aggressive approach to security he was on more solid ground. The policies of Roy Mason – with whom he got on very well, meeting with him regularly – proved effective, and there was no doubt that Neave would have continued the same approach with perhaps even greater vigour. It is now accepted that by the end of 1978, the IRA and INLA were on the defensive and suffering badly, demoralised by arrests, arms seizures and the knowledge that their ranks were riddled with security-forces informers.

As 1979 dawned, it seemed increasingly likely that Neave would soon be in charge of the continuing anti-terrorist campaign. The Callaghan government had been badly damaged by months of public-worker strikes which challenged the notion that only Labour could manage the unions. The party's three-seat majority had disappeared within a year of the October 1974 election and it relied on minority parties to survive.

On 28 March, Margaret Thatcher tabled a motion of no confidence in the government, which was passed by one vote. A general election was now inevitable. Ulster had played a part in Labour's downfall. It was claimed later that Neave's regional council scheme had emboldened the Official Unionists to abandon their support for the government.[54] Neave's death meant that the extent to which this played a part in the drama was never resolved, though Diana revealed that he spent some time on Tuesday 27 March, 'busy in the House of Commons talking to Ulster Unionists'.[55]

He had given his first and last big political job his all, bringing to it the thought, dedication and energy that he applied to all the work of his life. To some of the younger Tory aides in the Thatcher team, that energy seemed to be failing and Neave was a peripheral figure who belonged to the past. Matthew Parris, the leader's correspondence secretary and to whom Neave had been kind, finding him a job with Central Office when he decided to leave the diplomatic service, did not regard him as 'part of the central driving machine'.[56] His political adviser, Alistair Cooke, felt him to be 'far from robust. [He] walked slowly, talked slowly. Everything about him was slow.'[57] Yet as was often the case with Neave, this impression was deceptive. There was work to be done and he was eager to do it.

Just after the government fell, he met Michael Dobbs, then a young adviser to Mrs Thatcher, in her office under Big Ben. He recalled, 'I sat with him on the sofa in her office for two hours and we just talked … It was the plans for the future, what was going to happen, how we were going to … transform the country.'[58] After all the setbacks, snubs and disappointments, his career was going to end on a high note. He had one last job to do.

To Richard Ryder he confided how much he was 'looking forward to becoming Secretary of State for Northern Ireland … after that he was going to retire.'[59]

13

'The Perfect Target'

The bomb went off two minutes before Big Ben struck 3 p.m. The blast sounded in the Commons chamber, where a handful of members were debating the Credit Union Bill, but with a sangfroid of which the victim would have approved, they carried on business regardless. Richard Ryder had spent half an hour with Airey a few hours previously, 'just chatting' in his Commons 'cell', 202 Star Chamber Court. He heard 'this massive explosion ... a mammoth explosion' and ran to the window of Mrs Thatcher's office, which overlooked New Palace Yard. Directly below, on the exit ramp of the underground car park, he saw 'this car – just blown to smithereens ... I knew this car. I'd been in it. But I didn't put the two together.'[1]

The bomb removed Neave's right leg, two inches below the knee, and shattered the bones in the other. According to the medical report to the coroner, there were 'lacerations on the back of the left elbow and multiple small punctuate lacerations with scorching under the chin and on the face under the nose and over the left eye and cheek. The hair was singed ...'

It took time for ambulancemen, medics and firefighters to free him. A policeman, PC Peter Dickens, retrieved a wallet which contained 'correspondence in the name of Airey Neave MP'. There was another delay while the wreckage was checked for further bombs before an ambulance took him, alive but unconscious, to the resuscitation room at Westminster Hospital. There, at 3.45 p.m., on Friday, 30 March 1979, 'life was pronounced extinct.' The pathologist's report found death to be due to 'shock following bomb blast injuries of the legs'.[2]

That morning, John Chilcot, principal private secretary to the Home Secretary, Merlyn Rees, had dictated a memo concerning security arrangements for politicians in the coming general election. It stated that he had 'specifically asked the Commissioner [of the Metropolitan Police] to consider questions of personal protection, including not only the coverage of those ministers who already enjoy it (including the Leader of the Opposition and two ex-Prime Ministers) but also extended coverage to other political personalities who might be especially vulnerable during an election campaign (with special reference to Mr Whitelaw and Mr Airey Neave).'[3]

The Commissioner, Sir David McNee, had 'taken delivery of this', while reminding Chilcot of the 'manpower implications of any significant extension of coverage'. He went on to tell him that 'there is no present reason to foresee assassination threats of political personalities during the campaign.' However, the Metropolitan Police had 'the matter very much in mind'.

McNee's assurance appears odd in the light of the murder of the British ambassador to the Netherlands eight days before. Sir Richard Sykes had been shot dead, along with his manservant, as they left the residence in The Hague to go to the embassy on the morning of 22 March, apparently by the IRA.

Given Neave's history of hostility to Republican paramilitaries, it now seems extraordinary that he did not already have a police bodyguard. McNee later said that he had pressed him to accept 'a personal protection officer because of the known threat to his life'.[4] The offer had been rejected: 'He made it clear that if as an Englishman he could not walk the streets of London freely, life for him was truly not worth living.' McNee 'understood and respected his view', which was not unique to Neave. The Home Office files reveal that the former Prime Minister Lord Home (Alec Douglas-Home) had also turned down police protection. Official documents confirm McNee's story. One Home Office report states that 'Special Branch had been in touch with [Neave] for some years, in fact since

1975, and that he did not want tight personal protection but had been in regular consultation over his weekly programme.'[5]

Airey Neave was a soft target for the gunmen, who had observed his progress towards power with alarm and mounting hatred. In town, his way of life broke every rule of basic security. His London address was listed in *Who's Who*. Patrick Neave remembered that 'in those days, Westminster Gardens was a community of quite a few people who you knew, and that was your protection. They had very old porters who knew you, but apart from that, nothing.'[6] His father's daily routine was fairly predictable. Each morning he usually set off for the Commons or to the Bloomsbury offices of Northern Engineering Industries (as Clarke Chapman had been renamed), where he was a non-executive director. The company provided him with a light-blue Vauxhall Cavalier, which he drove everywhere. Residents of Westminster Gardens used a service road at the side of the block as a car park. There was no gate and no CCTV cameras.

Joy Robilliard's statement to the coroner's inquest held in October that year said that the car park at Tavistock House (East), Woburn Walk, WC1, where NEI had its offices, was 'not a secure one and open-air. I know that Mr Neave on one occasion left his car open there and I understand it is customary to leave keys in the front-rank cars so that they can be moved by an attendant.'[7] Her boss on occasion left 'identifying correspondence in his vehicle'. In her statement to the police, Diana said that her husband was a creature of habit and, on returning at night to Westminster Gardens, he was 'likely to park in his usual place in the service road'.

Neave was perfectly aware of the dangers. According to William, 'My father knew he was taking some immense risks.'[8] Why such insouciance? 'He wasn't a healthy man,' reflects William. 'He must have being saying to himself, "What is my life span here? I can afford to take these risks." I think that must have been the thought that went through his mind.'

Perhaps his brave words to McNee were a flourish of the spirit that had sustained Britain through the war, a declaration that he was still a soldier at heart and prepared to accept the mortal danger that went with service. Whatever was behind it, it made the killers' job less complicated. According to a detective involved in the subsequent investigation, 'He was the perfect target,' and killing him 'was a pretty basic event'.

Within a few hours of the bombing, the INLA had acknowledged it was their operation. The male caller to the *Irish Independent* newspaper in Dublin provided details not yet in the public domain to give credence to the claim, which was soon accepted by the authorities.[9] Five days later, the facts known to the security services were laid out in a report to the outgoing Prime Minister, Jim Callaghan. It stated:

1. It now appears almost certain that the Irish National Liberation Army were responsible for the murder of Airey Neave on 30 March. The results of forensic tests seem to confirm the details given by the Irish National Liberation Army when they claimed responsibility for the attack. They claim that the bomb comprised a mercury detonator device attached to one kilo of TNT. Later intelligence reports also indicated that the bomb had been attached to the car using a magnet. Forensic science tests have now revealed traces of mercury and pieces of magnet in the debris but have failed to find traces of residual explosive, which tends to confirm the claim that TNT was used, rather than any other explosive.

2. The bomb is thought to have been attached to Mr Neave's car while it was parked outside his home. This view is supported by the fact that Mr Neave did not normally attend the House on a Friday: a carefully planned attempt to assassinate him is unlikely, therefore, to have relied upon a chance visit. The device would probably not have been visible to the porter at the block of flats where Mr Neave lived who claims to have checked the car. Indeed had he seen it it is unlikely he would have recognised [it] for what it was. Rocking the car, as he claims to have done, would not necessarily have activated the

device since the remains of a watch found amongst the debris suggest that a device was fitted with a delayed arming mechanism.

3. It seems unlikely that the attack was carried out by a team permanently based in Great Britain. There is a small Irish Republican Socialist Party 'support group' in this country but its members are not thought to have been involved in the attack. They have, however, been interviewed and have provided the police with useful information about the organisation of the IRSP.

4. Intelligence reports received after Mr Neave's murder have suggested that a team of 6 INLA members was sent to Great Britain to carry out attacks. The names of the six men are known and the identity of four of them has been established. They have not yet been located.

5. The police are pursuing their enquiries and are following up any leads provided by the public. It seems likely, however, that intelligence reports will prove to be the most fruitful source of information.[10]

As was almost always the case, the intelligence the police were working on had come from the Royal Ulster Constabulary's Special Branch, who were in constant contact with the Special Branch of the Met. According to one of the investigating officers, it was they who provided the names and identities of the suspects. The strong likelihood is that these were supplied by an informant or informants.[11] The officer revealed that the RUC were also able to provide the address of a terraced house in Hampstead which had been rented on a short-term lease by two of the team, one of whom, despite the information in the report, was a woman. When the house was raided soon after the bombing, it was empty and 'clean. They'd disappeared.' A check of airports and seaports showed the couple had flown from Heathrow to Dublin on the early evening of the previous day. The detectives leading the inquiry concluded that all the perpetrators had left the country within a few days of the attack. The Irish police, the Garda Siochana, were alerted. Despite claims from sections of the media and some politicians to the contrary, relations between the Met and the Irish police were good. The investigating team 'did at one time consider extradition', but with no evidence on which the Irish could act, the Director of Public Prosecutions decided not to proceed, as although the suspects were known, there was no chance of a conviction. The detective involved in the inquiry 'agreed with him'.

However, the enormity of the crime demanded that the investigation was seen to be being pursued with the utmost vigour. Over the coming weeks left-wing supporters of the IRSP were arrested under the Prevention of Terrorism Act but subsequently released. The appeal for witnesses resulted in the issue of photofit images of four suspects on 10 April, ten days after the murder. Suspect number one ('aged 25–26 and 6 ft 1 in tall') had been noticed in the Westminster Arms, a pub near the Neaves' flat, on the evening before the attack.[12] The second ('age 36–42, about 5 ft 9 in') had been seen in the Westminster Gardens service road where Airey usually left his car, at 6.45 the following morning, having parked a yellow Fiat in Marsham Street, on which the block stood. The third ('about 34, 5 ft 7 in–5 ft 8 in') and fourth ('age about 28, 6 ft–6 ft 1 in') had also been spotted waiting near the service road at 11.30 the previous evening. All had been heard speaking with Irish accents. The head of the Anti-Terrorist Branch, Commander Peter Duffy, who had returned from the United States to lead the inquiry, told a press conference, 'I believe one of these men to be the bomber.' Despite the fact that his team were sure the team had long gone, Duffy maintained that the bombers could still be in Britain.

With the murder, the INLA had achieved the notoriety it longed for. In Belfast, Ronnie Bunting was ecstatic when he heard the news. Arriving at a fund-raising social event in the IRSP's Falls Road offices in West Belfast, he threw his arms around Sean Flynn, brother of Harry, shouting, 'We did it!' That night the drinks were on the house.[13] A statement dated the day after the murder which appeared in the *Starry Plough* offered a different version of events to the police narrative. It read:

> The INLA successfully breached intense security at the House of Commons to plant the device, consisting of one kilo of explosive. After taking stringent precautions to ensure that no civilians would be injured the ASU [Active Service Unit] returned to base … Airey Neave was specially targeted for assassination. He was well known for his rabid militarist calls for more repression against the Irish people and for the strengthening of the SAS murder gang, a group which has no qualms about murdering Irish people.

In April, the Dublin magazine *Magill* carried an interview with the INLA's 'chief of staff and director or intelligence'. This stated that the decision to kill Neave had been taken by the 'Army Council several weeks ago and was reaffirmed more recently by the Headquarters Staff'. The final go-ahead was given following the no-confidence vote that brought down the government. It was again claimed that the 'active service unit which placed the bomb breached the security of the House of Commons on the day of the assassination. The bomb was placed under the driver's seat. The kind of device used was previously used twice in Northern Ireland, once in the killing of a UDR member and the other in the injuring of an RUC reservist.' Their intention was to 'mark time on the British front for the time being'. However, the team that carried out the attack 'was and is based in England' and could 'carry out any operation it is asked to undertake'.

In contacts with the media in the years that followed, spokesmen for the INLA would add further touches to their story. The basic account, though, remained the same. The police also stuck to their initial version of events. The point where the two versions diverge is on the question of where the bomb was planted. The Royal Arsenal bomb expert who examined the debris of the car, George Berryman, concluded that 'The device consisted of a charge of a high-performance explosive which had been initiated by an electric detonator, and incorporated a battery, a wristwatch and a mercury tilt switch.' The bomb had been 'attached under the car with the aid of a magnet'. The wristwatch 'was used as a delayed arming mechanism and the mercury tilt switch to activate the device when the car was accelerating and/or going up a gradient'.[14]

The mercury tilt switch was an INLA innovation – its great contribution to terrorism technology. According to a military bomb expert, 'Basically, it's a little perspex tube fitted with two little wires at one end and filled with a quantity of mercury. If the mercury touches the wires, it completes an electrical circuit and, if the device is armed, triggers the bomb.'[15] It was invented by a scientifically minded operative from North Armagh by modifying a switch available in radio spares catalogues.[16] In December 1978, a prison officer at the Maze was injured when a prototype of the device went off under his car. On 15 March, a member of the Ulster Defence Regiment, Robert McNally, died of injuries sustained in a similar bomb attack six days earlier.

The wristwatch timing device gave the bomber flexibility and reduced the chances of detection and arrest. According to the bomb expert, it could be set for periods of up to an hour, or twelve hours depending on whether the minute or the hour hand was used to arm the bomb. Once activated, as Berryman stated, the act of 'accelerating and/or going up a gradient' would set it off.

Neave would have had to accelerate away from traffic lights at least three times on the short journey from the flat to the Palace of Westminster. Thus, if the police version was correct, the very earliest the bomb could have been planted under the car at Westminster Gardens would have been 2.45 a.m. on Friday 30 March. Their story would thus be feasible if the planter was suspect number two, seen in the service road at 6.45 that morning.

It was, of course, in the propaganda interests of the INLA to claim that the bomb was planted inside the Palace of Westminster. It would demonstrate their ingenuity and magnify the joy of their supporters at having put one over on the British. In a later version, given to Jack Holland, an Irish journalist, by Ronnie Bunting in

1979, it was claimed that as the Callaghan government fell, 'information unexpectedly came to the INLA from a political source in England.' Holland and his co-author Henry McDonald wrote that 'The source feared that Neave was preparing a right-wing backlash, with Thatcher as his chosen "front".' Thanks to their informant, 'the INLA had the access and the information necessary to launch one of the most daring assassinations in British political history.'[17]

The team, whose size Bunting did not disclose, 'penetrated the House of Commons underground car park posing as workers, carrying the device in a tool kit.' The bomb charge was a sixteen-ounce chunk of Soviet-made penthrite-tolite (TNT) explosive, part of a second batch obtained from their PLO contacts in Lebanon the year before. Their source had told them that 'the security cameras inside the car park … were not monitored very strictly.' Conforming to movie cliché, there was a last-minute hitch. They discovered the timing device was not working properly. They replaced it with a wristwatch timer, scraping the plastic coating off the hands with sandpaper to ensure a proper connection to activate the countdown.

The claim of inside assistance generated a wave of rumours about the identity of the accomplice. According to one story, the intelligence was provided by someone who went on to become a prominent Labour party figure. The charge was repeated by provincial police officers who had been involved in investigating Republican terror attacks, when they were being questioned over corruption allegations, but was apparently not taken seriously.[18] It seems that although security at Westminster had been tightened up after the start of the IRA mainland campaign, it was still inefficient. Nonetheless, the INLA version seems implausible. Why would the team multiply their chances of being caught by targeting Neave in the Commons – attractive though the propaganda benefits might be – when they could plant the bomb virtually risk-free at Westminster Gardens? The story of inside help that reduced the hazard serves to make the INLA account more credible.

What is clear is that the assassins' task was far easier as a result of Neave's decision to decline police protection. The INLA team had clearly watched their target for some time before they struck. Any competent officer would surely have noticed that Neave was under surveillance. Nowadays, the killers' movements would have been tracked every inch of the way by CCTV. Then, the technology was in its infancy, and when the team disappeared, the chances of them ever being brought to justice soon became vanishingly small.

The Metropolitan Police files are closed until 2079, under a rule that keeps the details of unsolved cases secret for a century after they occurred. The justification is that the emergence of new information might result in the investigation being reopened. Any interim examination of the papers would create the possibility of the file being tampered with. Access is also denied to the Home Office material covering the murder. Both this author and family members have made a number of requests under the Freedom of Information Act to examine the relevant files. Each one has been rejected on several grounds. A characteristic response was that given by the Metropolitan Police Service official dealing with the request: 'Whilst I acknowledge the importance of transparency with the general public, particularly as this request concerns the murder of a public figure, I have found that the public interest lies in favour of refusing your request. In view of the fact that the investigation into Mr Neave's murder remains unsolved and the release of the police file would prejudice the ability of police to conduct any further investigation, I have found that release is not in the public interest. Furthermore, I have also found that the release of the information within the file that was provided in confidence to police, would have an adverse effect upon the ability of the MPS, and the Police Service as a whole, to obtain information in connection with future investigations. For these reasons, I have found that the public interest lies in refusing your request. I have accordingly refused your request in its entirety.'[19] A further reason given for maintaining silence is that allowing access to the files would be 'harmful to the ability of those involved in safeguarding national security'.

Information from Republican sources has revealed the identity of one of the team: Patsy O'Hara, from Londonderry, who subsequently was the fourth man to die in the 1981 hunger strikes launched in a futile attempt to restore 'political status' for Republican prisoners. It was O'Hara who smuggled the bomb materials into Britain, arriving via France.

Although the police were aware almost immediately of the identities of the perpetrators, in the absence of evidence, a confession or the testimony of a 'supergrass', there was no realistic hope of obtaining a conviction. In 1986, however, events in France raised official hopes that the police might lay hands on a leading INLA figure closely connected to the operation. Two years earlier, INLA had forged a relationship with representatives of the PLO based in Prague. Through them they arranged a shipment of anti-tank rockets, rifles, machine guns and mortars. The consignment was due to be delivered to them in France. In July, an INLA man, William 'Boot' Browning, was identified by French police when he arrived and followed to Paris, where Harry Flynn (the Belfast-born founder member of the INLA who escaped from the Maze in 1976), George McCann and John Gormley were waiting for him. On 25 July, they were arrested near the Cité Universitaire, a campus housing foreign students in the south of Paris, and charged with illegal possession of arms and explosives.[20]

The development caused a flurry of excitement in London and Belfast. The memos and letters that sped back and forth between the Home Office, the Northern Ireland Office, the Foreign Office and the British Embassy in Paris showed that the arrest of Harry 'Basher' Flynn – as he was often now referred to in official documents – was seen as an event of the highest importance.[21] The Northern Ireland Office urged the Paris embassy 'to keep us in the closest touch possible with developments'. Officials were little interested in the fate of the other defendants and, as one document put it, 'in all of this the NIO's principal target is Flynn.'

He was remanded in Fresnes prison near Paris while the French authorities took their leisurely time to prepare their case. The British Embassy appears to have given them every assistance. The documents reveal that at some point 'highly classified intelligence information' supplied by the RUC was handed over to the state prosecutor. The inference is that the material was intended to emphasise the importance of at least one of the defendants. It had been handed over on a confidential basis and the RUC was horrified to learn that it had been shown to both the prosecution and defence lawyers.

Flynn's arrest opened the way to a possible extradition to Britain. A formal request was drawn up, to be issued in the event of the French court acquitting him or delivering a light sentence that meant that, given the time he had spent in custody, he would be freed immediately. The wording and procedure for delivering it were combed over by legal experts and even run past the French authorities to iron out possible glitches.

The charges it contained hardly seemed to justify the extraordinary effort. They dated back to the April 1975 Belfast bank robbery for which he was being held when he made his escape from the Crumlin Road courthouse. He was charged with stealing £3,339.91 from the Northern Bank Ltd and possession of a Luger pistol, a sawn-off shotgun and four cartridges. A similar extradition request had been made to the Republic in 1978 and been rejected by the High Court in Dublin on the grounds that the crime was 'political'.

On 16 September 1987, three weeks before the trial, a meeting was convened in Belfast to review 'the possible extradition of Harry Flynn'. The list of those present makes it clear that what was at stake was far more important than the clearing-up of a minor bank heist twelve years previously. The attendees included the Crown Prosecutor, senior intelligence and Home Office officials, and, most significantly, a detective superintendent and sergeant from the Metropolitan Police.

A 'brief line to take for ministers' was prepared to deal with anticipated questions as to why so much fuss was being raised over such relatively insignificant crimes, committed a dozen years previously:

Q. Isn't that a long time ago?

A. No. Flynn is an active member of the INLA and our extradition request will demonstrate our commitment to bring terrorists to justice for serious offences.

When the trial opened on 8 October, NIO officials stood by to inform their chief, Tom King, of the outcome 'immediately'. The proceedings lasted only a day and the results were only moderately satisfactory. The Paris court sentenced Harry Flynn to five years in prison, of which two were suspended. The time he had spent on remand, plus remission for good behaviour, meant he was freed the following summer. When Britain made a formal application for his extradition on release, it was rejected on the same grounds as those cited by the Irish court. Flynn returned to Dublin to carry on life unmolested.

For Ronnie Bunting, events did not go so well. At 3.30 on the morning of 15 October 1980, eighteen months after Neave's assassination, he and his wife Suzanne were asleep in the house in West Belfast where they lived with their three children. They were woken by the sound of the front door being smashed open with sledgehammers. Two masked men with handguns ran up the stairs to their bedroom. In the mayhem that followed, Suzannne was badly wounded. Ronnie and an IRSP colleague, Noel Lyttle, were shot dead. Suzanne described the killers as wearing green, military-style pullovers and ski masks. They seemed professional and unhurried.

There were immediate claims that the gunmen were either members of the SAS or that the security forces had assisted Loyalist assassins to carry out the hits. The fact that the Buntings' house at 7 Downfine Gardens was in the heart of a Nationalist area which would have been dangerous for Protestant paramilitaries to penetrate was cited as proof of official collusion. Ken Wharton, an ex-soldier who has produced the most comprehensive and minutely detailed account of the Troubles, believed that 'The truth was far more prosaic … The Loyalist UDA/UFF contained a fair number of Protestants who had once served in the British Army – and other

Armies, for that matter – and were trained to exacting professional standards.'[22]

Furthermore, 'a glance at the topography of the Bunting family home reveals that Downfine Gardens leads directly into Norglen Gardens, which is then a short burst to the Monagh Link and then straight on to the A55, Monagh By-Pass; this is then a fast drive to either the Upper Springfield Road and escape into the countryside, or the Springfield Road proper and over to Woodvale or Ballygomartin: safe Loyalist territory.' Wharton did 'not believe that it was the SAS whom the IRSP and INLA leadership were quick to point the finger of suspicion at'.

By then the memory of Neave's killing was dwindling fast. Given his prominence and the shocking circumstances of his death, it seems surprising now how quickly it disappeared from the front pages. This was partly due to the excitement created by the election campaign and the arrival in power of Britain's first woman prime minister. Mrs Thatcher did not allow the tragedy to divert her from the pursuit of victory. 'She was definitely very fond of Airey,' remembered Caroline Ryder, who saw Thatcher up close in the private office. 'She was definitely appalled and shattered by his death. But she was incredibly practical and she had a hell of a lot on her plate. And she got on with it.' Her stoutest supporter and most fervent admirer would have wanted nothing less.[23]

In her first public reaction to the news, Mrs Thatcher said that 'People will remember him for a lot of things – perhaps most of all for the fact that he got out of Colditz.' However, it was his private qualities that she chose to emphasise, and 'the many kindnesses he did'. He was 'a wonderful person, of tremendous inner strength'. Then, for a moment, the anger showed. 'Some devils got him,' she said. 'And they must never, never, never be allowed to triumph. They must never prevail. Those of us who believe in the things that Airey fought for must see that our views are the ones which continue to live on in this country.'[24]

In the days that followed, she met with all the family. 'She was superb,' remembered Marigold. 'She was very motherly, in a way.'[25] With Airey's departure, Diana lost half of herself. To an extraordinary degree, the pair had lived a complementary life in which happiness and sorrow, success and failure were experienced equally. The children sensed that the gigantic void that now opened before her should be filled as soon as possible. The antidote to sorrow was action. There was an immediate suggestion that she should take Airey's place in Parliament. Both the family and Margaret Thatcher herself were hesitant, worried about the consequences of the inevitable drive and conscientiousness that Diana would bring to the role. By taking on the task, wrote Margaret, five days after the murder, 'you may overtax your strength and do lasting damage to your health.'[26] Instead, 'On the assumption that we win on May 3rd, I would like you to take your place in the House of Lords.' As Baroness Airey of Abingdon, Diana spent thirteen years on the red benches, loyally pursuing Airey's causes, before dying in 1992 of a stroke which the family believe was brought on by overwork.

As Margaret Thatcher arrived at 10 Downing Street on the afternoon of 4 May, she remembered the man who had done so much to get her there. After the famous reference to St Francis of Assisi, she finished by saying, 'Finally, one last thing. In the words of Airey Neave, whom we had hoped to bring here with us, "There is now work to be done."' In the policies that the government followed in the succeeding years, however, there was little that bore the mark of Neave's thinking. The proposal for regional councils carried in the election manifesto came to nothing. His principle that there could be no negotiating with the IRA until their military defeat was slowly abandoned, and men he regarded as terrorists and gangsters gained respectability, power and honour in the eyes of the world.

With the coming of peace, the cell doors opened and men who had committed terrible crimes were free to walk again among those they had terrorised. Others, who had never been brought to justice while the Troubles were raging, could relax in the knowledge that now the likelihood was they never would. Among them was Harry Flynn. After further adventures, he left Ireland for the resort town of Santa Ponsa on the island of Mallorca.

There, from about 1998, he ran a pub called the Celts Well, popular with holidaymakers who did not know or did not care about his past. Following publication of this book early in 2019 the bar became the focus of widespread publicity. 'INLA Fugitive Suspected of Murdering Tory MP Airey Neave 40 Years Ago Found Running Celtic Pub in Majorca' ran the headline in the *Sun* of 14 March. The report described the decor as 'littered with pro INLA slogans, IRA references, republican propaganda and Irish flags'. When asked if he 'had any regrets over Mr Neave', Flynn declined to answer.

The coverage coincided with the announcement that a British paratrooper known as 'Soldier F' was to be prosecuted for the shooting of unarmed protesters in Londonderry during 'Bloody Sunday' in 1972. It prompted Ulster Unionist MP Jeffrey Donaldson to declare: 'The fact that an INLA suspect is living openly in Spain and doesn't appear to have been actively pursued by the UK authorities is yet another example of the unbalanced approach that has been taken to dealing with the legacy of our troubled past.'

Donaldson announced he would be writing to the Home Secretary, Sajid Javid, 'to enquire what steps he intends to take to pursue the extradition of this suspect from Spain to stand trial in the United Kingdom in connection with the murder of Airey Neave'.

Javid had already been asked by Greg Hands, Member of Parliament for Chelsea and Fulham, to reopen the case following a meeting with William Neave who lives in the constituency. In a letter to Hands, Javid said 'new work' was being done. 'I have reviewed the case and can confirm that extensive searches have been carried out, including by the Metropolitan Police, into the circumstances of the murder,' he wrote. He went on: 'I do not want to raise hopes of progress, but following my review of the case new work has been commenced by the police and the investigation is open. Should any potential leads come to light they will be scrutinised by the police to see if those responsible can be brought to justice.'

Epilogue

Hinton Waldrist

St Margaret of Antioch is the sort of church you expect to find in an old English village. It is small and plain, with a slate roof and a castellated tower, and the tussocky grass of the churchyard is studded with gently subsiding headstones. It feels unchanging and timeless, and despite the reminders of death there is a sense of continuity. Airey Neave is buried here. Diana lies beside him. His life is commemorated in a stained-glass window behind the altar. Set in the left-hand pane is an image of Colditz. The church stands opposite the Old Rectory, in a wing of which the Neaves spent the last four years of their lives together. The tableau is completed by Hinton Manor, which lies behind the church. Taken together, they form a stone, brick and mortar symbol of Tory England.

After Neave was laid to rest, the Conservative leader he had helped to power began a reformation of the party that in turn transformed the country itself. Had he lived, it seems likely that there would have been much he found disquieting in the new Britain that took shape under his heroine. Airey's relationship with Margaret had been marked by mutual respect. In the early days of her leadership he was a comforting and protective presence. According to Tom King, she was 'nervous of the gentry … Carrington, Whitelaw and Soames.*

---

* Christopher Soames (1920–87), educated Eton and RMC, Sandhurst; Conservative MP for Bedford, 1950–66; Ambassador to France, 1968–72; European Commissioner for External Relations, 1973–77; married Winston and Clementine Churchill's youngest daughter, Mary, in 1947.

She had the feeling that they didn't think she was good enough. Airey was a sort of shield and protection against that.'[1]

When he spoke, she listened, showing due reverence for his war record and the debt of gratitude she owed to him. However, the intellectual distance between them was clear. 'He was ponderous compared to her,' said Caroline Ryder.[2] Caroline's husband and then boss, Richard, recalled that '[Margaret] was very fast … she would know within a minute what he wanted to say.' Their conversations were about practical matters, not high policy, and 'there was no ideological discussion between them. He wasn't interested in ideology at all.'

By 1979 his job was done. He cannot, then, be said to have played any significant part in forming the political creed that carries Margaret Thatcher's name. Nor did he have any influence on her thinking over Northern Ireland. The loyalty and affection she felt for him did not imply any obligation when she came to power to press on with the policies he had pursued in opposition. The new Northern Ireland secretary, Humphrey Atkins, dropped the regional council plan and Tom King, who served in the post from 1985 to 1989, judged that the Neave approach was 'pretty much the opposite of where we ended up, really'.[3]

With Thatcher's election, the old Tory guard were changing, to be replaced by men of a different stamp, who had not known active service. Neave belonged to a Tory tradition that was fundamentally shaped by the war and rested on a belief in consensus and cooperation. Admiring though many of its members were of Mrs Thatcher's courage and determination, they were less comfortable with the hostility to collectivism inherent in her outlook.

His political creed was instinctive rather than intellectual or ideological, based on concepts of right and wrong that were already looking old-fashioned when he died. It came with a certainty, a quiet conviction – 'decent, dedicated, diligent', in Richard Ryder's words – that carried him through his public and private life. At sixty-three, his ministerial career was unlikely to have lasted much more than one parliamentary term.

His departure was premature, robbing his wife and children of his love and company. But he died a soldier's death and, by going when he did, was spared the sight of men against whom he had fought the last battles of his life being hailed as heroes and peacemakers. Norman Tebbit said of him that, in his approach to life, 'Airey was utterly sure of the destination and was prepared to take the route to it, however difficult that might be.'[4] He did so with a determination that never flagged with age. The churchyard at Hinton Waldrist where he now lies brings to mind the lines that T. S. Eliot wrote when contemplating a very similar place: St Michael's, in the Somerset village of East Coker:

> Old men ought to be explorers
> Here and there does not matter
> We must be still and still moving
> Into another intensity …

Acknowledgements

My thanks go first to the Neave family – Marigold, Patrick, William and his son Sebastian – who gave me every assistance while leaving me entirely free to arrive at my own judgements. Beyond them lie a wide circle of family and friends who have shown great generosity in sharing recollections and reflections. I am particularly grateful to Tom Rhodes for setting the project in motion and to Michael Bottenheim for his enthusiasm, his insights and his energy in driving the work along.

The foundations of the book are Airey's own writings, public and private, but to build on them I have made use of the memories of some of those who knew him or came in contact with him, directly or indirectly. As well as his children, I would like to thank the following for their help: Jonathan Aitken, Lord Dobbs, Lady Antonia Fraser, John Giffard, the Earl of Gowrie, Billy Stirling James, Lord King of Bridgwater, Lord Lexden, Lord Lilley, Elizabeth Neave, Philippa Neave, Matthew Parris, General Sir Michael Rose, Lord Ryder of Wensum, Lady Ryder, Lord Tebbit, Hugh Tilney, Dame Veronica Sutherland, Richard Webb and Dame Jane Whiteley.

I was greatly helped by the contributions of others who offered information, expertise and advice on military, political and security aspects of the story. They include: Professor Richard J. Aldrich of the University of Warwick, Lord Bew, John Bunney, Christopher Clark, Alexander Creswell, Mary Creswell, Walter Ellis, Rebecca Fitzgerald, Clare Ireland, Dr Stephen Kelly of Liverpool Hope University, Mary

Miers, Sir Hugh Orde, Michel Robinson, Peter Taylor, Sir Kevin Tebbit, Barry Strevens and Ken Wharton. My gratitude goes to John Howes who has made a special study of the Pegasus operations in which his father was involved and who has generously shared his source material and knowledge. I am also indebted to Bob Cox, the Metropolitan Police press officer of the period, and Stewart Tendler, for many years the distinguished crime corrrespondent of *The Times*, for their assistance. I had direct knowledge of the conflict in Northern Ireland having worked there as correspondent for the *Observer* between 1979 and 1983. On revisiting those times, my understanding was helped by several sources on both sides of the line who prefer to remain anonymous. I would like to thank my friends Pirate Irwin and Xan Smiley for explaining Eton customs and practices for the benefit of an Old Wimbledonian.

Lord Anderson of Ipswich QC, Lord Carlile of Berriew QC and Greg Callus of 5RB kindly contributed expert advice in my efforts and those of the family to gain access to government and police files. We would also like to thank Greg Hands MP for his representations on behalf of the family in their attempt to learn more about the police investigation into Airey Neave's death. Susan Lord of Westminster Coroner's Court provided valuable records of the inquest.

My work was greatly helped by Sophie Butler of the Airey Neave Trust who patiently answered my queries and ensured good communications between myself and the trustees. I would also like to acknowledge the generous financial support provided by the Trust to help fund my researches.

Georgina Robinson of the Eton College archives and Andrew Robinson, House Master of The Timbralls, assisted my researches into AN's Eton schooldays. My thanks are due to Julian Reid and the staff of Merton College Oxford Library for showing me the material relating to his time there. I am grateful to the Fellows for permission to use the picture of the Myrmidons included in the plates.

Sergeant John Allcock and Captain Stephen King responded enthusiastically to my requests for details of AN's army service and I am particularly indebted to Captain King for unearthing and passing on to the family records that filled in many gaps in the story. I am grateful to Andrew Riley of the Churchill College Archives Centre, Cambridge, for his support.

I benefited greatly from the professionalism of the staffs of the London Library (with particular thanks to Mandy Southern), the National Archives, the British Library, the Linen Hall Library, Belfast, and the Imperial War Museum. In Paris, the staff of the Bibliothèque Nationale de France (François Mitterrand) and the information service of the Tribunal de Grande Instance were welcoming and efficient.

My brilliant niece Grace Ries transcribed many of the interviews, swiftly and painstakingly. I am grateful to the team at HarperCollins for their customary skill, patience and professionalism and in particular to Iain Hunt who oversaw the editing process. Leo Nicholls and Julian Humphries have surpassed themselves with a superb design for the cover. I was very fortunate to have as my copy editor Tim Waller. His corrections saved me from many errors and his suggestions were invariably gratefully accepted. A special word of thanks to Annabel Merullo, my friend but also my agent, for her unfailing support and sympathy. Annabel, you are a star.

This project had the happy effect of reconnecting me with my old tutor at Corpus Christi College, Oxford, where I studied history in the early 1970s. In those days Brian Harrison was a brisk young don with a refreshingly open attitude to what counted as history and how it should be addressed. He went on to become Professor of Modern History at the university and editor of the *Oxford Dictionary of National Biography*. Sir Brian, as he now is, kindly agreed to read and comment on the work while it was in progress. After a gap of more than forty years it was a bracing (and sometimes chastening) experience to have my efforts subjected once again to his keen gaze. His observations have improved the end result greatly. The shortcomings that remain are all my own.

Finally, to my darling wife Henrietta and beloved daughter Honor my thanks for your forbearance and support – as always.

Notes

PROLOGUE: 'SOME DEVILS GOT HIM'

1. Statement of Joy Robilliard to Detective Sergeant Ian McGregor, 31 March 1979.
2. Interview with Richard Ryder, 19 July 2016.
3. Interview with Jonathan Aitken, 22 January 2018.
4. Interview with Tom King, 8 September 2015.
5. Records of Tom Brown Ltd.
6. *Daily Mail*, 6 April 1979.
7. Hansard, HC Deb, 10 April 1987.

1: A QUESTION OF UPBRINGING

1. *Nature*, vol. 150, p. 205, 15 August 1942.
2. Airey Neave school diary (Neave family papers), 24 September 1931.
3. Ibid., 20 October 1931.
4. Ibid., 21 October 1931.
5. Jo Grimond, *Memoirs*, Heinemann, 1979, p. 43.
6. AN school diary, 24 October 1931.
7. Ibid., 11 September 1931.
8. Henri Le Caron, *Twenty-Five Years in the Secret Service*, William Heinemann, 1892, p. 37.
9. Ibid., p. 195.
10. Ibid., p. 196.
11. Paul Routledge, *Public Servant, Secret Agent: The Elusive Life and Violent Death of Airey Neave*, Fourth Estate, 2002, p. 106.
12. AN school diary, 5 November 1931.
13. Ibid., 30 September 1931.
14. Interview with Marigold Webb, 15 October 2015.
15. Airey Neave diary, 17 February 1973.
16. AN diary, 25 February 1973.
17. Airey Neave, *Nuremberg: A Personal Record of the Trial of the Major Nazi War Criminals in 1945–6*, Hodder & Stoughton, 1978, p. 20.
18. Grimond, *Memoirs*, p. 45.
19. Neave, *Nuremberg*, p. 19.
20. Ibid., p. 20.
21. Ibid., p. 21.
22. Ibid., p. 22.
23. Neave's *Dictionary of National Biography* entry, by Sir Brian Harrison, makes mention of it, and the Marquess of Reading (Michael Isaacs) recalled 'Airey winning a political essay prize, about 1933, on Germany'. There is also a reference to it in Leonard Cheshire's 1980 appreciation of Neave in the Merton College magazine *Postmaster*, but extensive efforts have failed to turn anything up.
24. *Sixpenny: Stories and Poems by Etonians*, no. 4, 13 July 1934.

25. Robin Maugham, *Escape from the Shadows*, Hodder & Stoughton, 1972, p. 78.
26. Obituary of David Tree, *Daily Telegraph*, 28 December 2009.
27. Marquess of Reading, 'Some Personal Recollections', *Eton Chronicle*, 31 May 1980.
28. Grimond, *Memoirs*, p. 45.
29. Leonard Cheshire, *Postmaster* (Merton College Magazine), vol. VI, no. 1, March 1980.
30. Airey Neave, *They Have Their Exits*, Leo Cooper, 2016, p. 7.
31. Ibid., p. 7.
32. Merton College Library.
33. Cheshire, *Postmaster*.
34. Merton Floats programme, Neave family papers.
35. Marquess of Reading, 'Personal Recollections'.
36. Neave, *Exits*, p. 7.
37. Ibid., p. 6.
38. Richard Morris, *Cheshire*, Viking, 2000, p. 29.
39. Neave, *Exits*, p. 7.
40. Ibid., p. 6.
41. Ibid., p. 4.
42. Marquess of Reading, 'Personal Recollections'.

2: BLOODED

1. Neave, *Exits*, p. 7.
2. Airey Neave, *The Flames of Calais*, Coronet, 1974, p. 34.
3. Neave, *Flames*, p. 35.
4. Ibid., p. 15.
5. Ibid., p. 55.
6. Ibid., p. 39.
7. Ibid., p. 45.
8. Neave, *Exits*, p. 8.
9. Neave, *Flames*, p. 46.
10. Ibid., pp. 46–47.
11. Ibid., p. 94.
12. Ibid., p. 106.
13. Ibid., p. 106.
14. Ibid., pp. 130–31.
15. Ibid., pp. 131–32.
16. Ibid., pp. 139–43, for the full account of this action.
17. Ibid., p. 113.

18. Ibid., p. 164.
19. Ibid., p. 161.
20. Ibid., pp. 211–12.
21. Ibid., p. 213. In *Exits* (p. 10), Neave says it was a bottle of wine – an example of the minor discrepancies that occur in his various accounts of his exploits.
22. Ibid., p. 227.

3: 'IN THE BAG'

1. Neave, *Flames*, p. 74.
2. Ibid., p. 18.
3. Ibid., p. 137.
4. 'Nicholson, Claude', www.winchestercollegeatwar.com.
5. Neave, *Flames*, p. 216. Rifleman Matthews of the 2KRRC was awarded the Distinguished Conduct Medal for his bravery.
6. Airey Neave, *Saturday at MI9*, Hodder & Stoughton, 1969, p. 26.
7. Neave, *Flames*, pp. 232–33.
8. Imperial War Museum Documents 25969.
9. Neave, *Saturday*, pp. 27–29, for full account.
10. Ibid., p. 59.
11. Lt Colonel J. M. Langley, *Fight Another Day*, Collins, 1974, pp. 50–53.
12. Ibid., pp. 19–20.
13. Airey Neave, 'New Confidence in Ulster', *Spectator*, 17 December 1975, p. 16.
14. Neave, *Saturday*, pp. 27–29.
15. Neave, *Exits*, pp. 10–14.
16. Neave, *Saturday*, p. 29.
17. Neave, *Exits*, p. 13.
18. P. R. Reid, MBE, MC, *The Colditz Story*, Hodder & Stoughton, 1952, p. 84.
19. Ibid., p. 106.
20. Neave, *Saturday*, p. 29.
21. Neave, *Exits*, p. 13.
22. Ibid., p. 15.
23. The National Archives 40/2449.
24. William Ash (with Brendan Foley), *Under the Wire*, Bantam, 2005, p. 172.
25. Reid, *Colditz*, p. 17.

26. Ash and Foley, *Wire*, p. 153.
27. Aidan Crawley, *Escape from Germany: The Methods of Escape Used by RAF Airmen During the Second World War*, HMSO, 1985, p. 5.
28. Neave, *Exits*, p. 16.
29. Ibid., pp. 12–25, for full account.
30. Ibid., p. 17.
31. Ibid., pp. 26–40, for full account.
32. Neave, *Saturday*, pp. 32–33.
33. Neave, *Exits*, p. 42.
34. Interview with William Neave, 16 May 2016.
35. Peter Taylor, *Beating the Terrorists? Interrogation at Omagh, Gough and Castlereagh*, Penguin, 1980, p. 332.
36. Neave, *Exits*, p. 43.

4. THE ESCAPING CLUB

1. Neave, *Exits*, pp. 51–81, for full account.
2. Interview with Norman Tebbit, 18 May 2016.
3. Neave, *Exits*, p. 56.
4. Ibid., p. 63.
5. Ibid., p. 65.
6. Ibid., p. 67.
7. Reid, *Colditz*, p. 106.
8. Neave, *Exits*, p. 69.
9. Reid, *Colditz*, p. 98.
10. *Daily Mail*, 31 March 1979.
11. Neave, *Exits*, p. 71.
12. Reid, *Colditz*, p. 123.
13. Neave, *Exits*, p. 84.
14. Anthony 'Tony' Luteyn, IWM Sound Archive 21768. All subsequent quotations are taken from this source.
15. Neave, *Exits*, p. 78.
16. Ibid., pp. 81–95, for full account.
17. Ibid., p. 86.
18. Ibid., p. 87.
19. Ibid., p. 92.
20. Ibid., p. 93.
21. Ibid., p. 94.

5: HOME RUN

1. Luteyn, IWM Sound Archive 21768.
2. Neave, *Exits*, p. 97.
3. Neave, *Saturday*, p. 39.
4. *Daily Mail*, 31 March 1979.
5. Luteyn, IWM Sound Archive 21768.
6. There are several minor discrepancies between the two principal accounts Neave left of this period: *They Have Their Exits* (1953) and *Saturday at MI9* (1969). The essentials of the narrative, though, are consistent.
7. Neave, *Exits*, chap. 9 passim.
8. Neave, *Saturday*, p. 40.
9. TNA WO 208/4242.
10. Neave, *Saturday*, p. 41.
11. M. R. D. Foot and J. M. Langley, *MI9: Escape and Evasion 1939–1945*, Biteback Publishing, 2011, p. 132.
12. Interview with Christopher Clark, 17 January 2018.
13. Foot and Langley, *MI9*, p. 63.
14. In *Exits* (p. 105), it is a 'small' cemetery; in *Saturday* (p. 45), a 'large' one. Another example of the discrepancies Neave was prone to, surprising perhaps in an intelligence officer who might be expected to be punctilious about details.
15. Neave, *Saturday*, p. 45.
16. Foot and Langley, *MI9*, p. 63. The book is jointly authored, but the sentiments are surely Langley's. Foot too was a wartime escaper, but his third attempt came to an end when a Breton farmer's son beat him up, injuring him severely.
17. Neave, *Exits*, pp. 109–10.
18. Ibid., p. 111.
19. www.conscriptheroes.com.
20. Oliver Clutton-Brock, *RAF Evaders*, Grub Street, 2009, p. 42.
21. Foot and Langley, *MI9*, pp. 35–36.
22. Donald Darling, *Secret Sunday*, William Kimber, 1975, p. 9.
23. TNA KV2/415.
24. Darling, *Sunday*, p. 31.
25. Neave, *Saturday*, p. 83.
26. Clutton-Brock, *Evaders*, p. 77.
27. TNA KV2/415.
28. Neave, *Saturday*, p. 85.
29. Neave, *Exits*, p. 130.

6: ROOM 900

1. Neave, *Saturday*, p. 57, and passim.
2. Neave gave two different versions of what happened next. In *Exits* (p. 141), they shared a taxi to the Berkeley Hotel. In *Saturday* (p. 59), they said their farewells there and then. Another example of the discrepancies in Neave's published recollections.
3. Neave, *Saturday*, p. 62.
4. Neave, *Exits*, 143.
5. Neave, *Saturday*, p. 82.
6. Neave, *Exits*, 144.
7. AN diary, 8 October 1973.
8. Elisabeth Luard, *My Life as a Wife*, Bloomsbury, 2013, p. 16.
9. Neave, *Exits*, p. 144.
10. Patrick Cosgrave, obituary of Diana Neave, *Independent*, 1 December 1992.
11. Interview with Marigold Webb.
12. *Independent*, 1 December 1992.
13. Interview with Hugh Tilney, 16 November 2018.
14. Darling, *Sunday*, p. 19.
15. Neave, *Saturday*, p. 69.
16. The MI9 historian and wartime intelligence officer M. R. D. Foot has also claimed that Cavell was a British spy, as, after research in the Belgian archives, has the former head of MI5 Stella Rimington, though AN maintained otherwise.
17. Neave, *Saturday*, p. 70.
18. Ibid., p. 62.
19. Interview with Alexander Creswell, 18 May 2018.
20. Neave, *Saturday*, p. 132.
21. Darling, *Sunday*, p. 34.
22. Clutton-Brock, *Evaders*, p. 116, and TNA HS6/223.
23. Interview with Alexander Creswell.
24. Clutton-Brock, *Evaders*, p. 112, and TNA AIR 2/5904.
25. Papers of John Howes.
26. Neave, *Saturday*, p. 91.
27. Clutton-Brock, *Evaders*, p. 206.
28. Neave, *Saturday*, p. 150.
29. Ibid., p. 158. Other accounts say they were French.
30. TNA 7446.
31. Neave, *Saturday*, p. 148.
32. There are other versions of the story – e. g. Clutton-Brock, *Evaders*, p. 207 – but the overall picture remains the same. Jean-François Nothomb risked visiting flats used by the network after Frédéric de Jongh had been arrested, and it was only by sheer luck that he did not share his fate.
33. Neave, *Saturday*, p. 151.
34. Ibid., p. 152.
35. Ibid., p. 189.
36 She remained disarmingly haughty and unrepentant till the end, as can be seen in this YouTube clip: https://www.youtube.com/watch?v=XH8Vr4HpAC4].
37. Neave, *Saturday*, p. 190.
38. Ibid., p. 192.
39. Subsequently it was alleged that Lindell's 'unconventional ways' went further than mere eccentricity. In 2015, Marie-Laure Le Folon, a French historian, published *Lady Mensonge: Mary Lindell, fausse héroïne de la Résistance*. According to her researches, which included the testimony of surviving resisters, Lindell was something of a fabulist, hence the soubriquet 'Lady Lie'.
40. Neave, *Saturday*, p. 195.
41. Ibid., pp. 151–52.
42. Ibid., p. 314.

7: FROM NORMANDY TO NUREMBERG

1. Neave, *Saturday*, p. 242. All quotations are taken from pp. 241–300 unless otherwise indicated.
2. Ibid., p. 264.
3. Papers of Michel Robinson.
4. Neave, *Saturday*, p. 277.
5. Ibid., p. 283.
6. Telephone interview with Antonia Pinter, 27 December 2017.

7. Captain Peter Baker, *My Testament*, John Calder, 1955, p. 146.
8. I am indebted to John Howes for his exhaustive researches into this incident and the whole Pegasus episode.
9. Neave, *Saturday*, p. 293.
10. 'Arnhem Men Drove Through German Lines in Lorries', *News Chronicle*, 20 November 1944.
11. The full story is contained in Airey Neave, *Nuremberg: A Personal Record of the Trial of the Major Nazi War Criminals in 1945–6*, Hodder & Stoughton, 1978.
12 Neave, *Nuremberg*, p. 44.
13. Ibid., p. 79.
14. Ibid., p. 264.
15. Neave family story.
16. Rebecca West, foreword to Neave, *Nuremberg*, p. 5.

8: THE LONG MARCH

1. *Daily Herald*, 24 June 1953.
2. *Daily Mirror*, 29 June 1953.
3. Interview with William Neave.
4. Interview with Marigold Webb.
5. AN diary, 7 January 1974.
6. AMS Neave army file, in possession of family.
7. AN diary, 8 May 1974.
8. Ibid., 30 July 1973.
9. Interview with Dame Veronica Sutherland, 18 October 2017.
10. AN diary, 27 October 1973.
11. Ibid., 25 July 1974.
12. *Birmingham Daily Post*, 3 July 1953.
13. Hansard, HC Deb, 29 July 1953.
14. Hansard, HC Deb, 1 March 1954.
15. Hansard, HC Deb, 17 November 1953.
16. Interview with Sir Peter Hordern, 23 August 2018.
17. Hansard, HC Deb, 29 May 1956.
18. Interview with Marigold Webb.
19. Interview with William Neave.
20. Interview with Patrick Neave, 20 October 2016.
21. Interview with Philippa Neave, 6 March 2018.

22. Interview with John Giffard, 24 January 2018.
23. AN diary, 31 March 1973.
24. John Campbell, *Edward Heath: A Biography*, Cape, 1993, p. 101.
25. AN diary, 22 August 1973.

9: DARKEST HOUR

1. AN diary, 9 March 1973.
2. Ibid., 10 March 1973.
3. Hansard, HC Deb, 7 February 1969.
4. Hansard, HC Deb, 29 October 1965.
5. Neave, *Nuremberg*, p. 78.
6. AN diary, 10 June 1973.
7. AN was a director of Dawson and Barfos from July 1972 and worked for Edwin McAlpine.
8. Margaret Thatcher, *The Path to Power*, HarperCollins, 1995, p. 270.
9. Greville Wynne, *The Man From Odessa*, Panther, 1984, 41–42.
10. AN diary, 31 October 1973.
11. Ibid., 30 August 1974.
12. Ibid., 30 January 1974.
13. Campbell, *Heath*, p. 36.
14. AN diary, 1 August 1973.
15. *Daily Telegraph*, 1 January 2007.
16. AN diary, 24 May 1974.
17. Ibid., 29 May 1973.
18. Ibid., 17 March 1973.
19. Interview with Veronica Sutherland.
20. AN diary, 27 August 1973.
21. Ibid., 1 June 1973.
22. Ibid., 4 June 1974.
23. Ibid., 26 October 1973.
24. Ibid., 1 June 1973.
25. Ibid., 11 May 1973.
26. Ibid., 3 January 1974.
27. Ibid., 9 January 1974.
28. Ibid., 23 March 1974.
29. Ibid., 25 January 1973.
30. Ibid., 21 April 1973.
31. Ibid., 7 August 1974.

10: 'A PERFECT WOMAN, NOBLY PLANNED'

1. Charles Moore, *Margaret Thatcher*, vol. 1, *Not for Turning*, Allen Lane, 2013, p. 125.
2. John Campbell, *Margaret Thatcher*, vol. 1, *The Grocer's Daughter*, Jonathan Cape, 2000, p. 89.
3. AN diary, 9 June 1973.
4. From a modest Welsh background, Marshall gained a first in mathematical physics at Birmingham University before moving to Harwell.
5. AN diary, 6 July 1973.
6. Ibid., 4 January 1973.
7. Ibid., 19 July 1973.
8. Ibid., 15 July 1973.
9. Ibid., 22 October 1974.
10. Interview with Veronica Sutherland (née Beckett), 18 October 2017.
11. Neave, *Nuremberg*, p. 75.
12. AN diary, 30 December 1973.
13. Ibid., 29 April 1973.
14. Thatcher, *Path*, p. 270.
15. Interview with Jonathan Aitken.
16. AN diary, 15 September 1973.
17. See Campbell, *Heath*, pp. 561–73.
18. AN diary, 13 December 1973. Thanks to the magazine *Private Eye*, 'tired and emotional' had become a euphemism for 'drunk'. According to some accounts, the pressures of dealing with Northern Ireland had led Willie Whitelaw to turn to the bottle. See Moore, *Thatcher*, p. 244.
19. Ibid., 3 January 1974.
20. Ibid., 20 February 1974.
21. Ibid., 23 February 1974.
22. Ibid., 1 March 1974.
23. Moore, *Thatcher*, p. 248.
24. AN diary, 2 March 1974.
25. Ibid., 20 March 1974.
26. Ibid., 25 March 1974.
27. Ibid., 13 June 1974.
28. Ibid., 6 April 1974.
29. Ibid., 26 March 1974.
30. Ibid., 9 May 1974.
31. Ibid., 7 May 1974.
32. Ibid., 26 May 1974.
33. Ibid., 2 July 1974.
34. Diana Neave diary, 2 July 1974.
35. Interview with Marigold Webb.
36. AN diary, 3 July 1974.
37. Ibid., 14 July 1974.
38. Ibid., 26 July 1974.
39. Ibid., 24 September 1974.
40. Campbell, *Heath*, p. 639.
41. AN diary, 21 September 1974.
42. Ibid., 12 October 1974.

11: THE ARITHMETIC OF VICTORY

1. AN diary, 13 October 1974.
2. Ibid., 17 June 1974.
3. Ibid., 14 October 1974.
4. Ibid., 15 October 1974.
5. Interview with Sir Peter Hordern.
6. AN diary, 15 October 1974.
7. Ibid., 15 October 1974.
8. Ibid., 21 October 1974.
9. Ibid., 29 October 1974.
10. Ibid., 31 October 1974.
11. Ibid., 6 November 1974.
12. Ibid., 14 November 1974.
13. Ibid., 18 January 1975.
14. Ibid., 5 December 1974.
15. Ibid., 15 September 1973.
16. Ibid., 21 September 1973.
17. Ibid., 22 September 1973.
18. Ibid., 10 April 1974.
19. Ibid., 18 July 1974.
20. Ibid., 31 July 1974.
21. Edward Pearce, obituary of Edward du Cann, *Guardian*, 7 September 2017.
22. Moore, *Thatcher*, p. 273.
23. Thatcher, *Path*, p. 270.
24. AN diary, 28 November 1974.
25. Ibid., 6 December 1974.
26. Ibid., 28 November 1974.
27. Moore, *Thatcher*, p. 278.
28. AN diary, 1 December 1974.
29. Ibid., 19 December 1974.
30. Ibid., 31 December 1974.
31. Ibid., 'Personal Notes', 1975.
32. Ibid., 1 December 1974.
33. Ibid., 23 December 1974.
34. Ibid., 3 January 1975.
35. Ibid., 12 January 1975.
36. Thatcher, *Path*, p. 272.
37. AN diary, 16 January 1975.

38. Ibid., 18 January 1975.
39. Ibid., 20 January 1975.
40. Tam Dalyell, obituary of Arthur Palmer, *Independent*, 26 August 1994.
41. AN diary, 23 January 1975.
42. Ibid., 27 January 1975.
43. Ibid.
44. Quoted in Moore, *Thatcher*, p. 289.
45. AN diary, 27 January 1975.
46. Ibid., 26 January 1975.
47. Ibid., 27 January 1975.
48. Ibid., 28 January 1975.
49. Interview with Richard Ryder.
50. Interview with Norman Tebbit.
51. Interview with Billy Stirling James, 14 November 2018.
52. Campbell, *Thatcher*, p. 298.
53. Interview with Jonathan Aitken.
54. Moore, *Thatcher*, p. 291.

12: WARRIOR IN A DARK BLUE SUIT

1. Moore, *Thatcher*, p. 297.
2. Interview with Marigold Webb.
3. Moore, *Thatcher*, p. 587.
4. Interview with William Neave.
5. Interview with Caroline Ryder, 19 July 2016.
6. Interview with Grey Gowrie, 28 June 2018.
7. Interview with Lord Lexden, 25 January 2016.
8. Interview with Richard Ryder.
9. AN diary, 12 August 1973.
10. Ibid., 26 November 1974.
11. Ibid., 6 March 1974.
12. Ibid., 23 May 1974.
13. Interview with Peter Lilley, 15 March 2018.
14. Peter Lilley, Geoffrey Warhurst, John Wilkinson MP and Rochfort Young, *Do You Sincerely Want to Win?*, Bow Publications, 1972.
15. Figures taken from Ed Moloney, *A Secret History of the IRA*, Penguin, 2007, pp. 671–72.
16. Ibid., p. 672.
17. Hansard, HC Deb, 14 July 1975.
18. Hansard, HC Deb, 27 June 1975.
19. Merlyn Rees, *Northern Ireland: A Personal Perspective*, Methuen, 1985, p. 324.
20. Neave, 'New confidence in Ulster', p. 16.
21. Hansard, HC Deb, 24 November 1975.
22. Interview with Lord Lexden.
23. Neave, 'New confidence in Ulster', p. 16.
24. For a comprehensive and insightful analysis, see Stephen Kelly, '"No textbook solutions to the problems in Northern Ireland": Airey Neave and the Conservative Party's Northern Ireland Policy, 1975–1979', *Irish Studies in International Affairs*, 2018, 1–24.
25. Interview with Peter Lilley.
26. Kelly, 'No textbook', p. 2.
27. Hansard, HC Deb, 28 Oct 1976.
28. Airey Neave, 'Bridging the Ulster gap', *Guardian*, 3 May 1978.
29. TNA CJ 4/2642.
30. Ibid.
31. Ibid.
32. Neave to Mrs Winifred A. Walker, 3 April 1978, Parliamentary Archives AN/461, quoted in Kelly, 'No textbook,' p. 9.
33. Neave, 'New confidence'.
34. Lord Lexden, Conservative Home website, 30 March 2014.
35. 'Roy Mason', Wikipedia.
36. Neave, 'New confidence'.
37. Interview with Michael Rose, 26 March 2018.
38. Neave, 'New confidence'.
39. Interview with Michael Rose.
40. Interview with Patrick Neave.
41. Diana Neave, statement to DI John Holmes, 31 March 1979
42. See Jack Holland and Henry McDonald, *INLA: Deadly Divisions – The Story of One of Ireland's Most Ruthless Terrorist Organisations*, Torc, 1994, pp. 98–104 for full details.
43. TNA FCO 87/2566.
44. Walter Ellis, *The Beginning of the End: The Crippling Disadvantage of an Irish Childhood*, Mainstream, 2006, p. 157.

45. Ibid., p. 228.
46. Ibid., p. 223.
47. Private information.
48. Holland and McDonald, *INLA*, p. 105.
49. Ibid., p. 121.
50. Ibid., p. 106.
51. Ibid., p. 130.
52. TNA CJ 4/2642.
53. Ibid.
54. See Moore, *Thatcher*, p. 593.
55. Diana Neave, statement to DI John Holmes, 2 April 1979.
56. Interview with Matthew Parris, 27 June 2018.
57. Interview with Lord Lexden.
58. Interview with Michael Dobbs, 25 April 2018.
59. Interview with Richard Ryder.

13: 'THE PERFECT TARGET'

1. Interview with Richard Ryder and statement of Joy Robilliard to Detective Sergeant Ian McGregor, 31 March 1979.
2. Report of M. Rufus Crompton to Westminster Coroner's Court.
3. TNA HO 287/2627.
4. David McNee, *McNee's Law: The Memoirs of Sir David McNee*, Collins, 1983, pp. 136–7.
5. TNA HO 287/2627.
6. Interview with Patrick Neave.
7. Statement of Joy Robilliard to DS Ian McGregor, 31 March 1979.

8. Interview with William Neave.
9. Routledge, *Public Servant*, p. 314.
10. TNA CJ 4/3134.
11. Private information.
12. *Daily Mail*, 11 April 1979, p. 17.
13. Holland and McDonald, *INLA*, p. 140.
14. Statement of George Berryman to Westminster Coroner's Court.
15. Interview with military bomb expert, 17 April 2018.
16. Routledge, *Public Servant*, p. 312.
17. Holland and McDonald, *INLA*, pp. 137–38.
18. Private information.
19. Email from Damion Baird to the author, 23 June 2018.
20. Holland and McDonald, *INLA*, pp. 250–53, and AP report for 25 July 1976.
21. TNA FCO 87/2566.
22. Ken Wharton, *Torn Apart: Fifty Years of the Troubles 1969–2019*.
23. Interview with Caroline Ryder.
24. YouTube, 'The Death of Airey Neave'.
25. Interview with Marigold Webb.
26. Margaret Thatcher to Diana Neave, 4 April 1979. Neave family papers.

EPILOGUE: HINTON WALDRIST

1. Interview with Tom King.
2. Interview with Caroline Ryder.
3. Interview with Tom King.
4. Interview with Norman Tebbit.

Image Credits

Airey aged about seven months with his mother Dorothy. (*Neave family*)

As a seven-year-old schoolboy. (*Neave family*)

Airey with his siblings, Averil, Rosamund, Digby and Viola. (*Neave family*)

Merton College dining club the Myrmidons, 1937. (*Fellows of Merton College*)

British troops march into captivity, Calais. (*Chronicle/Alamy Stock Photo*)

AN shortly after arriving at Spangenberg. (*History and Art Collection/Alamy Stock Photo*)

Colditz Castle. (*Wikipedia*)

Francis Blanchain, Mario Prassinos, Hugh Woollatt, AN and Louis Nouveau, Quai Rive Neuve, Marseilles, 1942.

Jimmy Langley, 1944.

AN with Albert-Marie Guérisse ('Pat O'Leary') after the war.

AN and Diana marry after a whirlwind courtship, 29 December 1942. (*Neave family*)

Michael Creswell on a shooting holiday during his stint as a diplomat in pre-war Germany.

Harold Cole. (*Cumbria Archive Service*)

Andrée de Jongh.

Jean Greindl, Jean-François Nothomb, Peggy van Lier and Florentino Goïcoechea.

Mary Lindell, aka La Comtesse de Milleville.

AN towards the end of the conflict. (*Neave family*)

Evaders await rescue in the Fôret de Fréteval.

British troops move through the burning streets of Arnhem. (*Pen & Sword/SSPL/Getty Images*)

Nuremberg trial.

Margaret Thatcher and Airey Neave. (*Roger Jackson/Central Press/ Hulton Archive/Getty Images*)

AN and Diana Neave at the Watchfield Free Festival, August 1975. (*Paul Fievez/Associated Newspapers/REX/Shutterstock*)

Edward du Cann, chair of the 1922 committee, 13 October 1974. (*Ronald Spencer/Associated Newspapers/REX/Shutterstock*)

INLA operative Patsy O'Hara.

Harry Flynn in 1976. (*Pacemaker Press*)

The wreckage of AN's car on the exit ramp of the car park. (*PA/Ian Showell/PA Archive/PA Images*)

Margaret Thatcher at AN's funeral in Oxfordshire. (*Ball/Keystone/ Hulton Archive/Getty Images*)

Index